THE YOGA OF KNOWLEDGE

JÑĀNAYOGA

To Amber
have a good read

THE YOGA OF KNOWLEDGE

JÑĀNAYOGA

Patrick Mulvey

P. Mulvey
24.05.2019

The Estcourt Press

Published by the Estcourt Press 2019

First Published in Great Britain in 2019
The Estcourt Press
Winchester SO23 8EA

British Library Cataloguing-in-Publication Data
A CIP catalogue record for this book is available
from the British Library.
Mulvey, Patrick
The Yoga of Knowledge
1. Philosophy
2. Eastern Thought
3. Yoga
4. Religion
I. Title

ISBN: 978-0-9522961-3-3

Printed and Bound in Great Britain

CONTENTS

Preface

The vision of Shri Madhvacarya contemplated each individual thing in its uniqueness as much as in its existence as a member of a class. His vision is thus, primarily, of what is real. He saw the imposition of the object in a category as a secondary operation. This operation is to some extent the decision of each individual mind; and we can place any one object of perception and thought, under a myriad of different categorical headings.

Shri Madhvacarya was what we call a 'realist'. He thought of God as a true creator, creating existences whose being was separate from Himself. Shri Madhva taught the actual reality of the material universe; and he taught the real existence of individual souls. His vision is *dvaita*, or dual.

The vision of Shamkara is 'non-dual' [*advaita*].

Shamkara taught that the world and souls were just dreams in the mind of God. Somehow the souls became separated from God; forming their own illusions of themselves, conceiving their own worlds, but ultimately disappeared again into the only Self.

Like Shri Madhvacarya, other important Indian thinkers also accepted our first sense that the world is real; and that each of us experiences his own permanent being. This book is a tribute to the sanity of such thinkers: Ishvarakrishna and Jaimini; Udayana and Swatmarama.

***

I would like to thank my brother Christopher, for endlessly listening to my ideas on philosophy. Christopher basically takes a practical, John Stuart Mill/A. J. Ayer view of things; but he has been, as a university teacher, an academic master, encouraging so many students to develop their own ideas. I must again thank my brother Roderick for directly contributing to my text in the chapter, 'Yoga'.

Above all I would like to thank my wife Amelia, and my daughters, Florence and Marianne, for the greatest encouragement of loving patience.

Once when Florence was twelve, I was walking about our garden with my hands joined, shaking a tube of red car repair paint. Florence came into the garden and said, 'Dad, are you doing your eastern thought?' Yes, Eastern Thought is about humour, patience and, therefore, sanity.

Patrick Mulvey
Whitstable, 2019

CHAPTER 1

BEING

Rig Veda 10:129 Creation Hymn (Nāsadīya)

Nor aught nor naught existed; yon bright sky
Was not, nor heaven's broad woof outstretched above.
What covered all? what sheltered? what concealed?
Was it the water's fathomless abyss?
There was not death - hence was there naught immortal,
There was no confine betwixt day and night;
The only One breathed breathless in itself,
Other than it there nothing since has been.
Darkness there was, and all at first was veiled
In gloom profound, - an ocean without light. -
The germ that still lay covered in the husk
Burst forth, one nature, from the fervent heat.
Then first came Love upon it, the new spring
Of mind - yea, poets in their hearts discerned,
Pondering, this bond between created things
And uncreated.
Comes this spark from earth,
Piercing and all-pervading, or from heaven?
Then seeds were sown, and mighty power arose -
Nature below, and Power and Will above.
Who knows the secret? who proclaimed it here,

Whence, whence this manifold creation sprang? -
The gods themselves came later into being. -
Who knows from whence this great creation sprang? -
He from whom all this great creation came.
Whether his will created or was mute,
The Most High seer that is in highest heaven,
He knows it, - or perchance e'en He knows not.

Ancient man asked himself questions about the world around him. These questions prompted a sense of wonder, which enriched his experience of that world. They developed an understanding through love, and an appreciation through joy.

Poetry and philosophy were born when men expressed their reflections. Metaphysics came to be when they painted a picture of what seemed to be the world's origins.

The creation Hymn from the Rig Veda [*ṛg veda*] is an early philosophical poem. The Rig Veda describes the origin and nature of the universe according to the experience of mystical vision. It offers this experience as an answer to the questions of the wondering man. Indeed, in the mystical vision, question and answer are one: just as, in metaphysical truth, origin is nature.

The Rig Veda [Sanskrit *ṛg veda*, from *ṛc* 'praise, shine' and *veda* 'knowledge'] is an ancient Indian collection of hymns. It is one of the four canonical sacred texts [*śruti*] of Hinduism, known as the Vedas.

The Ten Thousand Things

The Chinese called the universe the 'ten thousand things'.

The ancient Indian wondered at the myriad number of beings around him; and conceived that thousands of bodies in the heavens were individual, whole worlds. He also saw that each individual thing, because it is a being, has a likeness to, and a fellowship with, any other thing in the universe: and thus, that the universe is one.

He decided that it is this oneness of the universe, rather than its divisibility, that is the ultimate truth. The vision of countless individual things and events, he thought, was a secondary truth. For individual beings are continually coming to be and fading away. They occur, persist for a moment, decay and then disappear. He decided further that this coming to be and declining of things and events is the way the universe appears to our individual consciousness. He called this secondary vision of his individual consciousness: '*māyā*'.

The Greek philosopher Heraclitus taught that nothing in the world is permanent. 'All is flux,' he said. He also said: 'You cannot step into the same river twice.' He taught that everything is made of fire.

Parmenides lived four centuries before Christ and shortly after Heraclitus. His city was Elea, on the Turkish coast of the Aegean. Elea was a trading port between civilisations; and perhaps, an emporium of religious and philosophical ideas.

Parmenides thought that there must be a permanent being, which lay underneath all beings we perceive. Every existent thing that we perceive is born and dies — it comes to be and fades away — it therefore cannot be the source of its own substance. In modern terms it is unsustainable.

The permanent being, which lies underneath everything else, he called the 'One'. He described it as a 'blessed god'.

This ultimate substance — we might think of it as atomic; or as a very rarefied substance — a kind of subtle energy — who knows? The Dao De Ching says:

> We look at it but do not see it;
> We name this the 'minute'.
> We listen to it but do not hear it;
> We name this the 'rarefied'.
> We touch it but do not hold it;
> We name this the 'level and smooth'.
>
> These three cannot be examined to the limit.
> Thus they merge together as one.
> 'One' – there is nothing more encompassing above it,
> And nothing smaller below it.
> Boundless, formless. It cannot be named,
> And returns to the state of no-thing.

Thus ancient man had a sense of an ultimate substance underpinning the material world. Was it water, bottomlessly deep? This substance presented paradoxes. How many times can we divide a drop of water? These paradoxes were accepted, rather than arbitrarily resolved in one direction. Meditation upon these paradoxes pointed further and beyond; to the mysterious and the infinite. Again this substance, albeit One thing, must contain, within, the means of producing the variety we perceive. A common and somewhat paradoxical view was that the primary substance, while being wholly one, was somehow also, within itself, tripartite.

Indian sages have always seen the material universe as emanating from a primary cosmic vibration [*ākāśa*]. Akasha is sometimes translated 'ether'; sometimes as 'subtle sound'. It is the mysterious fifth element from which precipitates the other four material elements of earth, water, fire, and air. It is an energy, conceived as a vibration to be felt or heard, as well as light to be seen. Akasha is both 'space' and that which fills 'space'. Stephen Hawking said that space is no more than events, being just the dimension of events (where they happen); and time is no more than events, being the measurement of the linear sequence, of before and after, that events have (when they happen). Energy can be regarded, both as a quality that objects possess, and as a stuff of which objects are made. Indeed, we can think of energy both as the cause of the objects we perceive and as those very objects themselves. Thus akasha is the sounds [*śabda*] and vibrations [*spanda*] in all space and all time. As well as being a vibration, akasha is both the medium that vibrates and also the vacuous totality of space-time, where and when the vibrations occur.

The Gunas

When they thought of that primal energy field as Nature, and as the cause of the nature we see, the sages called it *prakrti*. They also saw that, in order to manifest herself as the manifold variety of creation, the primal energy of *prakrti* must possess three qualities [*guna*]. These gunas may be seen as three different kinds of energy, or three aspects of energy; but they are not independent constituent elements. Nor are these gunas just subsidiary attributes of the underlying, and more real, cause. They are that cause. In the realm of the unmanifest [*prakrti*], just as in the realm of particle physics, object and quality, cause and effect, are not fully distinguished. Quality and quantity are likewise not to be separated. The gunas, or three qualities, can be imagined as three groupings of vibrations: heavy and slow [*tamas*], medium [*rajas*] and fast and light [*sattva*]; corresponding to the way notes can be played on the instrument, called the sitar, to the scale of a *rāga*. As these gunas blend and separate in an eternally varied kaleidoscope of combinations, so the myriad things of the universe come to be and disappear. The gunas are what the Unmanifest is said to be made of, to possess, or, if you will, to be.

How does the One of *prakṛti* become the Many of the visible universe? The major Indian philosophies make a primary division between the Conscious and the Unconscious. In the beginning Prakṛti, the Unconscious, lies dormant; and is One. When the presence of Consciousness, or the witness [*puruṣa*], stirs her energy the Prakṛti divides itself into two forms: sound [*śabda*] and vibration [*spanda*]. Through the separation and the blending of the gunas, the *spanda,* or vibrations and movements, form the material objects that we can see and touch. These objects are either heavy with *tamas*, or they are mobile with *rajas*. The *śabda* partly becomes the sound we hear; and partly remains in its subtlest *sattva* form as *ākāśa*.

Subtle sound [*ākāśa*] is the most sattvic aspect of material, unconscious, or objective being. From akasha, mind [*manas*] is formed; and with mind the meanings [*sphoṭa*] of our words come to be. Our mind is the dwelling place of the Purusha; but it is the Purusha who is conscious, not *manas*.

The spirit [*purusa*] does not possess these gunas. Therefore He is stable, unchanging, blissful and pure. He does not need the experience of association with Prakṛti, which is the cause of his illusion of sadness. He is without any need at all. He is perfect [*sat*] in the bliss [*ānanda*] of his consciousness [*citt*]; the bliss of his Self-being [*svabhāva*]. He is substantial.

The Rig-Veda contains a poem to Cosmic Heat. Here we have a different concept of the origin of things. This vision neither begins with nor depends on duality. There is no distinction between the matter of the heat and its force; but there is simply an energy and a fire, which is sacred. The heat [*tapas*] has aspects of matter and spirit; and of that which forms, and that which is formed. Does the 'arranger' arise from *tapas*; or is it an entirely separate being? This original One, without the primary division of Purusha and Prakṛti, may be an idea from an earlier period of India before the Vedas.

Again visions have survived in India where the One is female; an all-creative Mother goddess, both conscious and unconscious. Or again, the One is seen as the Cosmic Serpent, Kundalini—the half-personification of the primal cosmic energy, which is envisaged as spiral in form. It has a vast body and a small head. This One is neuter; and it is seen as the origin both of consciousness and unconsciousness. Consciousness [*puruṣa*] is not, in these views, a primary being. Instead, each stage of the world's evolving is a semi-conscious being — a god. There is mind in all things. All things are sacred.

> 1. From Fervour [*tapas*] kindled to its height Eternal Law [*ṛta*] and Truth [*satya*] were born: Thence was the Night produced, and thence the billowy flood of sea arose.
> 2 From that same billowy flood of sea the Year was afterwards produced, Ordainer of the days nights, Lord over all who close the eye.
> 3 Dhātar [the arranger], the great Creator, then formed in due order Sun and Moon. He formed in order Heaven and Earth, the regions of the air, and light.

Order [*ṛta*] and *satya* [Truth], are rooted in the nature of Being. The primal cosmic energy [*tapas*] manifests order [*ṛta*] as we can see from the movements of the stars. In so far as this order illuminates our minds it is Truth [*satya*].

Periodically, in the ancient Hindu world picture, the cosmos returns to the state of primal cosmic energy and then emerges again. As with the cosmos, so with man, the microcosm. In deep sleep all his inner faculties return to the elemental breath [*praṇa*]; which they all really are.

> Now with reference to the body. Breath (*praṇa*) is indeed the end of all. When a man sleeps, speech goes into breath, so do sight, hearing, and mind. Breath indeed consumes them all.

Sound

Before all, the vision of early India is a vision of beauty, of poetry. Art in Indian thought is the response of the mind and feelings to the true nature of a situation. Sound [*śabda*] is the primary form of cosmic vibration of which all that we experience is formed. The subtle version of sound [*ākāśa*] is that of which our mind, senses and imagination are made. Just as the material world is composed of the three gunas, so the subtle, inner world of our imagination is composed of the six 'tastes' or 'flavours' [*rasa*]. The Sanskrit meaning of *rasa* is: sap, juice, or the finest part. Rasa is the experience of the subject; but the subjective rasa is no less true than the objective actuality of the gunas. As seen from the point of view of the audience of a drama, the gunas of Prakṛti become the *rasa* of music, poetry, dance and painting. In music, and in all the arts, rasa is the basis of art and of true emotional response. To tell a story in music is to tell the emotional truth of it. Through the perfect verse, which expresses the emotional content of a scene at the turning point of a drama, the poet gives the audience the detached experience of '*rasa*'. Rasa, in this secondary sense of detached experience purely felt, is what, in the west, we call 'the aesthetic'. But 'the aesthetic' is an abstraction. In Rasa theory, Indian thought reveals deeper reals, rather than abstractions.

In Rasa theory the poet, or the singer (the dancer, the painter and so forth), is the Guru: the hearer, or the critic, is the Swami. The poet has the vision and the true emotional response; he has a purer being, because his sensibility is less tainted by impurity [*dośa*] due to the residue of bad, or unfortunate deeds [*karman*]. The listener needs the help of the poet to achieve this truth of response. The poet and the listener then begin to recognise 'Maya', as maya.

avidyā

Thinking that Maya, the material universe, is totally self-supporting and real is called, in Sanskrit, *avidyā* – 'blindness'. In a spiritual sense *avidyā* is not seeing, not understanding. It is the mistaking of the Maya of *prakṛti*, for the Purusha.

An over confident view of the solidity of material things, leading to the unbalanced desire for power, riches and pleasure is thus named as 'blindness'. In early Indian thought hearing was considered the subtlest and truest of the senses. Intuition, or feeling in the darkness of reality, is often of more use that knowing. The figure of the *śabda bhidi*, the blindfolded archer, who can shoot at a sound, is a prominent symbol of the knower of the truth, both in the Upanishads and in the later epic, Mahabharata. Ordinary vision thus can be spiritually 'blind'. In the gentle experience of rasa, the elements of a situation can be witnessed and felt in a more spiritually appropriate mode.

The ideas of philosophy also lead us to truth. When we take the final step on the journey to truth we will realise that the Purusha is the Purusha; and does not need the involvement with Prakṛti. Thus we will step beyond desire.

Reading the Upanishads creates an awareness of the transcendent — a feeling that there might be, or must be, a reality beyond the phenomenal world. The suggestion is of a reality, which is undivided into opposites, like substance and quality, or quality and quantity — a reality that is one and not many. This reality thus cannot be conceptualised or thought about; it perhaps can only be experienced.

The earth is seen as supporting all the meadows and mountains and seas, but earth is also made up of what it supports. Therefore there must be a support, truly, in principle, which is not made up of what it supports. A support, which is unsupported, cannot be perceived or even thought about. It cannot be an object. It may exist, yet it is no particular thing. It is the Transcendental.

Being

Indian thought, like Greek philosophy and mediaeval western thought, is ontological. Ontological philosophies arise from a vision of Being as existing as such. 'Ontology' means the science of Being. Some modern philosophies declare that the term 'being' has no object of reference. They do not see that there is 'being'; but only that there are beings. But, because individual things fade and merge, Being can be considered as existing as such. The One, in Indian thought, is the totality of things; at once considered as an abstraction and as a single individual existent.

Being is then regarded as a good beyond all the opposite, intermediate goods and evils. Being, for most early philosophies, is like 'Life' for the Russian writer, Boris Pasternak [1890-1960], the creator of *Doctor Zhivago*. Through the poetic vision of Yuri Zhivago, every moment of life, every joy and every pain is seen as part of the incomparable gift of existence.

If Being is good, the practical syllogism, i.e. the necessity of acting in certain ways because such and such is the case, is valid. If Being were valueless, and beauty were merely in the eye of the beholder, it would be illicit to say that 'is' can lead to 'ought'; illicit to say that any actual physical situation in the external world could indicate how one should act. Some modern western philosophers say either that Being does not exist, or, in any case, that it contains no pointer to ethical conduct. Thus they declare from their pulpits that values are subjective and, indeed, 'merely' subjective. Aristotle taught that the man has the duty to bring about the good situation. The argument that goes from a situation to a duty, from a person seeing a hungry child to experiencing the duty to feed it, he called 'the Practical Syllogism'. Some thinkers may claim that Aristotle's ethic is wrong; but their claim that his ethic is illogical is, itself, most illogical. Aristotle's ethic is derived from his ontology, not from the very different ontologies of his critics. To assume that everyone else is coming from where you are coming from, is the major error.

Dharma

'Natural' in Shakespeare's plays usually means 'virtuous', or living in accord with one's own being. 'Kind', in modern English, means acting in a loving way towards other creatures; a meaning derived from original meanings of 'type' and 'nature'. Here again we have a sense of an underlying goodness in things. Also in modern psychology and spirituality, being healthy, or being good, is seen as 'being oneself'; over against a superficial world that wants one to play some kind of role. This common sense and practical science is included in the Indian ideal of *dharma*. The idea of *dharma* has marked social connotations and includes the acceptance of personal religious codes; and *dharma* respects the emotional needs of individual and family. It is, as an Indian student told me, 'the good way to go'.

Some recent European thinkers have said that terms, like 'Being', which describe or refer to objects that we cannot perceive, have no meaning. Ludwig Wittgenstein [1889–1951], the Cambridge philosopher, taught that the notion that terms have 'meanings' at all is an illusion. When we need to ask for meaning of a word, he said, we should ask for a word's use. He also taught that the totality of things cannot even be referred to; that sounds such as 'reality', 'world' and 'universe' not only, like all words, have no meaning, but also have little use.

Before he died Wittgenstein exclaimed, 'I have had a wonderful life!' And then added, 'Alas, I die with contradiction on my lips.'

Friedrich Ludwig Gottlob Frege [1848–1925] the German mathematician, logician and thinker taught that, within a system of mathematical formulae, no one formula, could refer to the whole system of formulae.

But, nevertheless, in spite of the relative truth of these pronouncements on the conceptual level, we are still vaguely aware of the totality. Even those who deny the totality seem to think that they understand what they are denying; thus admitting that the idea of 'Being' is partially, if paradoxically, conceivable. It is Indian philosophy, however, that is true to our experience.

The Vedas contain all points of view. They hold that the consideration of all possible philosophical positions is necessary for the balanced attainment of truth. All the stages of the development of mankind's ideas about the universe are preserved to this day in Indian mythology and thought.

The Chandogya Upanishad is a dialogue where pupil and teacher enquire into the nature of things. By question and answer, pupil and teacher arrive at knowledge of ultimate Being. The innocent, clear vision of the child, who so purely desires truth, is as much valued as the wisdom of the old man. It is the teacher who asks the questions and the child who answers, while both regard one another with love and respect.

Chandogya Upanishad, VI. xii. 1-3.

'Bring hither a fig from there.'
'Here it is, Sir.'
'Divide it.'
'It is divided, sir.'
'What do you see there?'
'These rather fine seeds, Sir.'
'Of these please divide one.'
'It is divided, Sir.'
'What do you see there?'

'Nothing at all, Sir.'

Then he said to him: 'Verily my dear, that finest essence which you do not perceive – O verily my dear, from that finest essence, this great Nyagrodha [sacred fig] tree thus arises.'

'Believe my dear,' said he,

'That which is the finest essence, — this whole world has that as its Self:

That is the Reality. That is *Atman.* That thou art, Savetaketu!'

CHAPTER 2

THE HARRAPAN CULTURE AND THE ARYAN INVASIONS

The Indus Civilisation

The Indus civilisation, or Harappan culture, flourished from 2500 BC to 1500 BC; and it stretched beyond the Indus valley — from Balochistan, on the Persian border in the West, to Uttar Pradesh in the central Northern plain, where the tributaries of the Ganges flow. In the North it reached the Himalayas and in the South Gujurat. The political organisation was not centralised but was rather a network of city-states, across an area greater than ancient Egypt. The two most important archaeological sites are Harappa and Mohendro-daro in present-day Pakistan.

These excavations reveal the regional centres of a highly organised society. Streets and lanes were laid out in a set, mathematical plan. At another site in the Indus valley, Kalibangan, the lane width followed a set ratio: while the lanes were 1.8 metres wide, the streets in multiples of the lane width were 3.6, and 7.2 metres wide.

The citadel at Mohendro-daro contained imposing buildings, all made of kiln-burnt bricks: the great bath, the stupa, the priests' college, the granary and the assembly hall. The main town contained many large houses. The average house comprised of four to six living rooms around a courtyard, with a bathroom and a kitchen. Some great houses had up to thirty rooms, with staircases indicating other stories. There were brick sewers with regular manholes. The area of the granary was 55 by 37 metres. On the lowest floor rows of brickwork podia supported the wooden floor of the storage hall and allowed air to circulate. What was probably the assembly hall covered an area of over 750 square metres. It has twenty massive brick piers in four rows of five. The workingmen's quarter of the city had regular rows of living quarters with small working platforms. The area had its own granary. This regularity of design and of architecture suggests that the population was extremely regulated.

At Lothal on the Gulf of Cambay, there is a huge brick-lined dock, 216 metres by 37. Probably a channel (7 metres wide) connected the dock to the Bhogavo River, now 2 kilometres away. A large spill-channel was also provided. Objects of lapis lazuli, jade and turquoise, materials not native to India, have been found. These items, along with the Indus seals found in other west Asian sites, indicate a flourishing sea and land trade at that time.

Pottery, made of red slip, coloured with black pigments, has been found on every site. Scenes and animals were painted; especially the short-horned bull. There are sculpted stone statues and many, beautifully executed, tiny, clay figurines. The craftsmen were also expert workers in bronze: making knife-blades, short-swords, spears, arrowheads, sickles, chisels, razors, pins, tweezers and fishhooks. Furthermore beautiful statuettes have been found, as the famous dancing girl from Mohendro-daro. The finest craftsmanship is found in the seals cut out of steatite. On these seals the brahmani bull frequently appeared. The seals were inscribed with a sign language of 400 signs. Portrayals show a man wearing a dhoti, as in India today. Among the ornaments, the *bīja* — hollow, conical earrings — were found.

Skeletal remains indicate that the culture embraced several racial types. Proto-Australoid remnants are common. This type, related to the Australian aborigine, still lives in India today. The languages of this early civilisation may have given rise to the non Indo-European languages of southern India. A language, related to languages spoken by this far away southern group, is still spoken in Pakistan today.

Artefacts found indicate the worship of a mother goddess and of nature spirits. Some are shaped like the *linga* or the *yoni*; and there are portrayals, on seals, of a god like Shiva — *paśupati*, lord of the animals.

The valley cultivation was rich: wheat, barley, bananas, melons and peas were grown. There is evidence that people ate fish and all meats. The inhabitants of the area seem to have been the first people in the world to cultivate cotton.

The decline of the Harappan civilisation was due to several causes. There was severe flooding in some areas, disease became widesread and finally the Aryans invaded from the north. There are also signs in the west of the region of the drying up of great rivers and of the extension of the desert.

The Aryans moved gradually from further north, into the plain of the Ganges, which lies to the south of the foothills of the Himalayas. The plain is bordered on the west by the desert of Sind and on the southeast by the jungle of the Ganges Delta and by the Bay of Bengal. The great rivers of north India, rising in the Himalayas, water the vast region of tropical grasslands and scattered forests. The cow and the bull grazed the plain and were the basis of the northern economy throughout history. These animals were the symbol of nature's sustaining power; and thence of the divine itself. The forests provided hunting for the rajas, sanctuary for the hermits and medicines for the healers. But the tiger of the forests became the symbol of royal rule; and that most extraordinary beast of burden, the elephant, was the symbol of the fertility of the earth and of the power of the people to produce, if managed gently. Rice could be grown in the irrigable zones beside the rivers. These paddy fields were fertilised annually by inundation after the monsoons. The economy of rice production required vast numbers of workmen with a very simple skill. It has been said that it took a hundred peasant families of planters and cowherds to support one family of soldiers, of craftsmen, or of scholars. The soldiers then defended the raja's power; while the craftsmen provided him with refined and ritual objects; and the scholars supported his rule with the arguments of law. It had been said that a society based entirely upon the simple agriculture of rice cultivation, did not develop the full lower feudal hierarchy of labourers, ploughmen, blacksmiths and other village craftsman — a stable class of wealthier working people — as did medieval europe. It was for this reason that Karl Marx [1818-1883], the theorist of society and social economics, did not think that oriental history would so clearly illustrate the structure of the dialectic of the class struggle, as did the history of Europe. Oriental societies, he thought, were inclined to be static rather than evolving. The common view of all eighteenth-century European thinkers was that India and China were basically rice economies; and that this type of economy led to a rule by cultivated despots, preventing economic growth and legal development; and thus keeping society and polity static.

During the early nineteenth century this simple view was supported by John Stuart Mill [1806-1873], the empirical philosopher who was the proponent of utilitarianism. Mill held that the lack of private property in oriental society was stultifying. A despotic administration, he thought, combed all the surplus wealth from the villagers, who worked the irrigation systems, and gave it to the fabulous courts of the rulers.

All this was questioned by the economist Richard Jones [1790-1855] who held the chair of economics at the East India College, Haileybury. Jones was an economist who was always in contact with the world of business and manufacture. He never formed theories until he had collected an amount of data; he was very much an inductive thinker. His study of history made him aware of the large number of particular economies that had to be studied separately and in detail in order for economics to be understood. He rejected the notion of the Enlightenment that there is an abstract 'economic man'; the course of whose activities could be predicted *a priori*. His work at Haileybury brought him into direct contact with the Indian subcontinent and its enormous variety of societies and sub-societies. He was aware that the powerful local economies of the city-states, in India, had existed through the epochs. Richard Jones realised that there are no classic economic models. Thus the notion of the despotic oriental economy; and therefore of a standard type eastern despotic society; was a cultural myth of the west.

After about 1500 BC, the numbers of Aryan people in the Indian subcontinent greatly increased. There was not one sudden invasion, but large numbers of migrants settled in the area of the Punjab. Gradually the Indo-Aryan language, Sanskrit, which is closely related to European languages, replaced the ancient Dravidian dialects. Languages of the Dravidian group are still spoken today in southern India. There is one area in Pakistan, Balochistan, where a Dravidian language, Brahui, is still spoken; but the vast majority of peoples of the north and the centre of the Indian subcontinent speak tongues derived from Sanskrit. Hindi is spoken by 258 million people and is the language of Indian national government.

These Aryans had originally separated from the main group in southern Russia and begun to make their way into central Asia. A related group migrated to the Baltic, probably at the same epoch. Today, Lithuanian is the closest modern language to Sanskrit, the Aryan language. As the Aryans moved towards central Asia, the Hittites, another related group, settled in Asia Minor. Modern Turkish is in no way related to Sanskrit; but the small groups in the area of Turkey, Georgia and Cyprus, speaking the Armenian language and preserving its culture, are remnants of the ancient Hittites. Another group close to the Indo-Aryan was the Indo-Iranian – the words Aryan and Iranian are derived from the same Sanskrit word, *aya*, meaning: man, or life giving. The Iranians entered the Persian region about 1000 BC. The two languages, Avestan (old Persian) and Sanskrit have similar vocabularies.

Sanskrit	Avestan
yajña [sacrifice]	*yasna*
sapta [seven]	*hapta*
himā [winter]	*zyam*

The Sanskrit *hima* means basically: cold and frost. We may remember the Latin for winter, *hiems*, and we may think of the Himalayas. Sir Monier-Monier Williams [1819-1899], the great Sanskrit scholar, however, gives *himalaya* as 'abode of snow', in his dictionary.

ṛta [cosmic order]	*arta* (Old Persian)
vinda [finding]	*viṇden* [they found]
vak [speaking]	*vācim* [voice]
aham [I]	*azem*
asti [there is]	*asti* [is]
pati [husband]	*paitīm* [lord]
mādhya [middle]	*maidīm*

The two peoples had a common mythology. They both cultivated fire worship and also the mystical drug soma. The god Mithras [*mithra* in Vedic India] spread his worship all over the Roman empire. I well remember, when I was at secondary school, that the London temple of the late Roman god was being excavated.

The Aryans were a pastoral people. They were warlike. The Vedas, the hymns and poems about the cosmos and the gods, were composed between 1300 BC and 1000 BC. These poems do not describe an invasion; which must have been, therefore, earlier and, perhaps, gradual. They describe a culture, which was partly developed outside India; though there is no actual memory of the prehistory of this culture beyond the Himalayas. The story is, however, of a continual struggle with the *dasyu*. The meaning of *dasyu* is 'enemies of the gods'; these *dasyu* were the native inhabitants of India. The war-god of the invaders, Indra, was known as *puraṁdara* – destroyer of cities. Agni, the fire god, was also regarded as an ally in that destruction. The Aryans were superior in the military field because of their light war chariot. The cities were abandoned almost entirely and a pastoral culture was developed. There is no archaeological evidence, however, that cities were destroyed on the scale of a cataclysm.

The Aryans set up small kingdoms of tribal villages. The houses and furniture in the tribal villages was made of wood. The *kulapati* headed the family, *kula*. The *kula* was the smallest unit of society. The kulas made up the *grāma*, or village, which was in turn part of the *viṣ*, or tribal unit. The *jana* was the tribe; and the *rāśṭra*, or king, ruled one or more tribes. He was assisted by the chief priest, *purohita*, and by a military commander, *senānī*. The Welsh tribes at the time of the Mabioniog also had two chiefs: an older man, who was a sort of legal ruler and administrator, and a younger man, who was a war leader.

The attitude of the Vedic poets to the *dasyu* was utterly hostile, even associating them with evil. The Vedic religion was one of sacrifice. It was considered that the creation, maintainance and destruction of the world were the phases of the cosmic sacrifice. Sacrifices marked every season and every aspect of Aryan life; sometimes at vast expense and taking a great length of time. Rituals enacted the relationship of man to the cosmos and to the gods; emphasising family ties and duties and other relationships. There developed a caste, or class system. The two senior castes of Aryan society were *dvijā*, or twice born. They were the warrior and ruling caste – *kśatriya*; and the priestly and scholarly caste – *brahman*. The subject peoples formed the two lower castes – the farmers and traders were *vaiṣya*; and the manual workers were *ṣūdra*. The Sanskrit word for caste is *vana*, meaning 'colour'. Originally the invaders of India were of fair complexion. An aspect of the caste system was that a man was born to a trade within the lower castes. Trade, or sub-caste, is *jaṭi*. These lower castes may have been the primitive tribes of the forest, or they may have been a remnant of the city dwellers, who had better relations with the Aryans and who came to dwell on the edge of their society.

Homes were built of wood or of reeds. Barley was the staple diet; milk was made into ghee, and vegetables and fruit were eaten. Strong intoxicants, *surā* and *madhu*, were brewed.

A study of agricultural words in the early Sanskrit reveals a number of words of proto-Dravidian origin, used for agrarian implements and practices. This indicates that agriculture and ploughing were very developed in pre-Vedic India.

Indian historians in the late nineteenth century favoured the identification of race, caste [*vaṛna*] and language. They thought that the ruling class of India was descended from a separate white or pale race of people who spoke Sanskrit, conquered India and introduced 'civilisation'. Nowadays, in a more democratic era, Indian historians emphasise the indigenous origins of Indian culture and society and the contribution to civilisation of the darker races.

Asoka

Between 400 BC and 200 BC the great Indian Epics, the Ramayana and Mahabharata, were written. These epics assemble a vast number of individual stories from the different peoples of the sub-continent of India into coherent and artistic forms. The epics are compendia of philosophy, science and religion. They set out the spiritual, social and political ideals of mankind. Their historical reference is many layered. The story is at once about the Aryan conquest of India, about the Hindu civilisation of the seventh century BC, when the ideals of Hindu civilisation were fought for and achieved. By slight yet significant references the epics clarify these ideals of life against the ideals of Buddhism and Jainism, which were, at that time, developing into separate religions and philosophies.

After 322 BC, Chandragupta Maurya began the expansion of the kingdom of Magadha. Magadha lay on the plain of the Eastern Ganges. A civil war among the successors of Alexander, the Greek conqueror, gave Chandragupta the opportunity to conquer the North Indian plain as far west as the Punjab. His rule developed the system of land taxation that he had taken over from the Nandas, who had previously controlled the East Ganges plain. Workmen were organised into guilds. The Arthasastra, the earliest Indian text on administration and economy, was said to be written by Kautilya, the great administrator of the Mauryan Empire. Chandragupta died in 297 BC.

Ashoka Maurya [272-232 BC] conquered central and most of south India. After the defeat of Kalinga in the east [64 BC], at which final battle he is said to have deployed 9,000 elephants; he decided that war must cease. He is said to have become a Buddhist. He softened the harsh laws of his predecessors and forbade the slaughter of animals for sacrificial purposes. On stone pillars about his kingdom he proclaimed his *damma* of beneficient rule. Some of these monuments have survived. They proclaim harmony and peace between people of all religions.

The Dravidian Culture

South of Goa the linguistic culture of Sanskrit and its derivative languages did not extend. But the Vedic religious culture did eventually predominate in the south; taking in innumerable local gods and developing the literary and artistic culture of ancient Tamil. Tamil was the chief Dravidian language of Southern India. By the fifth century AD there were versions of the Epics and Puranas in Southern Indian languages. There was also a special, native cult of court poetry: love poetry – *agam* – considered to be subjective; and heroic, or martial poetry – *puram* – considered to be objective. Poems of unrequited or of forced love were often considered as *puram*.

The ancient Telagu and Kanada languages also produced versions of the Ramayana and the Mahabharata. There was a culture of love poetry. After the fall of the Northern Gupta Empire, powerful Southern kingdoms arose. They encouraged these cultures. They developed a unique and popular cult of Shiva, which gave birth to the *agama* poets of the Middle Ages. There were ashrams of many schools of philosophy; some of which were influenced by Christianity. The greatest of all of the Southern poets, Kalidasa, however, wrote in late (sixth century) Sanskrit. His great spiritual love poem, 'The Cloud Messenger', was translated into German during the eighteenth century; and influenced the European Romantic movement.

CHAPTER 3

THE VEDAS AND GOD

The Being of a God

The religion of the Aryans was one of great, open-air sacrifices, preceded by long ceremonial chants. The chants were called Mantras, or hymns. The Mantras are visions of the glory and joy of God, of the universe and of man. They are the work of the poet rather than of the theologian or of the philosopher. Veda (from the root *ve* — weave; and thus, recite, or compose) means that which has been spoken, in the sense of pronounced and given. Thus it means 'knowledge'. The Sanskrit language was seen as perfectly reflecting, and thus revealing, reality, when it was perfectly used. Again the authority of the Vedas was not seen as primarily the authority of men, but as the Truth of the perfect word. There are four collections of mantras, or chants, called Vedas.

The Rig Veda is the oldest collection of mantras. The root *ṛc* means 'praise'. The verses are true *sūkti* – 'poems' – verses not necessarily connected with the sacrificial and the ritual. It is the earliest and most original of the four collections of mantras. The Rig Veda may date from before the eleventh century BC. The mantras of the Sama Veda and the Yajur Veda were written later. These chants are decidedly liturgical. The Sama Veda contains the low key, rhythmic chants of the priests to the moon. The Atharva Veda, the last of the four collections, was probably written, or at least collected, as late as the fifth century BC. Many of the hymns of this last Veda originate in the earlier religions of pre-vedic India. The collection includes chants, charms and hymns to all sorts of forces and spirit beings. These verses had been incorporated gradually by the Vedic religion from local animist, or pagan, religions. The genius of Hinduism has been its ability to absorb opposing religions into the vast corpus of its ceremonial and the kaleidoscopic genealogy of it families of gods. Throughout the ages intellectual reformers have opposed many of these cults as impure.

Sarvepalli Radhakrishnan [1888–1975] was born at Tiruttani, near Madras, to poor brahmin parents. He attended the Christian college in Madras and he wrote his degree thesis on the ethics of the Vedas, defending the Vedas against the charge of not teaching an ethic. Radhakrishnan believed that the philosopher had a crucial role in the development of India. He taught that the philosopher could reach into the past and thus prepare for the future. In 1936 he was invited to fill the Chair of Spalding Professor of Eastern Religions and Ethics at Oxford. In 1939, he was appointed the Vice Chancellor of Banares Hindu University. After Independence he became India's ambassador to the Soviet Union. There he confronted Stalin with his oppression and tyranny.

In 1962 he was made President of India. His appointment as President was hailed by Bertrand Russell, who said, 'It is an honour to philosophy that Dr. Radhakrishnan should be President of India and I, as a philosopher, take special pleasure in this. Plato aspired for philosophers to become kings and it is a tribute to India that she should make a philosopher her President.' The birthday of

Radhakrishnan in September became Teacher's Day. In India the highest profession is considered that of the teacher.

The philosophy of Sarvepalli Radhakrishnan has always given prominence to the study of ethics. He developped an understanding of the ethical teaching of the Vedas. In metaphysics he blended the thought of Immanuel Kant with the philosophy of Shamkara. More recently he described the charms, spells and chants to inanimate things of the Atharva Veda as corrupt and uncivilised. Where they appear in the Rig Veda, he regarded them as inessential and later additions.

There are commentaries on the Rig Veda, called 'Brahmanas', from the Sanskrit *brāmaṇa*, meaning: pertaining to the priests. The Brahmanas contain instructions on the ritual for the carrying out of ceremonies and for the recitation of the Vedas. They also contain explanations of the poems. The explanations of the Brahmanas were written many centuries after the original poems, for a society that no longer fully understood them; a society that could no longer immediately grasp the metaphors of the verses and spontaneously act on their inspiration. Later, during the seventh century BC, purely philosophical commentaries followed the Brahmanas. These were called 'Upanishads'. The Upanishads discuss metaphysical issues; exploring ideas of being and substance, analysing consciousness and enumerating its levels. By the time the Upanishads were written, brahmin society had become analytic and speculative. The Upanishads, however, always accept the tradition of the Vedas as truth. The vision of the poet-seer [*ṛsi*] is regarded as pure and undeniable experience.

It is said that the Vedas are the vision of poet, that the Brahmanas express the sacrificial calling of priesthood, and that the Upanishads are the works of philosophers. However, the original verses of the *ṛsi* in the Rig Veda are, at once, poem, priestly instruction and philosophical disquisition.

Generally speaking, the commentaries and chants that were written after the Vedas are called *vedanta* — meaning simply 'derived from the Vedas', or 'about the Vedas'. The veda/vedanta distinction occurs in many religions. In Christianity the equivalent of the Veda is the Bible: the Commentaries of the Holy Fathers are the Vedanta. Because of the superior excellence and originality of the Rig Veda, and also because of the commentatory and adaptive nature of the other Vedas — the Sama Veda, the Yajur Veda and the Atharva Veda — they are frequently considered to be Vedanta rather than Veda.

The Rig Veda is the collection of poems praising the gods and the beauty and power of nature. Each god, or cosmic personality, is distilled from an aspect of the cosmos, land and climate. If we take the god of dawn, for example, he is certainly the actual individual dawn we see on a particular morning. But, then again, since dawn endlessly recurs, the myriad of individual dawns becomes the one of 'Dawn'. Modern thought would regard this oneness of 'Dawn' as a logical construct; a mere way of referring to the collectivity of individual dawns. Mediaeval western thought would have regarded 'Dawn' as a universal; an abstract form, or pattern, of all dawns. Of course the dawn is an aspect of the sun's movement, seen from our point of view. It is an accidental effect of the sun's power. But early man would have seen each dawn as a conscious experience — a special sort of self, renewing its own being each day. The conscious experience of freshness, of a newness, and thus in a sense, of a new time and a renewed universe, is one with its object, the visible dawn. The world and being were seen as conscious; and not as separated and different from the consciousness of each individual man. In the radiant dawn, the universal becomes a beautiful individual. Again, the feeling aspect of our experience was regarded as having a factual validity equal to that of the visible. Thus feelings were considered objective; or a witness of real aspects of the external world. Where an individual was exhausted, lazy or hung over, he might shun the dawn. In that case his individual consciousness has become separated from the joy of the common consciousness, which is objective; and has degenerated into something purely personal and subjective, and therefore sad. This sadness is true subjectivity. From the earliest times the positive nature of Indian thought has taken the bliss component of the universe as real; as it has asserted the objectivity and empirical nature of all experience; very much including the inner experience of the *ṛsi*.

To the poet of earlier aeons, the power that makes the dawn is a consciousness. It might be thought of also as an essence in the Aristotelian and scholastic sense. But firstly it is an individual and even a person that you meet every morning, filling you with understanding and inspiration. These individual personalities or powers of the universe such as the sun or the sky, earth or night were seen by the worshipper in turn as the central aspect of universe; the totality, the One. These major Gods, the Sun, the Sky and Indra, or the land of India, and so forth, were each worshipped in turn as the Great God Himself. This religious phenomenon is called, not monotheism, but henotheism. Rather than polytheistic, or monotheistic, the vision of Vedic India was henotheistic.

Dawn, as any cosmological phenomenon might in ancient times, had male and female aspects. There was a goddess of Dawn; but more interestingly the male aspect was portrayed as a pair of twins together riding a chariot, or, sometimes, a horse.

Asvins

1 ASVINS, what praise may win your grace?
Who may be pleasing to you both?
How shall the ignorant worship you?
2 Here let the ignorant ask the means of you who know
— for none beside you knoweth aught —
Not of a spiritless mortal man.
3 Such as ye are, all-wise, we call you. Ye wise, declare
to us this day accepted prayer.
Loving you well your servant lauds you.
4 Simply, ye Mighty Ones, I ask the Gods of that —
wondrous oblation hallowed by the mystic word.
Save us from what is stronger, fiercer than ourselves.

The verse begins with the special praise of the Asvins; that praising of them brings grace. They are very important helpers of human beings. Grace purifies us and therefore we pray we will be pleasing to them. But their special twin aspect of the twin gods is that they bring knowledge and bliss. Thus, seated on their mount, the horse, the classic animal of that pastoral, warrior civilisation, they together incarnate the three aspects of divine being: Being [*sat*], Knowledge [*cit*] and Bliss [*ānanda*]. Dawn is the time of the first ritual prayer of the day, so the Asvins are the gods of prayer and ritual.

Of the Asvins Shri Aurobindo has written:

> The two Riders on the Horse; lords of the joyous upward action of the mind and the vital powers; twin divine powers whose special function is to perfect the nervous or vital being in man in the sense of active enjoyment, but they are also powers of Truth, of intelligent action, of right enjoyment.

Aurobindo Ghosh [1872–1950] was perhaps the foremost Indian thinker of the twentieth century. He took part in the movement for Indian independence, but then retired to lead the mystical life, to reflect and to write on the philosophy of man's transition.

In their role as knowers the Asvins are the enlightening dawn. They are *cit*, which means, in the Rig Veda, 'precise, or focused knowledge'; and then 'understanding'. There is really no Sanskrit word for 'consciousness' as such; but *cit* was later used in this sense in the Mahabharata (loc. Xviii, 74). When we know, we know that we know; and when we enjoy, we are aware that we enjoy; thus together the closely twinned *cit* and *ānanda* (joy) imply consciousness. Vedic philosophy is a whole philosophy; and the converging, not-wholly separable, quality of its ideas defies total analysis. And consciousness itself is one of these ideas. That consciousness is one, but has different aspects, which are graspable by conceptualisation, and which then become part of a whole understanding, is the mystery of Vedic thought. That Being is both one and many is the mystery of Being: that knowledge is clear, simple and yet various is, in its turn, the mystery of knowing.

The following verses emphasise the roles of the Asvins as recipients of the sacrifice, and thus patrons of religion, as fertility gods, and thus as providers of the harvest; and finally as the encouragers of enjoyment, which is the purpose of everything.

> 3 Juice in the wide room hath been prepared to feast you; for you the grass is strewn, most soft to tread on.
>
> With lifted hands your servant hath adored you. Yearning for you the press-stones shed the liquid.

The Asvins are also healers.

> 6 Thrice, Asvins, grant to us the heavenly medicines, thrice those of earth and thrice those that the waters hold.
>
> Favour and health and strength bestow upon my son; triple protection, Lords of Splendour, grant to him.

According to my Sanskrit dictionary, *āśvina* means — 'like riders or horsemen', i.e. 'swift'. The Asvins are described as protectors in danger, as rescuers and as aids of soldiers in battle. The reader might wonder at the spectrum of activities that the twins cover. But this is how mankind moves from animism, and belief in a myriad of spirits, to polytheism. Polytheism recognises a few gods as superior to these other spirits. Then man moves from polytheism to the henotheism of the Rig Veda; the celebration of one god as being more important than the others. Finally man arrives at the theism of devotional Hinduism.

Like Shri Aurobindo and the majority of Indian thinkers since Vedic times, Hindus have considered their thought to be derived from the Vedas. One might say the contrast between Veda and Vedanta is like the difference between the acorn and the oak. The different schools of philosophy are like the branches of the oak, which tend to struggle against and even break one another when the storm rages; but the acorn is one, solid whole.

Other Vedic Gods

An early Vedic god was Indra. The idea of creation; the idea of India, the land; the event of the Aryan peoples' invasion of India; are all fused into a vision of Creation. The idea, which, like any idea, is a modification of consciousness and a moment of consciousness, then becomes a personality. The action, in which this hero, Indra, expresses his being – his personality – is the killing of the dragon, Vṛta.

Indra — the Killing of Vṛta

RIG VEDA 1.32

> 1 Let me now sing the heroic deeds of Indra, the first that the thunderbolt-wielder performed. He killed the dragon and pierced an opening for the water; he split open the bellies of mountains.
>
> 2 He killed the dragon who lay upon the mountains; Tvaṣṭṛ (smith of the gods) fashioned the warring

thunderbolt for him. Like lowing cows, the flowing waters rushed straight down to the sea.

3 Wildly excited like a bull, he took the Soma for himself and drank the extract from the three bowls in the three-day Soma ceremony. Indra the Generous seized his thunderbolt to hurl it as a weapon; he killed the first-born of dragons.

4 Indra, when you killed the first-born of the dragons and overcame by your own magic the magic of magicians, at that very moment you brought forth the sun, the sky, and dawn. Since then you have found no enemy to conquer you.

5 With his great weapon, the thunderbolt, Indra killed shoulderless Vṛta, his greatest enemy. Like the trunk of a tree whose branches have been lopped of by an axe, the dragon lies flat on the ground.

6 For, muddled by drunkenness like one who is no soldier, Vṛta challenged the great hero who had overcome the mighty and who drank Soma to the dregs. Unable to withstand the onslaught of his weapons, he found Indra an enemy to conquer and was shattered, his nose crushed.

7 Without feet or hands he fought against Indra, who struck him on the nape of his neck with his thunderbolt. The steer who wished to become the equal of the bull bursting with seed, Vṛta lay broken in many places.

8 Over him as he lay there like a broken reed the swelling waters flowed for man. Those waters that Vṛta had enclosed with his power – the dragon now lay at their feet.

9 The vital energy of Vṛta's mother ebbed away, for Indra had hurled his deadly weapon at her. Above was the mother, below was the sun; Dānu lay down like a cow with her calf.

10 In the midst of the channels of the waters, which never stood, still or rested, the body was hidden. The waters flow over Vṛta's secret place; he who found Indra an enemy to conquer him sank into long darkness.

11 The waters who had Dāsa for their husband, the dragon for their protection, were imprisoned like the cows imprisoned by the Paṇis. When he killed Vṛta he split open the outlet of the waters that had been closed.

12 Indra, you became hair of a horse's tail when Vṛta struck you on the corner of the mouth. You, the one god, the brave one, you won the cows; you won the Soma; you released the seven streams so that they could flow.

13 No use was the lightning and thunder, fog and hail that he had scattered about, when the dragon and Indra fought. Indra the Generous remained victorious for all time to come.

14 What avenger of the dragon did you see, Indra, that fear entered your heart when you had killed him? Then you crossed the ninety-nine streams like a frightened eagle crossing the realms of heaven and earth.

15 Indra, who wields the thunderbolt in his hand, is the king of that which moves and that which rests, of the tame and of the horned. He rules the people as their king, encircling all this as a rim encircles spokes.

The poem is filled with seminal images; and from these seeds have grown the later metaphysical doctrines of creation and existence. Of course, Indra is a god, as much as God; and as a god (with a small 'g') he has to have an opposite, Vṛta. Vṛta represents the chaotic forces of nature, which are brought under the control of intelligence. In Aristotelian terms, Vṛta is matter to Indra's form. Again Vṛta is the 'Other' of war and opposition and destruction; not the harmonious, 'doppelganger' twin of the Asvins. But without Vṛta, Indra cannot create.

The Sky is an early symbol of spirit or the divine. Earth is of course 'matter'; and a clear symbol of Matter, in the metaphysical sense. In the early Greek cosmology *Ouranos* [Sky] and *Gaia* [Earth] are the primary beings from which everything was born. In Sanskrit, the root *vāra* means, among many other things, 'covering'. Varuna is the name of the Vedic god of the sky. Because the sky appears over against earth, it is the light by which we see; and then, by transposition of meaning, a sort of eye. That which covers all becomes that which witnesses everything. The Sky is the witness of all earthly activity. Varuna is, thus, an ethical deity. He is the witness of all our deeds, however, secret. He is the guardian of Ṛta; and the automatic workings of Ṛta bring retribution.

Charles Dickens [1812–1870] rarely emphasised in his tales the part of organised and formal religion. His novels, however, show a powerful sense of an overlying cosmic providence and a justice implicit and deep at the heart of things. For Dickens murder is the archetypal crime, as it is in the Book of Genesis. There is a religious sense of the sanctity of every life; and the greatest sacrilege is the shedding human blood.

In *Oliver Twist*, Bill Sykes murders his wife, Nancy, in a fit of violent rage. The crime is not immediately witnessed, yet it is hardly concealed. Sykes has been seen walking away from his lodging. He is pursued by a mob and caught, with inevitability.

In *Martin Chuzzlewit*, Jonas Chuzzlewit poisons his father and kills his business partner with a stake. Both crimes are ingeniously concealed, but at each crucial juncture the murderer has been seen and recognised by an onlooker, quite accidentally; and thus his crimes are uncovered.

In both of Dicken's epics the guilty consciousness of the murderer takes on a cosmic quality. There is a mystical sense of his being seen by a thousand eyes because of the wickedness of his crime, which is magically converged by the passionate writing of Dickens into a single sense of *nemesis*, or cosmic justice.

It is thus that the poem of 'The Deeds of Varuna' ends with a prayer for forgiveness; the reciting of which is an act of reconciliation like the Christian Sacrament of Penance. The bonds from which we seek release are those of the very sin itself, as well as the other bonds, which are the punishment of the god. For man, the laws of hospitality [*aryaman*] and of domesticity [*mitra*] on the social level are the equivalent of the regulation of the stars by Ṛta, on the cosmological scale. Sin, in this early vision, is essentially not following one's path of social duty. But in this early cosmological vision sin can be a blind act, rather than a free and conscious choice of wrong. Acts against the code incur bondage, whether conscious or unconscious, intended or unintended — that is Karma. Karma is rather like the laws of physics.

The Deeds of Varuna

RIG VEDA 5.85

1 For the emperor I will sing a splendid, deep prayer, one that will be dear to the Famous Varuna who struck apart the earth and spread it beneath the sun as the priest who performs the slaughter spreads out the victim's skin.

2 He stretched out the middle realm of space in the trees; he laid victory in swift horses and milk in the dawn cows, intelligence in hearts and fire in the waters. Varuna placed the sun in the sky and Soma on the mountain.

3 Over the two world-halves and the realm of space between them Varuna has poured out the cask, turning its mouth downward. With it the king of the whole universe waters the soil as the rain waters the grain.

4 He waters the soil, the earth, and the sky. Whenever Varuna wishes for milk, the mountains dress themselves in cloud and the heroes, brandishing their power, let them loose.

5 I will proclaim the great magic of Varuna the famous Asura (sky god), who stood up in the middle realm of space and measured apart the earth with the sun as with a measuring-stick.

6 No one has dared this great magic of the most inspired god: that these shimmering torrents, pouring down, do not fill the one single ocean with their water.

7 If we have committed an offence against a hospitable friend like Aryaman or a close friend like Mitra, or against one who has always been a comrade, or a brother, or a neighbour – one of our own or a stranger – loosen that offence from us Varuna.

8 If we have cheated like gamblers in a game, whether we know it or do not know it, O god, cast all these offences away like loosened bonds. Let us be dear to you, Varuna.

The poem began with the act of creation. This act is identified with the deed of the sacrificing priest. Both in the act of creation and in the deed of sacrifice, there is seen to be a division, a duality, a riving apart of being, or of matter. The sky is then seen as pouring the waters of life over the earth and supplying the cosmos with life-giving energy. The act of creation is eternal because the ocean or void can never be filled up.

Here the ocean is a depersonalised, neutral opposite, which has negative infinity like the *materia prima* of Aristotle and the *chora* of Plato.

The splitting of the carcass yields the sacramental meal. In a sense every meal we eat is just an act of personal re-creation. However, the ritual meal of Vedic sacrifice is not a mere meal; nor again is it just an exercise of cosmic power, or magic. The essence of the act of the sacrificing priest is sacramental. He is enabling the onlookers to share in the sacredness of the act of God's creation for the joy and blessing — the sheer worthwhileness of it. He is raising men onto a higher spiritual plain.

The Sanskrit *brahman* means a member of the priestly caste, or simply a priest. The brahmins officiated at the Vedic open-air sacrifices. They chanted the series of prayers. They presided over ceremonies and festivals. They were the custodians of the traditions and laws of their society. They were the thinkers and advisers to governments, but frequently not the rulers. The druids had exactly the same functions in western, Celtic society, in ancient times. The Druids drank yarrow tea and, in a trance, told future events. The brahmins drank a drug called 'soma': to revive their spirits, lift their hearts and to help them meditate.

For me also the sky always has a presence. For primitive man, as for some mystics and saints, every being is conscious. For the ancient Indian the ultimate ground of the universe was Being beyond the distinction between consciousness and unconsciousness. It is thus an easy step to make a god of some natural event or phenomenon. Personality, like all other qualities, is the product of the ultimate ground of the universe — why should not the essence of the sun, or the moon, or the sea appear, again, as a man or a woman? I once dreamed I visited a cave, under the sea or by the sea, and in it sat an old man who was the sea. In the midst of the dream the experience seemed natural and to make entire sense. The unconscious presence of the sea transformed itself into the conscious presence of the old man. Since then the idea of 'a god' has been intelligible to me. But the dream was an experience rather than a series of concepts, or an argument. It can be difficult to convey this sort of experience to someone else.

In the Vedic hymn to Surya, the sun is said to be the eye of Varuna. The sun is worshipped as the greatest of the natural phenomena; as the greatest god; and therefore, virtually, as God.

In verse eight, the sun is said to be the wheel of the chariot that carries the sun god, on his daily journey across the sky.

The Ancient Greeks cherished the same image of the solar deity, Helios, crossing the sky on his chariot. His son Apollo was the god of intelligence and enlightenment. The young Apollo once stole his father's chariot but could not control the temperamental steeds.

They reared and plunged and dragged the chariot all over the sky. At one time the sun came far too near to the earth and the island of Crete was burned from one end to the other.

When intellect is precocious and tries to take control of the cosmic forces without the guidance of wisdom and the self-control of maturity, the result is catastrophe.

The Sun, Sūrya

RIG VEDA 1.50

1 His brilliant banners draw upwards the god who knows all creatures, so that everyone may see the sun.

2 The constellations, along with the nights, steal away like thieves, making way for the sun who gazes on everyone.

3 The rays that are his banners have become visible from the distance, shining over mankind like blazing Fires.

4 Crossing space, you are the maker of light, seen by everyone, O sun. You illumine the whole wide realm of space.

5 You rise up facing all the groups of gods, facing mankind, facing everyone, so that they can see the sunlight.

6 He is the eye with which, O Purifying Varuna, you look upon the busy one among men.

7 You cross heaven and the vast realm of space, O sun, measuring days by nights, looking upon the generations.

8 Seven bay mares carry you in the chariot, O sun god with hair of flame, gazing from afar.

9 The sun has yoked the seven splendid daughters of the chariot; he goes with them, who yoke themselves.

10 We have come up out of darkness, seeing the higher light around us, going to the sun, the god among gods, the highest light.

11 As you rise today, O sun, you who are honoured as a friend, climbing to the highest sky, make me free of heartache and yellow pallor.

12 Let us place my yellow pallor among parrots and thrushes, or let us place my yellow pallor among other yellow birds in yellow trees.

13 This Āditya has risen with all his dominating Force, hurling my hateful enemy down into my hands. Let me not fall into my enemy's hands.

This is a prayer for healing against jaundice and diseases of the eye. But of course eye trouble and blindness are images of intellectual error in the Sanskrit culture. Again in this culture the higher realms of being are not opposed to the material. The light of the sun is an emanation of the higher light of the Truth. But some western commentators have wrongly interpreted this harmony of levels as a doctrine of monism, or a doctrine of pantheism, where God and the universe share the same substance. The Vedas are always subtle; and they support the higher and more ethical view.

The hymn to the All-Maker [*viśvakarman*] presents a clear and simple idea of God as Creator. Vishvakarman is the creator God of religion. If, however, we regard him as emanating from the ultimate Brahman, and then if, further, the world emanates, in its turn from the All-Maker; then Visvakarman is the philosophical equivalent of that intermediate cosmos-maker of the Greek philosopher Plato, the Demiourgos. The poem asks what existed before the act of creation and out of what was the universe made.

The first verse points out that creation is the first sacrifice. By the words, the prayers, of God, the priest, the world comes to be – Name and Form [*namarupa*]. The second verse asks what is named and thus divided, what chaos is made sense of by the divine, creative description. The third verse refers to the legend of Brahma waking from the ocean of Being, looking round and, seeing the emptiness on all sides, creating.

The All-Maker – Vishvakarman

RIG VEDA 10.81

1 The sage, our father, who took his place as priest of the oblation and offered all these words as oblation, seeking riches through prayer, he entered those who were to come later, concealing those who went before.

2 What was the base, what sort of raw matter was there and precisely how was it done, when the All-Maker, casting his eye on all, created the earth and revealed the sky in its glory?

3 With eyes on all sides and mouths on all sides, with arms on all sides and feet on all sides, the One God created the sky and the earth, fanning them with his arms.

4 What was the wood and what was the tree from which they carved the sky and the earth? You deep thinkers, ask yourselves in your own hearts, what base did he stand on when he set up the worlds?

5 Those forms of yours that are highest, those that are lowest, and those that are in the middle, O All-Maker, help your friends to recognise them in oblation. You follow your own laws, sacrifice your body yourself, making it grow great.

6 All-Maker, grown great through the oblation, sacrifice the earth and sky yourself. Let other men go astray all around; let us have here a rich and generous patron.

7 The All-Maker, the lord of sacred speech, swift as thought – we will call him today to help us in the contest. Let him who is the maker of good things and is gentle to everyone rejoice in all our invocations and help us.

The Sanskrit word *brahman* means: growth, evolution, outpouring or effusion, and prayer. Brahma (neuter) is the supreme, impersonal spirit. Brahma (the masculine form of the word) means the personal God, the creator. Towards the end of the Vedic period, there is increasing awareness both of Brahman, the supreme spirit, and of Brahma, the creator.

Brahman, the supreme, impersonal spirit, gave rise to the golden egg, according to another vision of creation in the Rig Veda. Hiraṇyagarba means, 'egg (seed, womb, or embryo) of gold'. It is the seed from which the universe is reborn in a new phase of time [*kalpa*]. The Rig Veda commands that Hiraṇagarba be worshipped as a god. Brahma (masculine) is the god who should be especially worshipped by the oblation of sacrifice; because sacrifice represents him; and represents the process of his coming to be.

The Unknown God, the Golden Embryo

RIG VEDA 10.121.

1. In the beginning the Golden Embryo arose. Once he was born, he was the one lord of creation. He held in place the earth and this sky. Who is the god whom we should worship with the oblation?

2. He who gives life, who gives strength, whose command all the gods, his own, obey; his shadow is immortality – and death. Who is the god whom we should worship with the oblation?

3. He who by his greatness became the one king of the world that breathes and blinks, who rules over his two-footed and four-footed creatures – who is the god whom we should worship with the oblation?

4. He who through his power owns the snowy mountains, and the ocean together with the river Rasā, they say; who has the quarters of the sky as his two arms – who is the god whom we should worship with the oblation?

5. He by whom the awesome sky and the earth were made firm, by whom the dome of the sky was propped up, and the sun, who measured out the middle realm of space – who is the god whom we should worship with the oblation?

6. He to whom two opposed masses looked with trembling in their hearts, supported by his help, on whom the rising sun shines down – who is the god whom we should worship with oblation?

7. When the high waters came, pregnant with the embryo that is everything, bringing forth fire, he arose from that as the one life's breath of the gods. Who is the god whom we should worship with oblation?

8. He who in his greatness looked over the waters, which were pregnant with Dakśa, bringing forth the sacrifice, he who was the one god among all gods – who is the god whom we should worship with the oblation.

9. Let him not harm us, he who fathered the earth and created the sky, whose laws are true, who created the high shining waters. Who is the god whom we should worship with the oblation?

10. O Prajāpati, lord of progeny, no one but you embraces all these creatures. Grant us the desires for which we offer you oblation. Let us be lords of riches.

Scholars have identified Dakśa as the male principle, or seed — in Vedic cosmology one principle devolves another, or indeed, one entity is another, from a subsequent point of view.

From the poetry of the Rig Veda three visions of God, or of the ultimate reality, are derived.

1. The Creator God — the lord of the sacrifice of the priest and of formal religion.
2. The personal God of love — friend of the devotee.
3. Brahma — the Supreme Being of Philosophy — from whom the levels of reality emanate.

The Golden Embryo is all of these. The mysterious poem points to the transition from the religion of sacrifice to that of devotion [*bhakti*], but equally points to the development of the philosophic view.

When we have breathed out we must then breath in. Hiranyagarba is the seed from which the cosmos grows, but it is also the seed to which the world returns at the end of each Kalpa, or cosmic period. Thus the movement of creation is followed the movement of dissolution. And with our individual lives the Karma of our deeds taints the seed-remnant of our being, at our dissolution; so that our spirits seek flesh once more and we are reincarnated.

CHAPTER 4

THE UPANISHADS

During the seventh century BC, there was a flowering of society in the North of India. The Vedic period of Indian history passed away. Kingdoms were established, cities flourished, and a greater social harmony was brought about by the welding of the different races into the cast system. From the groups of hermits dwelling in the forest, innumerable ashrams developed. They were often located near villages or towns and provided education for the young and training in scholarship, meditation and philosophy, for men and women of all ages.

From this period date the earliest Upanishads – the philosophical commentaries on the Vedas, painting a metaphysical picture of God and the Universe. The Ashrams, where they were written and studied, cultivated an exploration of consciousness of self; and an awareness of reality founded upon meditation and breath control, upon the study of philosophy and on discussion and upon the practice of austerity. Those who lived in the ashrams were pupils and teachers, rather than congregational priests. They were usually brahmins who had advanced, in youth or in old age, to the later stages of *vānaprasthya*, or *sāmnyasa*. Attendance at festivals and public ceremonials, long recitations of prayer, were not considered necessary. To this day there can be heated debate about the relative merits of the different approaches to the Ultimate; but the ashrams were always wholly part of the Hindu religion. The Hindu temple and the Hindu cult always have a philosophical aspect; just so the ashram has a religious aspect.

The prayer at the beginning of the Aitareya Upanishad sets out the ideal of the Ashram: to find God through the quest for truth and through adherence to the Veda; also through honesty between pupil and teacher. It may date from a later period — perhaps the fifth century BC.

Aitareya Upanishad – Prayer

> May my speech be based on the mind: may my mind be based on speech. O Self-effulgent One, reveal Thyself to me. May you both (speech and mind) be the carriers of the Veda to me. May not all that I have heard depart from me. I shall join together day and night through this study. I shall utter what is verbally true: I shall utter what is mentally true. May that (Brahman) protect me; may that protect the speaker (i.e. the teacher), may that protect me; may That protect the speaker – may That protect the speaker.
>
> Om Peace! Peace! Peace!

The Mandukya Upanishad is a metaphysical explanation of being and consciousness, experienced through meditation on Om.

Mandukya Upanishad

Om. This eternal Word is all: what was, what is and what shall be, and what beyond is in eternity. All is Om.

Brahman is all and Atman is Brahman. Atman, the Self, has four conditions.

The first condition is the waking life of outward-moving consciousness, enjoying the seven outer gross elements.

The second condition is the dreaming life of inner-moving consciousness, enjoying the seven subtle inner elements in its own light and solitude.

The third condition is the sleeping life of silent consciousness when a person has no desires and beholds no dreams. That condition of deep sleep is one of oneness, a mass of silent consciousness made of peace and enjoying peace.

This silent consciousness is all-powerful, all-knowing, the inner ruler, the source of all, the beginning and end of beings.

The fourth condition is Atman in his own pure state: the awakened life of supreme consciousness. It is neither outer nor inner consciousness, neither semi-consciousness, nor sleeping-consciousness, neither

> consciousness nor unconsciousness. He is Atman, the Spirit himself, that cannot be seen or touched, that is above all distinction, beyond thought ineffable. In the union with him is the supreme proof of his reality. He is the end of evolution and non-duality. He is peace and love.
>
> This Atman is the eternal Word Om. Its three sounds, A, U and M, are the first three states of consciousness, and these states are the three sounds.

As a small child, I was fascinated by the fact that I was conscious, that I had a mind and could think. I wondered that I could see the world as it is, and could also imagine it as I would like it to be. I would look in mirrors and behind mirrors and wonder at the experience of a 'me' that had the limitation of a single point of focus. I remember asking myself, 'Why am I 'Me'?'

I remember some years later, making an imaginary mark in the pointing of the wall of Saint Winefride's Church in Kew, and deciding that I would always remember that event. I suppose it was as a celebration of consciousness and existence – a trivial and arbitrary action, which, in some strange way, asserted my conscious existence as something greater than any other individual experience I could have.

And I remember, many years later again, as a young man, I stood in Richmond Library looking at the philosophy bookcase. On the top shelf was a large volume with a title, such as, 'On the nature of Being'; and I thought to myself: 'That's what I really want to study.'

At King's College, London, I delighted in the Philosophical Meditations of Descartes [1596–1650]. Descartes said: 'Cogito ergo sum' — 'I think, therefore I am.' Modern British philosophers of the analytic school have written much about this statement. Some have said it is a valid inference and some have said that it is not. Some have said that it is a meaningful statement and some have said it is not meaningful. To me 'the Cogito' was never a tautology and no mere clever remark; but an utterance of the profoundest philosophical truth. Perhaps I had a dim awareness that my own existence was, in some way, prior to any experiences I could undergo. The experience of Descartes, falling asleep exhausted, during a military campaign, in that chair by the fire of a peasant's cottage, when he dreamed he was sitting in an armchair by the fire; his waking confusion as to whether he was then asleep or awake; and the meditation that then engrossed him, are important events in the development of the thought of the Western World.

I was enthralled by the brilliant and deep lectures of Professor J. N. D. Findlay [1903–1987] on Descartes, Kant and Hegel. His lectures on Meinong, Bretano and Husserl were equally rich, but I could not follow his huge intellect into the depths of Phenomenology (or the philosophy of consciousness and experience.) Perhaps these depths would have helped me to grasp and enrich my own consciousness, which was what I was really seeking from philosophical studies.

I very much enjoyed my tutorials with Dr R. Ashby, our logic teacher. Under his guidance I made a slow and careful study of *Some Main Problems of Philosophy* of G. E. Moore, the Cambridge philosopher [1873–1958]. I was influenced by that thinker's careful, honest, analytic approach to his experience. I tried to write my essays in that style, assuming as little as possible; weighing the meaning and usage of each word. Moore questioned the assumptions of common sense, but always with the greatest respect. Philosophy remained, with him, a civilised discussion about how the world seems, and how it must, be.

Dr Ashby was a specialist in logic, but had a similar approach to philosophy, as did Dr G. Vesey. Dr Vesey's lectures were a model of commonsense analysis and careful use of words. Dr Pole lectured on modern British Philosophy. He conveyed a sense of the immediacy of personalities like Wittgenstein and Russell. That was very exciting indeed. Though possibly a follower of the school of logical analysis himself, Dr Pole always hid his own view. He had a brilliant awareness of the shortcomings of that school and of the difficulties of trying to look at the world without a sense of the beyond.

I remember reading *The Blue and Brown Books* of Ludwig Wittgenstein in early summer before finals in 1966. I was sitting on a bench in Kew Gardens. The clarity of what I read, and its detachment from any assumption, made me experience my experience, for some time, in a richer way.

After the years at King's, linguistic analysis and modern philosophy began to seem increasingly dry. I enormously missed the intellectual stimulus, the affection and the fun of the Philosophy department.

A few years later my father, Dominic Mulvey, met an Indian family in Kew, through his teaching of yoga. They gave him an article by Rabindranath Tagore [1861–1941], the poet and philosopher of Bengal, for me to read. I was struck by the deeply human and spiritual reaction to the West, and to technology, that the article evinced.

For some reason I did not read more of Tagore until years later still. I was tutoring the son of Dr Chatterjee who was a surgeon at the Hereford Hospital. Dr Chatterjee's grandfather had been a friend of Tagore. After lessons we talked for hours of philosophy and spirituality. He said that I would like Tagore's thought as it was similar to my own and that I would find Hindu thought sympathetic. He obtained for me a copy of 'Gitanjali'. 'Gitanjali' enthralled me and seemed poetry beyond poetry.

The thought of Tagore is steeped in the thought of the Vedas, where philosophy and poetry are one.

After reading his *Reminiscences* and his book, *Philosophy*, I began to study Hindu thought. One day I came across an excerpt from the Chandogya Upanishad, where the old man points out to the boy the minute space at the heart of the Nigrodha seed and says: *'tatt tvam asi'* –'That thou art'. It was a draught of refreshment from the everlasting font of knowledge; knowledge of consciousness and being; knowledge of the soul and God.

The Mundaka Upanishad sees the being of Brahman as a truth to be attained beyond all that can be called knowledge; and by other means than normal waking observation, or rational enquiry. Brahman is more real than the aggregates of energy points that make up ourselves and the objects of which we are conscious. The

Mundaka Upanishad sets out the aim of the student who meditates on 'Om', the sacred syllable [in Sanskrit *aum* – the neuter plural of 'all'].

Mundaka Upanishad
Part I
Chapter 1

Now there was a man whose name was Saunaka, owner of a great household, who approaching one day Angiras with reverence, asked him this question: 'Master, what is that which, when known, all is known?' The Master replied: 'Sages say that there are two kinds of wisdom, the higher and the lower.

The lower wisdom is in the four sacred Vedas, and in the six kinds of knowledge that help to know, to sing, and to use the Vedas: definition, grammar, pronunciation and poetry, ritual and the signs of heaven. But the higher wisdom is that which leads to the Eternal.

He is beyond thought and invisible, beyond family and colour. He has neither eyes nor ears; he has neither hands nor feet. He is everlasting and omnipresent, infinite in the great and infinite in the small. He is the Eternal whom the sages see as the source of all creation.

Even as the spider sends forth and draws in its thread, even as plants rise from the earth and hairs from the body of man, even so the whole creation arises from the Eternal.

By *tapas*, the power of meditation, Brahman attains expansion and then becomes primeval matter. And from this comes life and mind, the elements and the worlds and the immortality of ritual action.

From that Spirit who knows and sees all, whose *tapas* is pure vision, from him comes Brahma, the creator, name and form and primal matter.

Part II

Chapter 1

This is the Truth: As from a fire aflame thousands of sparks come forth, even so from the Creator an infinity of beings have life and to him return again.

But the spirit of light above form, never born, within all, outside all, is in radiance above life and mind, and beyond this creation's Creator.

From him comes all life and mind, and the senses of all life. From him comes space and light, air and fire and water, and this earth that holds us all …

Chapter 2

Radiant is his light, yet invisible in the secret place of the heart, the Spirit is the supreme abode wherein dwells all that moves and breathes and sees. Know him as all that is, and all that is not, the end of love – longing beyond understanding, the highest in all beings.

He is self-luminous and more subtle than the smallest; but in him rest all the words and their beings. He is everlasting *Brahman*, and he is life and world and mind. He is truth and life immortal. He is the goal to be aimed at: attain that goal, O my son!

Take the great bow of the Upanishads and place in it an arrow sharp with devotion. Draw the bow with concentration on him and hit the centre of the mark, the same everlasting Spirit.

The bow is the sacred Om, and the arrow is our own soul. Brahman is the mark of the arrow, the aim of the soul. Even as an arrow becomes one with its mark, let the watchful soul be one with him.

Perhaps the best-known British philosopher of the twentieth century was Bertrand Russell. He was actually born in 1872 and died in 1970.

When Bertrand Russell began writing, the view that material particles were the foundation of all phenomena was very popular. The then recent discovery of molecular particles and atomic elements, and contemporary research into sub-atomic particles, seemed to give enormous credence to the materialistic vision. Everything was made of atomic particles. The soul was considered to be the brain; the brain, a sort of biochemical calculator. Philosophy was merely a matter of polishing up the operations of that calculator, where it appeared to have got confused. This philosophy was often known as Positivism.

Russell was dissatisfied with positivism because he saw that it could never satisfactorily explain the phenomenon of consciousness. In *Analysis of Mind* and *Analysis of Matter*, he proposed his own theory of neutral monism.

According to this theory, the universe is made of innumerable minute points of view. The distinction between consciousness, or spirit, on the one hand, and matter, on the other, comes about as follows.

If some of these points of view are organised in one way we get a sense of a permanent subject which perceives, or sees, these points of view; or has them as its own experience. If another set of points of view are organised in another way we get a sense of an object, or a thing, which is permanent, and which has a history of being, seen, perceived or observed in various ways by various subjects. Every 'percept', as he called these points of view, occurs in at least one subject set, and at least one object set. From this we built notions of our individual selves and of the things we perceive.

Immanuel Kant [1724–1804] lived at Koenigsberg on the Baltic Sea and, for most of his life, he taught philosophy at that renowned University. He was one of the great luminaries of Europe.

Two important aspects of our seeing of things dominated his thought.

1. Any object we consider is divided into: a supporting substance or underlying object which possesses the qualities and dimensions we perceive, but which is not any one of those qualities or dimensions; and a set of qualities and dimensions which enable us to recognise and think about the object.
4. If I consider my own self, I immediately see a distinction between all the thoughts and feeling and experiences I have had, and the 'Me' which has had those thoughts, feeling and experiences. The 'Me' itself is somehow colourless and indescribable.

The Object we assume to be there, on an everyday basis, Kant called the Phenomenal Object. The self we accept as there while we are awake he called the Phenomenal Self.

He argued that there must be a Transcendental Self, whose laws of receiving information governed the way we see things and provided the regularity and the necessity we observe in the universe.

Beyond the Phenomenal Object, beyond the universe we know, he thought that there must be a Transcendental Object. He called this the 'transcendental *x*'.

The obvious necessity that there are these entities he called 'The Transcendental Argument'. This argument he considered not to be scientific or a logical proof, as normally understood. It did not yield information. We cannot say that we know that there is a Self, or that there are substances; but we cannot deny them. I must say that I find this proposition confusing, and even, confused.

Chuang Tzu, the Daoist sage, lived during the fourth century BC. He was born in the village of Wei, in what is now Honan province of China. The sage made this aphoristic comment on the problem of the Transcendental Argument.

> Hence, as the ground which the foot treads is small, and yet, small as it is, it depends on the untrodden ground to have scope to range, so the knowledge a man needs is little, yet little as it is he depends on what he does not know to know what is meant by 'Heaven'.

The Prasna Upanishad clearly distinguished between the phenomenological self and the Transcendental Self, as did Immanuel Kant. It teaches that the phenomenological self is really the Transcendental Self.

Prasna Upanishad IV: 9.

> And this one is the seer, feeler, hearer, smeller, taster, thinker, ascertainer, doer — the Purusa (pervading the body and senses), that is a knower by nature. This becomes wholly established in the supreme, immutable Self.

The mystics in the Islamic tradition are called Sufis. Jami was a Persian Sufi who died in 1492.

The aspects of God as Self or *atman*, and God as creator, desiring beauty – the beauty seen in the Garden of Eden – are experienced in Jami's poem. This is clearly a mystical vision, where the coming-to-be of beauty is an aspect of God's own mysticism, rather than a causal act of creation:

From all eternity the Beloved unveiled His beauty
in the solitude of the Unseen;
He held up the mirror to his own face, He
displayed His loveliness to Himself.
He was both the spectator and the spectacle, no eye
but his had surveyed the universe.
All was One, there was no duality, no pretence of
'mine' or 'thine'.

CHAPTER 5

HINDUISM

The Personal God

From the Pantheon of many Gods, The Vedas gradually emphasised the idea of a personal God who was to be worshipped through ritual and who required ethical conduct.

During, perhaps, the eighth century BC, another solar deity, Vishnu became increasingly popular. The name may be that, not of a Vedic god, but of a native god of northeast India, whose personality has been fused with Varuna. Varuna was the Vedic God with the all-seeing eye, who especially recognises right and wrong actions. Vishnu also has a strong ethical force, punishing wrong.

His solar and celestial aspects developed in a very special direction. He became the god of appearances.

The Hebrew Bible speaks of 'The face of God'. That is the aspect of God intelligible to mankind. Like Brahman, God in Himself, in the Bible, is unknowable. Like the ultimate Dao, Jaweh is unnameable. He is, however, able to present a special aspect of Himself to men — to reveal Himself.

The Hindus speak of Vishnu as 'the Personality of the Godhead.'

The poem 'The Three Strides of Vishnu' is one of the later hymns in the collection of the Ṛig Veda. Vishnu is seen as the celestial deity of a cattle tribe. Yet his 'three strides' are that: in first stride he steps over, or encompasses earth; in the second stride he steps over heaven; and, in the third stride, he steps over whatever is beyond heaven. Thus he is God.

The ideas involved in the three strides refer to the rich philosophical developments which were taking place and which led to the writing of the Upanishads.

The Three Strides of Viṣṇu.

RIG VEDA1.154.

1 Let me now sing the heroic deeds of Viṣṇu, who has measured apart the realms of the earth, who propped up the upper dwelling place, striding far as he stepped forth three times.

2 They praise for his heroic deeds Viṣṇu who lurks in the mountains, wandering like a ferocious beast, in whose three wide strides all creatures dwell.

3 Let this song of inspiration go forth to Viṣṇu, the wide-striding bull who lives in the mountains, who alone with but three steps measured apart this long, far-reaching dwelling-place.

4 His three footprints, inexhaustibly full of honey, rejoice in the sacrificial drink. Alone, he supports three-fold the earth and the sky — all creatures.

5 Would that I might reach his dear place of refuge, where men who love the gods rejoice. For there one draws close to the wide-striding Viṣṇu; there, in his highest footstep, is the fountain of honey.

6 We wish to go to your dwelling-places, where there are untiring, many-horned cattle. There the highest footstep of the wide-stepping bull shines brightly down.

Vishnu was associated with Brahma and Shiva in what is known as the Hindu trinity. Vishnu is the conserver; just as in nature the sun nurtures and preserves life. Brahma is the creator. Shiva is the destroyer. And, as in nature the sun enables us to see, Vishnu is the god of appearances. The Hebrew Bible has an equivalent in the concept of 'The Face of God'– that aspect of the supreme Being which enables us to see, or perceive Him.

Vishnu is known as the personality of the godhead. He can assume any form he wants. He can cause a vision in the mind of anyone. He can create a thought form which appears to be a human being and which can carry out actions in the world, but which is an illusion. He can be born, when he wishes, as a real human being, yet perfect. These perfect human beings are called avatars. When the world goes astray Vishnu appears in the world to lead men to truth. Narada, the first Hindu sage, is considered an avatar. Rama is an avatar. Arjuna, the hero of the Mahabharata, is considered an avatar.

For the Hindu, however, the greatest of all these incarnations is Krisha. Krishna, hero, sage and divine lover of mystics, is included in the Hindu trinity thus:

Brahma – Vishnu – Shiva

|

Krishna

Brahma is the god of prayer, of priests, and the creator of the universe. Vishnu (Krishna) is the god of appearances, the preserver of the universe and the punisher of evil. Shiva is the destroyer of the universe, the god of penance and austerity, and the bringer of death.

Brahma, who rose from the sea of being, woke up and looked around him, saw that there was nothing, was lonely, and created, corresponds to waking consciousness.

Vishnu, who appears, corresponds to dreaming sleep.

Shiva, the bringer of peace who terminates existence corresponds to dreamless sleep.

The deep sea of consciousless Being, blissful but unknowable, is Brahman. That is the silence surrounding 'aum' after the three syllables have been uttered, as the Mandukya Upanishad tells us.

The three persons of the Hindu trinity also correspond to the three gunas or metaphysical qualities of nature, according to Indian thought from time immemorial. Brahma is *sattva*, the happy contemplative principle – awake and looking about and bringing about existence. Vishnu is *rajas*, the active principle; because he intervenes in the affairs of men and preserves the world. Shiva is *tamas*, the dark, dull principle, because he brings death and unconsciousness.

Purana

During second century BC written collections of stories, shorter than the epics, appeared. These collections are called Puranas [*pūraṇa*]. They make the essence of Vedic teaching available to the common man. They provide endless versions of the creation and the destruction of the universe; and they also provide histories of kings and stories of the saints.

A Purana also contains many descriptions of the duties of the various castes. It also contains details of sacrifices, of festivals, of pilgrimages and all matters of religious concern.

Traditionally eighteen Puranas are recognised. Among the most important is Srimad Bhagavatam.

During the period of the Puranas, the building of temples began. The Greek invasion increased the influence of Hellenistic culture; and statues were made of the gods. The Vedic religion of open-air sacrifice and nature worship, and, indeed the religion of tribal membership, was finally transformed into the Hindu religion of temple services and rituals of image worship, which were carried out by temple congregations, or by families in homes.

The images of Shiva became increasingly important and the Puranas contain stories where Shiva appears as his own image, or *linga*. Sometimes the *linga* in these stories is simply a solid column of stone. In the later poetry of the sixth century AD, the linga could be a small stone worn around the neck of the devotee. Thus the ancient worship of standing stones was incorporated into the modern ritual and into the practice of meditation — that stone representing that aspect of ourselves, and, indeed, of the cosmos, which is most potent, most creative, and utterly unchanging.

In the Greek legend Atlas, the giant, stood on earth and supported heaven on his shoulders. He tried to trick the hero, Heracles, into taking on his burden. He failed, but Zeus, to console him, turned him into the Atlas Mountains, so that he might bear the weight of heaven more easily. In the Vedic poem, Purusha, the cosmic man, stands between heaven and earth and pushes them apart. The standing stones of Europe are visual forms of these legends. The standing stone also represents the conjugal union of heaven and earth, of male and female, as the heart of the process of creation.

The period of the Puranas is also that of the Sutras. Sutra, in Sanskrit, means, 'thread' — that which runs through things, supporting things and holding them together. The Sutras are books, which consist of a linked series of rules or principles. Different sutras view the world from quite different standpoints and they are the bases of different and contending schools of thought.

The Vaishesika Sutra was written by Kanāda about 300 BC. He studied a kind of alchemy [*rasavādam*]. The Sutra sees reality as made of eternal and indivisible atoms, known as the small [*anu*]. The atoms form basic molecules in twos [*dvyaṇuka*] and threes [*tryaṇuka*]. An ultimate being is denied, but the fact of consciousness is taken as evidence of a myriad of individual jivas, or spirits. The theory of Kanāda has been fully preserved and seems more advanced than the fragments we have of the Greek atomists. His interest is mainly in the material construction of reality, but he does not dismiss consciousness, as Democritus and Leucippus probably did.

The Nyaya Sutra is an investigation of logic, and the bases of knowledge. It was written by Gautama, probably during the third century BC. As Kanāda, Gautama did not believe in a supreme God, but in a myriad of individual, everlasting consciousnesses. The Nyaya has been linked to the Vaisesika system. The two systems are traditionally taken together as a joint school.

Patanjali probably lived sometime during the fourth century AD. Little is known of his life. The Yoga Sutra of Patanjali, however, is a text that has survived in full. It combines three elements of Indian thought.

1. The Saṁkhya with its metaphysical system of evolving entities.
2. The Yoga system of austerity (tapas) meditation and breath control.
3. The devotion to Krishna, or the religion of Krishna.

Yoga is derived from the Sanskrit root, *yuj*, meaning: join, link, yoke, fasten; prepare, make ready, unite, conjoin (of planets); concentrate, meditate and unite with the spirit. To my father Yoga meant: 'joining body to soul and man to God'. This is an excellent translation for the Westerner; bearing in mind that there is not such a clear distinction between matter and spirit in Indian philosophy; indeed, not such a clear separation between the divine and the human minds. My father believed, in any case, that in the original Greek and Christian tradition also, body and soul formed a unity. He thought that modern man had lost sight of this unity; and that the best way for him to understand yoga was to begin by understanding the earlier European view of things — the view perhaps of Plato. The term *yoga*, in the following excerpt is used in the sense of the Bhagavad Gita, as loving devotion and surrender to, and union with, Ishvara, the Lord, and the personal God.

These three elements form the philosophical and the religious basis, taken with the cults of Vishnu and Shiva, of the great Hindu epics — the Ramayana and the Mahabharata. These elements are especially emphasised and synthesised in the Bhagavad Gita, which is the crucial theistic revelation within the Mahabarata.

Shrimad Bhagavatam

The Srimad Bhagavatam was originally written at about the time of Christ. It is the Purana, or storybook, which sets out the Samkhya philosophical system, blending that system with devotional theism. Following in the footsteps, imprinted in the soil of the Indian subconscious, by the Bhagavad-Gita, the Purusha, or consciousness, is identified with the personal creator God, who regards mankind with infinite love and mercy, and yearns for men's souls to know and love Him in return; so that they can be released from bondage. God desires this release for men because of His infinite goodness. He is indifferent; because the good of mankind cannot be of any benefit to God, who is already perfect. In this cosmological vision, however, God is not necessarily the creator of Prakṛti. A gross mass of inert and meaningless matter is seen as always having existed; and as existing forever.

In the passage that follows, Kapila, the legendary founder of the Samkhya system, enlightens his mother, Devahuti, as to the ultimate nature of things. Kapila knows all, because he has been 'born free'. Kapila is born in the state of *moksa* – release –through the merciful providence God; so that he can teach the men of the epoch of Kali, who live in the darkness of gross ignorance, the knowledge that had been lost. Kapila, in the Hindu belief, is an *avatar*. Whenever men lose the truth, Hindus believe that God sends an *avatar* in order to lead them back to the true way. The process of straying and returning is seen as endless. Modern Hindus often consider that the Buddha and Jesus Christ are avatars.

The light of inner consciousness, which exists as the self of man, is also known as Purusha. The Purusha is self-luminous, without beginning and without end, and entirely separate from Prakṛti, or matter. The universe of name and form is the outcome of Prakṛti – that is, when the non-Self becomes deluded in Avidya [*āvidya*] and his consciousness becomes finite. The Purusha is eternal witness, always free, and never the performer of actions. All actions proceed from the Gunas of Prakṛti, but because of super-imposition and identification, the Purusha thinks himself their performer, though in reality he is blissful and free. He seems bound by Karma, and he seems to remain subject to birth and death, and is either happy of sorrowful. In the Shrimad Bhagavatam Devahuti asks Kapila a question.

Devahuti:

I understand that Prakṛti is the cause of this universe – subtle and gross. But, tell me, what is Prakṛti?

Kapila:

Prakṛti is that which, though undifferentiated, has within itself the cause of all differentiation. Prakṛti consists of three Gunas – Sattva, Rajas, Tamas. When these Gunas are in equilibrium, in perfect balance, the state is known as Prakṛti, or nature quiet and formless. When the balance of Gunas is disturbed, then is the universe projected.

The Purusha is without form, without attributes, changeless; therefore he cannot be the performer of actions. As the sun, though reflected in water, is not affected by the attributes of water, so the Purusha, though living in the body, is not affected by the attributes of the Gunas of Prakṛti. But because, through ignorance, the Purusha identifies himself with the Gunas, he seems to be happy or sorrowful and thinks himself the performer of actions. Hence his bondage to Karma, which subjects him to birth and death in this world, with the result that he is born as beast, man, angel, or god.

As the mind is allowed to cling to the world and to the objects of the world, attachment grows, and there comes delusion. He who desires to rise above the world must learn self-control by the practise of non-attachment.

> Follow the path of the Yoga of meditation. Be steadfastly devoted to God, and with a concentrated mind dwell in the thought of God.

It is important to note that Devahuti says that; 'Prakṛti is the cause of this universe – subtle and gross.' In Indian philosophy, the distinction between consciousness and its object is prior to the distinction between matter and spirit. Brahman is ultimately the consciousness in all beings. The souls of creatures, as well as their bodies, are derived from Prakṛti. The body is sometimes described as the outermost sheath of Brahman. There are six other sheaths, one, as it were inside the other. The second sheath, inside the body, is the subtle body or, *linga ṣarīra.* The *linga ṣarīra* may enable to us to feel certain perceptions about the material world, which are more delicate than the sensations of colour, heat or weight. We all experience a rich variety of aesthetic sensations: many people experience the sensation of a subtler energy moving about their bodies while they are doing Tai Chi or Yoga. This subtler energy seems also to radiate from the standing stones, or to hover above certain landscapes!

CHAPTER 6

MAHABHARATA

The Saṁnyāsin and the Aśrama

The brahmins frequently left their homes to wander the roads of India, begging alms, or to live in the forests, as hermits. They no longer then took part in public ritual sacrifices. They did not take their sacrificial fire with them. Sometimes their wives accompanied them. They became *saṁnyāsin*, meaning: one who lays aside, abandons, or is an ascetic.

The *saṁnyāsin* were wandering monks, hermits, or holy men. They hoped for a speedier release from their *karman* through the yoga of meditation and philosophical speculation. By avoiding sacrifices they hoped to avoid the *karman* that, paradoxically, the sacrifices must also cause; because a sacrifice can almost never be carried out perfectly. They often formed groups and lived as hermits, building primitive huts, as dwellings, around a small compound. From these beginnings the ashrams grew, as places where the scriptures were studied and systems of asceticism and meditation were taught. The meaning of *aṣramaṇa* is 'indefatigable', i.e. ascetic.

I remember watching a television programme about the Abyssinian monks at their monastery in Jerusalem. I wondered at these dark men, barefoot with unkempt hair and beard, and dressed in rough leather skirts. Suddenly I realised that they were the earliest monks – men from more developed agricultural societies who had returned, for personal and spiritual reasons to live the hunter-collector life.

Sacrifice [*yajña*], in Indian culture, is the re-enactment of the whole process of the cosmos; from the creation of the universe until its final reabsorbtion in God. The time period of each universe is called a *kalpa*. Sacrifice is purifying. Sacrifice, again, is also the enactment of the birth and death of an individual human being. Sacrifice purifies us of our faults; and leads us to a better incarnation, or to final release. Most Hindus have always practised sacrifice; though those more spiritually advanced avoid sacrifice because sacrifice also has negative aspects. These latter follow a more direct way to spiritual release.

A key concept of the sacrifice, and indeed of the Hindu cosmic view, is that of *ucchiśta*. The meaning of *ucchiśta* is literally: rejected, stale, spat out, the leavings of a meal — and thus, polluted food. The leavings of the meal are inferior, because leavings of the human body have touched them, at least spittle; or they have been discarded, either to be touched by animals, or to putrefy. Food offered to the Gods, on the other hand, must be of the purest kind and must then be further sanctified by burning in the sacrificial fire. Thus the leavings [*ucchiśta*] of the sacrifice [*yajña*] are pure. By the derivative process of opposites, these special leavings are not only edible, but also spiritually beneficial. They are '*śeṣa*' [remainder]. Sesha, however, is also is the name of the serpent coil [*kuṇdhalinī*], which is left after the universe has been absorbed into Brahman at the end of a cycle of time, or *kalpa*. Sesha is a powerful god.

Thus each ritual sacrifice not only represents, but also in essence is, the absorption and recreation of the universe. It is the nature of all ritual that the thing, which represents, is identified with the thing represented; because of the oneness of form. This absorption [*pralaya*] of the world into Brahman is a cleansing and a new beginning. Literally, *pralaya* can mean, 'melting', as of snow. At the religious sacrifices, all of which are repeated periodically, the destruction of unresolved and bad *karman* takes place; for the period of time which has elapsed since the last ceremony. As with the cosmos, so with the religious sacrifice, a *sesa* is left, which is as pure or impure as the intention and meticulousness of the sacrificer and the participants. As with the old universe, this *sesa* contains *bīja* – seeds – of new *karman*. The intersecting lines of these *karman*, or causal deeds, constitute *dharma*. Each individual soul rolls through his *dharma* towards final release – *moksa*: perhaps visiting a heaven on the way, if one is of the Purva Mimamsa school of thought.

But not only the remains of food burnt before the gods are *sesa*. Food offered to ancestors, food given to brahmin guests, food given by the student [brahmacārin] to his teacher [ācārya], are all instances of sacrifice [*yajña*]. Thus pupils always beg food of the public. They then offer this food to their guru. After he has finished cooking and eating, his students eat the leavings. At home, the brahmin guest, or else the father of the household, always eats first. Thereby the rest of the meal becomes *sesa*. Thus home and ashram are places of sacrifice; and daily life is sacred.

The brahmin, who is the officiating priest at a temple, is usually a vegetarian. He may not eat food that has been touched by a non-brahmin, because for him that would be impure. Thus the ceremonial meal in a temple is always cooked by the officiating brahmin priest.

During the fourth century BC, the Laws of Manu were written down. To the Hindu, the Laws of Manu are the Ten Commandments and, to a certain extent, the equivalent of Leviticus, Numbers and Deuteronomy. (The Brahamanas, however, the priestly commentary of the Vedas, added over many centuries, give details of ritual prescriptions. These books are of greater length than those early books of the Bible.) The Laws of Manu lay down how life is to be lived by priest and by layman, if one may make that distinction and apply it to Hindu society.

These writings set out the four great aims of Hindu life: *dharma* or righteousness, *artha* or wealth, *karman* or enjoyment, and *moksa* or spiritual freedom. *The Code of Manu*, a metrical work of 2,685 verses, sets out these aims and the details of their accomplishment in a series of clear statements and firm commands. The Epics, at huge length, provide illustrations of these aims and inculcate them in the Hindu mind by means of image and story. And, thereby, the Epics have created Indian civilisation.

> The brahmins, according to the laws of Manu, lived in four stages:
>
> 1 Student – *brahamacārin*. One who has completed his studentship is a *snātaka*.
> 2 Householder – *gṛhastha*.
> 3 Hermit – *vanaprastha*
> 4 Wandering ascetic – *saṁnyāsin*.

The laws of Manu laid down prescriptions for brahmins who left home to dwell in the forests. These rules encapsulate all the stages of the evolution of monasticism at once. In the Christian and Hebrew worlds, the origins of modern monasticism can only be dimly perceived in the Bible and in the remnants of Abyssinian tradition.

The Forest-dweller

1. A twice-born *snātaka*, who has thus lived according to the law in the order of householders, may, taking a firm resolution and keeping his organs in subjection, dwell in the forest, duly (observing the rules given below).

2. When a householder sees his (skin) wrinkled, and (his hair) white, and the sons of his sons, then he may resort to the forest.

3. Abandoning all food raised by cultivation, and all his belongings, he may depart into the forest, either committing his wife to his sons, or accompanied by her.

4. Taking with him the sacred fire and the implements required for domestic (sacrifices), he may go forth from the village into the forest and reside there, duly controlling his senses.

5. Let him offer those five great sacrifices according to the rule, with various kinds of pure food fit for ascetics, or with herbs, roots, and fruit. …

28. Or the hermit who dwells in the forest may bring (food) from a village, receiving it either in a hollow dish (of leaves), in his (naked) hand, or in a broken earthen dish, and may eat eight mouthfuls.

29. These and other observances must a brahmin who dwells in the forest diligently practise, and in order to attain complete (union with) the (supreme) Self, (he must study) the various sacred texts contained in the Upanishads,

30. (As well as those rules and texts) which have been practised and studied by the sages (*ṛṣi*) and by brahmin householders, in order to increase their knowledge (of Brahman), and their austerity, and in order to sanctify their bodies; ...

These instructions are filled with the deepest respect that the Hindu has for his ancestors, and redolent with his very great appreciation of the delight of life in the forest.

The Indian consciousness has never lost the memory of the simplicity and goodness of the life of wild men; the memory of an existence closer to nature, closer to man's true self and, thus, closer to God.

As a species, our bodies, our senses and our minds evolved as forest hunters, and as collectors of food. Life in the forest enabled us to use the faculties of our human nature to the fullest possible degree.

That life provided perhaps the greatest satisfaction in living that mankind has ever experienced. The natural overflowing of man's soul with a sense of conscious fullness and delight – perhaps at a heightened moment of gratification or of satisfaction, or just at the end of each day – was the most perfect meditation or prayer. Our delight in the world that God has created and our deep happiness in existing, say to God a perfect 'thank you'. In modern religion, too much prayer and too many thanks are based on a sense of obligation, rather than of joy.

The delight of life in the forest is celebrated in the Indian epic, the Ramayana. In the following incident we visit a forest hermitage. Rama and his wife Sita have been banished from Ayodhya, the royal court of Rama's father, Dhrita-Rashtra. Rama has been the victim of his jealous stepmother's intrigue. Rama, Sita, and faithful brother Lakshman take refuge in the forest at the ashram of Valmiki. Valmiki is the legendary author of the Ramayana itself. Valmiki actually plays his part in the story he tells. In the following description the *ślokas* of Valmiki (late Sanskrit couplets) are rendered into English 'Hiawatha metres' by Romesh Chandra Dutt [1848–1909], the Victorian scholar.

Ramayana — Valmiki's Hermitage

And the wanderers from Ayodhya on the river's margin stood,
Where the unknown realm extended mantled by unending wood.
Gallant Lakshman with his weapons went before the path to clear,
Soft-eyed Sita followed gently, Rama followed in the rear.
Oft from tree and darksome jungle, Lakshman ever true and brave,
Plucked the fruit or smiling blossoms and to gentle Sita gave,

Oft to Rama turned his consort, pleased and curious evermore,
Asked the name of tree or creeper, fruit or flower unseen before.

How can we avoid a comparison (or a contrast) with the iambic pentameters of William Shakespeare? The pastoral life was a cherished theme of classical and renaissance literature in the west. In this description of the forest of Arden the mystical Duke Senior expresses that very early cosmic vision of universal consciousness.

As You like It
Act II Scene 1
The Forest of Arden.
Enter Duke Senior, Amiens, and two or three Lords, like foresters.

DUKE SENIOR: Now, my co-mates and brothers in exile,
Hath not old custom made this life more sweet
Than that of painted pomp? Are not these woods
More free from peril than the envious court?
Here do we feel but the penalty of Adam,
The seasons' difference, as the icy fang
And churlish chiding of the winter's wind,
Which, when it bites and blows upon my body,
Even till I shrunk with cold, I smile and say
'This is no flattery: these are counsellors
That feelingly persuade me what I am.'
Sweet are the uses of adversity,
Which, like toad, ugly and venomous,
Wears yet a precious jewel in his head;

And this our life exempt from public haunt
Finds tongues in trees, books in the running brooks,
Sermons in stones and good in everything.
I would not change it.

AMIENS: Happy is your grace,
That can translate the stubbornness of fortune
Into so quiet and so sweet a style.

DUKE SENIOR: Come, shall we go and kill us venison?
And yet it irks me the poor dappled fools,
Being native burghers of this desert city,
Should in their own confines with forked heads,
Have their own haunches gored.

Mahabharata

There are three phases in the development of the human ethic:

1. The code of revenge by which wrong is righted by one individual against another individual.
2. The code of justice whereby the king punishes wrongdoing on behalf of society.
3. The code of peace and forgiveness, which is the ashramic order.

The Mahabharata illustrates the three ethical orders together.

The forest life, as a life sought by a retiring brahmin, seems an idyll of peace and delight. But the consciousness of the earlier hunter-gatherer had had its darker side. The Brahamanas were priestly commentaries on the Vedas. They give insight into the meaning of the rituals. Their textual corpus is enormous, being many times longer than Deuteronomy. The Satapatha Brahmana gives us an amazing understanding of consciousness of an earlier phase of humanity; explaining the primitive idea of *karma* as the revenge of injured nature. The commentary tells how Bhragu, the son of Varuna, witnessed the vengeance, not only of animals, but also of trees, plants and waters. All, in this vision, appear as human beings. In the vision of ancient man consciousness is primary Being and all beings are conscious. Indeed, all beings were seen as men and women. All consciousness has equal status; all living things have equal status. Man at this point in the evolution of his view of himself had no superiority in the universe of Being. The universe and all things in it being conscious, man at this stage had no sense of God as separate from that universe. There was no idea of a personal God; but rather the vision of a personal cosmos. The guilty hunter felt that he outraged that cosmos and the beings in it. He felt watched. He had no fear of God; but nevertheless he was afraid. This dream story in the Satapatha Brahamana is an explanation of the *agnihotra* sacrifice. This sacrifice is one of the most important Hindu rituals. In the Hindu home today it can simply consist of an early morning recitation and the pouring of some milk onto the newly lit fire.

> Bhragu, the son of Varuna, thought he knew more than his father. Varuna noticed this and said, 'Go my son towards the east. When you have seen what you will have seen, go towards the south; then towards the west; then towards the north; then towards the northeast. And then come and tell me what you have seen.'

Bhragu, then, went to the east, and saw, O horror! Men who were dismembering men, tearing them limb from limb as they said: 'Here's one for you and one for me!' He said, 'What a horrible thing! Woe is me! These men here who dismember men, who tear them limb from limb!' They replied, 'This is how they treated us *(asacanta)* in the other world, now we are returning them the favour *(pratisacamahe)'*. Bhragu said, 'Is there no expiation *(prayascitti)* for this?' 'There is one'. 'What is it?' 'Your father knows what it is'.

To the south, he saw men who cut men into pieces.

To the west, it was men who, sitting silently, were devoured by other men sitting silently.

To the north, men who screamed, and were eaten by men who screamed.

To the south, west and north, Bhragu asked the same questions and received the same answers.

To the north-east, he saw two women, the one beautiful and the other surpassingly beautiful. Between these two women is a black man, with yellow eyes, who holds a stick in his hand. Seeing him, Bhragu is seized with terror. He returns to his father and sits down. His father says to him, 'Learn, then your Vedic lesson. How is it that you have not learned your lesson?' Bhragu answers, 'What is it that I should learn? There is

> nothing to learn anyway'. Then Varuna knows: 'Indeed, he has seen'. And he says to his son, 'The men you saw to the east were trees. When one throws onto the fire logs one has taken from trees, one becomes the lord of trees, and conquers the world of trees. The men you saw to the south were animals. When one makes an offering of milk, one becomes the lord of animals and conquers the world of animals. The men you saw to the west were plants. When one lights up the milk of the *agnihotra* with a flaming piece of straw, one becomes the lord of plants and conquers the world of plants. The men you saw to the north were the waters. When one pours water into the milk of the *agnihotra,* one becomes lord of the waters and conquers the world of the waters. Of those two women, the beautiful and the surpassingly beautiful, the beautiful one is Belief; when one offers the first libation of the *agnihotra,* one becomes master of Belief, one conquers Belief. The surpassingly beautiful woman is Non-Belief: when one offers the second libation, one becomes lord of Non-Belief and conquers Non-Belief. As for the black man with the yellow eyes, he is Wrath. When, after having poured water into the spoon, one pours the libation into the fire, one becomes the lord of Wrath and conquers Wrath. And, in truth, anyone who, knowing this, offers the *agnihotra*, becomes lord of all things and conquers everything.'

It is, thus, in Hindu thought that man became lord of creation and acquired a right to make use of its creatures.

Early man had a sense of guilt when using or harming other creatures. The Jaina philosophy is entirely pacific in nature and its adherents have always been strictly vegetarian. Buddhist monks are forbidden to carry out horticulture; it involves transplanting and culling the plants. The Buddhist laity are generally allowed to eat meat, but their grace before a meat meal thanks the animal for the gift of its life. These religions have involved a certain separation from everyday life and politics. To my knowledge there has never been, and I imagine there never could be, a Jaina state. When states have adopted the Buddhist faith the defence of the state has involved a compromise. Until the communist invasion in 1949, Tibet was policed by bands of strong monks armed with wooden staves. That was a remarkable achievement for an earlier type of society.

But the Hindu religion could never be separated from Indian society. It is that society. Some Hindus are celibate, some are married, and some have many wives. For a woman to have several husbands is normally utterly forbidden; but sects have been known where this was allowed. In the Mahabharata, Queen Draupadi marries all of the Pandava brothers. This is probably the memory of prehistoric custom. Such memories often occur in religious scriptures. Hinduism does not purge these memories; it respects all stages of human evolution. It does not seem to worry about scandal caused.

Since Vedic times until recently, a professional warrior class [*kśatriya*] has ruled India. The root *kśi* means: to possess, have power over, or rule. The *kśatriya* are those who possess supernatural or political power; who have dominion. Their religion was based on a code of honour and duty. Pride was a virtue. Their meditation probably included yogic exercises, which strengthened the physique [*āsana*]. They developed concentration through archery and the practise of arms. To revenge a wrong done to his family, to his tribe, or to his king was the first duty of the warrior.

The mystery of Hinduism is that it includes such religious and philosophical opposites. Just as the ritual is included with its opposite of philosophy, so both pacific approaches are then included with the diametrically opposed warrior cults. Religion cannot be here used in the western sense of universal church membership. Religion is the cult of a certain group, which has its own dharma — its own code of special duties. For the brahmin, whether ritualist or philosopher, non-violence was the essential way. For the *kśatriya* the willingness to fight was a necessity. For the *kśatriya* revenge was a virtue; it was the personal involvement in and the carrying out of the law of karma. And all these things were the warrior's dharma. The peaceful, and the contrasting, violent attitudes of Hinduism are its vision of cosmic harmony. Its acceptance of these extremes is the source of psychological balance for the individual and for society. Good and evil are aspects of Being, which, as One, is the ultimate Good.

Revenge is, in earlier Indian thought, a natural emotion and a worthy act.

> When a man has repaid the evil done him by another when he was in distress, by one who mocked him in hard times, it is, I think as if he were born again.

The tissue of the Mahabharata is woven from themes of revenge. There is no word that is equivalent to 'revenge' in Sanskrit. The epics contain terms like 'reaction' [*pratikāra*] and 'reward' [*pratikāriya*].

Retribution in the epics is considered a sacred duty and an essential human passion. Retribution in the stories is not a matter of fair combat but, often, of murder and treachery. The saga of the Mahabharata begins with resentment of the Kurus. This jealousy results in a horrid destruction of the Pandavas' wealth and position by the Kurus. The Kurus are cruel to the Pandavas' queen, and they abuse her. The murder or killing of a relative, even in an accident, necessitates revenge by another member of the family, or by one who owes loyalty to that family. Thus can develop a process of revenge and counter revenge that is endless.

The causality [*karman*] of these stories is, however, submitted to an account of the workings of society and to the total force of causality in the cosmos. Both of these ideas are included in the signification of the term *dharma*. The vicious behaviour of the individual is the symptom and, in turn, the cause, of the decline of the cosmological era, before its dissolution [*yugānta*]. The path of the individual is seen in relation to the totalities of family, society and cosmos. The Pandava princes, on a purely worldly level, lack the qualifications to rule. King Pandu prefers the forest life to the throne. Thus the final battle of the Mahabharata is the dissolution of the failing ruling families. A purified remainder [*sesa*] is left, by the arrangements of the gods, so that all things can begin again. These pure individuals are the *sesa* of society — just like the *sesa*, or remainder, of each meal; and again, just like at the *pralaya*, the *sesa* of the entire universe.

However worthy their motives as individuals, these Pandava princes have been disloyal to their original princely dharma, by adopting the way of renunciation, which is the ascetic life. The kshatriya is a ruler in essence. But the king himself is more than a kshatriya. He can rise above the warrior's code. He has the right to punish. Punishment is a higher and a more worthy act than revenge. The king may punish lightly or forgive. Advised by the brahmin, he can use his power to punish wrong and to purify his kingdom. But he cannot be entirely pacific.

The Laws of Manu lay down the role of the king, as the punisher of wrong. Yama is the king of the dead and the god of death. The meaning of *yama* is 'control', or 'repression'. Yama is the ancestor of the human race; that is why we all have to die. He is the personification of the dharma; and as his children we are part of, and are, the dharma. Thus death is seen as part of control; both social and cosmic — an aspect or *ṛta*, the ultimate principle of the cosmos. Yama has a son called Punishment [*dandha*]. When the king administers punishment, vengeance is regulated in accordance with the dharma, and it no longer threatens the cosmic process.

7.14 It is for the sake of the king, says Manu, that (in the beginning) the creator produced his son punishment [*dandha*], which is nothing other than *dharma*, and which consists of the flame of the *brahman.*

7.17 It is punishment that is truly the king, it is he who is the male, the leader, he who ordains, who is the guarantor of *dharma* for the four stages of life. It is punishment alone that governs all the creatures, who alone protects them, who alone watches over them while they sleep. The sages declare: punishment is *dharma*

1.20 If the king did not punish, without cease, those who deserve to be punished, the strong would fry the weak like fishes on a skewer; the mob would eat the sacrificial cake, the dog would come and lick the offerings, no one would be able to hold on to his possessions, inferiors would take the place of their superiors . . .

1.24 Every class would be corrupted and every barrier broken; every man would be enraged at every other man were punishment to go astray. But there where black punishment keeps watch with red eyes, there where he annihilates the evil ones, the people do not go astray, so long as he who inflicts punishment has the right perspective.

The meaning of *karma* is that every action of a man returns to that man as the doer of the deed. The directness of the return varies. The return may be immediate, later, or very much later; even in another incarnation. For this reason our use of the world necessitates vengeance. Not only do we fear revenge from the animals we kill or use and from other men we have offended, but our use of plants, of water and of the elements of the cosmos also deserves to be avenged. And again we have offended the gods. The ritual of sacrifice is fundamentally to assure, that he who eats in this world is not eaten in the next!

There are many levels in the Mahabharata, as in all Hindu scriptures. The Pandavas have betrayed their dharma as warrior kings, in refusing to revenge or punish and in taking to the peaceful life of the forest. But is this not an ethical advance? Is this not a truer step towards escape from karma towards release [*moksa*] from reincarnation? And furthermore does not the chaos brought about by the kings' following of a higher dharma actually speed the process of decline and make a new beginning for society possible. Shiva is lord of decline and equally lord of ascetics. This new social beginning coincides, in the epic imagination, with the rebirth of the cosmos.

An Indian pupil once told me that his father would take him for walks and tell him stories of the Mahabharata and the Ramayana. The family did not tell these stories in the home lest the harmony of home might be disturbed. I think that the Hindu religion has always been taught this way, before temples were built, or, indeed, whenever temples could not be visited.

The Mahabharata tells of the struggle between the sons of Pandu, who were called Pandavas, and their rivals, the Kurus.

> At one time king Pandu ruled the Kurus, but he died while his children were young; and his brother, Dhrita-rashtra succeeded to the throne. Dhrita-rashtra had one hundred

sons. He reared the Pandavas along with his own sons, under the tutelage of Bhisma, his brother; and under the instructions of Drona, the brahmin, who taught meditation and the mystical control of weapons.

Just as later, in the Zen monasteries of China and Japan, the art of the bow was practised, so, in ancient India, archery was the foremost method of teaching concentration, and thus meditation and spirituality, as well as the necessary management of the weapon itself.

Of all the princes the third son of Pandu, Arjuna, was the most godlike, the most strong and the most skilled in the use of weapons. He was really the son of Indra, the god. Yudhishthira, the eldest of Pandu's sons, excelled in courtesy, learning, self-control and princely virtue; but he had a fatal weakness for gambling – thus for dicing with fate, rather than following his dharma; and thus surrendering to the lower laws of the cosmos rather than reaching above. Bhima, another son of Pandu, was a stalwart fighter.

The five sons of Pandu thus won love and acclaim; but they also inspired jealousy.

The eldest son of Dhrita-rashtra was Durodhan. Durodhan was determined to succeed to the entire Kuru kingdom, the rightful inheritance of the Pandava brothers.

Hearing that the five princes wished to visit a great historic city in the East, Durodhan arranged for a huge palace of pure lacquer (clearly symbolising attachment to the ephemeral and something easily purged by fire) to be built there, to house them with there mother, queen Kunti. His plot was to burn them all alive. A counter-intrigue, however saved the Pandavas and queen Kunti. They all escaped into the forest.

Thus began, for the Pandavas, their first period of wandering, of destitution and of harmony with nature. It was a time of continual meditation and asceticism; arrived at in an unselfconscious way. It was a time of preparation of the spirit for the future struggle with their enemies and cousins, the Kurus; and on a deeper level, the struggle to realise themselves as free from the chains of causality which bring men into conflict with one another and which are called 'karma'.

Drupada, the king of the Panchalas, another powerful tribe, announced a great contest – a *svayaṁvara*. He offered the hand of his beautiful daughter, Draupadi, as the prise. The chief event of this *svayaṁvara* was the stringing of the giant bow and the shooting of five arrows through a golden ring, suspended by a fine thread from the bough of a giant tree, some distance away. Only the mighty Arjuna achieved this feat. He thus won the bride, Draupadi, for himself and, strangely, for his four brothers.

Thus the five sons of Pandu returned to live in civilisation. Their popularity became immense. Durodhan's jealousy increased. But Drona, the brahmin, and Bhisma, the uncle, who had reared both the Kurus and the Pandavas, persuaded Dhrita-Rashtra to give to the sons of Pandu the desert half of his kingdom.

The heroes organised their new kingdom with immense energy and skill. They irrigated the desert and laid out verdant champagnes; they encouraged and subsidised agriculture and industry, arts and crafts; and they built the magnificent city of Indra-prastha.

Prince Yudhishthira now feels that he should become king and that a coronation sacrifice should be held. His advisers enthusiastically agree; but lord Krishna alone engages him in the true dialogue where every aspect of the matter is considered and by which a monarch should prepare himself for such a decision. They discuss the state of the country and the state of the surrounding tribes; what rivals have to be defeated and what alliances have to be cemented before the kingdom is ready for the sacrifice.

The minute details of the sacrifice and their symbolic importances are carefully discerned and Yudhishthira determines that they should be carried out exactly. (This section of the epic is an exposition of statecraft and constitutional theory.)

When the preparations for the sacrifice are finally ready and the illustrious guests are arriving, there comes one called Narada and he has inner sight. Seeing Lord Krishna, Narada is blind to the glitter and the festivity and becomes lost in worship.

Bhisma also recognises Krishna as the Lord and as the incarnation of God. On his advice Yudhishthira offers homage to Krishna first; as one taking precedence over all the royal guests.

And so, at this sacrifice, Krishna was first recognised.

After the sacrifice Durodhan remained for many days as a guest in his cousins' palace. He enjoyed the many wonders of the buildings. Coming upon a room with a crystal floor, he lifted his clothes to bathe. He tried to walk through doors of glass and would not walk through open doorways. He walked into a pool of water with his clothes on, thinking that it was empty. He was much confused and became the butt of many jokes. He could not tell the difference between reality and illusion; because he could not tell the difference between God and maya; between his own true Self and his temporal, artificial self. But this only increased his jealousy of the sons of Pandu and his desire for revenge.

His adviser Sakuni, the evil brahmin, was full of wicked tricks. He was also a master with dice. Sakuni began to yearn for another victim in the game. He persuaded his master, Durodhan and the king, Dhrita-rashtra, after their return to Hastinapurna, to arrange a tournament of dice. Thus a royal challenge was sent to Yudhishthira.

Yudhishthira's advisers were dismayed when they heard of the challenge and who the players were to be. They begged their king not to take part. But regal pride and his thirst for the dice got the better of Yudhishthira. He accepted the challenge, saying,

'I think it is the call of fate.' And so he cast aside his freedom.

The court assembles at Hastinapurna and the guests arrive. After a ceremonial entry and a fanfare of trumpets, Yudhishthira sits down. He begins to throw the dice, in an atmosphere of solemnity. Sakuni's low cunning causes him to win throw after throw; but still Yudhishthira gambles on in a manic frenzy. He stakes all he possesses: treasures, chariots, horses, cattle, jewels, servants; and then he loses. He then stakes his kingdom and again he loses. He stakes his four brothers and himself and again he loses. Finally he stakes the queen, Drapaudi. And at last he has lost everything.

Dhrita-Rashtra at that point hears animals of ill omen, calling outside his palace: the jackal, the ass and the birds of death. Advised by Bhisma and Drona, he agrees to let the Pandavas keep their wife, their freedom and their kingdom, asking them to surrender only their possessions.

The five princes and their noble queen hand over all their possessions and set out on the road.

However, the vengeful Durodhan persuades the pliant Dhrita-Rashtra to allow a further game. If the Pandavas win, they will regain everything; if they lose they will live in the forest as free hermits.

Once again Yudhishthira cannot resist the fatal challenge. He returns to the palace at Hastinapurna and the court is reassembled.

Sakuni and Yudhishthira sit opposite one another and the chequered board is set out once more; this time ready for the players to throw only once each. In silence again the fatal dies are cast. Prince Yudhishthira loses.

Thus began the twelve years of banishment of the sons of Pandu, queen Drapaudi and queen Kunti, their mother.

The Mahabharata tells the story of the exile at length; incorporating many legends of appearances of Shiva and the other gods and explaining methods of asceticism and the achievement of just ends through prayer and sacrifice.

Of the five sons of Pandu, Arjun was the greatest warrior. He was also the holiest of the five. Arjun wished to obtain divine weapons in order to redeem the honour of his brothers and to end the tyranny of Durodhan. In the material world wickedness has an obvious advantage. In order for the just to succeed, divine help is always needed, however great the prowess and the intelligence of the epic hero.

An old hermit, who was really the god Indra, told Arjun that he must go to mount Indrakila, in the Himalayas, and pray and fast. Then he must sacrifice to a clay image of Shiva – a sort of standing stone, called a '*linga*'.

Arjun did as he was bid and fasted and prayed; till after three months he was able to live on air alone. For hours he stood on one leg and his face shone radiantly. The area around where he stood was warm with the energy of his '*tapas*'.

Arjun then made his *linga* and began to recite the special mantra. Suddenly a boar rushed out of the undergrowth; and, with the instant reaction of a hunter, Arjun leased a dart from his bow. But before his dart stuck home, another dart transfixed the animal. Looking up Arjuna saw a huntsman with his followers. The hunter had long black hair and rough leather garments. He appeared to be a mountain king. Arjun immediately fired all his remaining darts at his rival; but the body of the mountain king seemed to absorb them.

'Then we must wrestle,' said Arjun; and he grasped hold of the mountain king.

But the king stretched out his right hand and plunged it into the chest of Arjun. The hand squeezed Arjun's heart and he was suddenly filled with love. All desire to struggle ceased and Arjun immediately turned to carry on his devotion to the Linga. He decked it with a garland of white flowers. Immediately he saw that the king was wearing the garland. Arjun realised who the mountain king really was; and he prostrated himself in adoration. Shiva gave Arjuna the Gandiva, the divine bow, and other divine weapons, which would give a certain victory over the enemies of the Pandavas.

Eventually the long exile of the Pandavas came to an end. They gathered a large army of all their allies, of whom the most numerous were the Panchalas, and marched to fight the Kurus. All the threads of the long story meet and come to an end at the great battle. The karmas of all the characters in the epic come to a resolution. In the battle brother fights brother, nephew kills uncle and cousin slays cousin. Humanity is devastated because all the warriors are slain except the five Pandava brothers.

On the eve of the final day of the great battle the good Arjun sits in his chariot, in despair; seeing the sadness of the plight of all mankind. Arjun realises that whatever action is taken the outcome must be disastrous. Should the Pandavas refuse to fight, tyranny and impiousness would triumph: should the Pandavas fight and win civilisation would nevertheless be destroyed.

We now come to a late insertion into the epic. This addition from the second century BC is called the Bhagavad Gita. The Bhagavad Gita is an exposition of the Samkhya system of philosophical, ascetic and moral teaching. It leaves behind the Vedic religion of Sacrifice and priestly intercession and points the way to the later Hindu religion of personal service and devotion to God. The Bhagavad Gita is the revelation of Krishna to Arjun. The dialogue appears in later versions of the Mahabharata.

Hitherto the emphasis of religion in the epic had been the devotion to Shiva. Now the religion of Krishna appears.

> At the moment of Arjun's despair the god Krishna appears to Arjun and speaks to him the words of consolation which are the Bhagavad Gita. Krishna tells Arjun that even the noblest end of natural virtue that Arjun has achieved, that is the desiring of the good of mankind, is still a form of materialism, and indeed of selfishness. A man must act only because the action is right. He must not act in order to achieve a good direct causal result. Arjun must fight to defend his honour as a prince; and for that end only. The practical outcome, whatever it is, must be a matter of indifference. Arjun is thus relieved of his despair. He was defeated because he could not achieve the end of life that his human reason had conceived. He now sees that he can always achieve the supreme good, because that good is personal and spiritual. He must live a life of complete detachment from worldly aims and thus achieve true bliss. The truest way to achieve this is by the pure love of Krishna as a person—the yoga of devotion.

In the Mahabharata and in the Ramayana the emphasis is not on sin and guilt but upon blindness [*avidyā*] and *karman*. Dhrita-rashtra had in his youth made a fatal mistake. The sufferings of his descendants can be traced to this error. He had been a skilled archer and a redoubtable hunter. One day while out hunting in the forest he came upon a young bull elephant; and he pursued it to get a good aim. The bull elephant disappeared into a thicket. Dhrita-rashtra, seeing a branch moving and hearing a sound, drew back his bow and released the arrow at the exact spot. He was horrified to hear a human cry. He rushed through the bushes to where he found a young hermit dying, pierced by the arrow. Dhrita-rashtra was filled with pity and did what he could to help. The young man, with glazed eyes, begged Dhrita-rashtra to find his aged parents and to tell them what had happened, and then he lay back and died. Dhrita-rashtra did as he was bid. He found the parents outside their simple hut in a small clearing of the forest, spread with kusa grass; and piteous was the cry of the aged pair when they realised they had lost their only support. He expressed his sorrow for what he had done and promised them to be their son instead. But nothing could change what had happened; and the evil effects of the misdeed ran their course. Thus the Pandavas were ill fated. Dhrita-rashtra was guilty of the crime of killing a hermit.

Blindness of course is the human condition. In a sense Dhrita-rashtra could not help what he had done. Wrong in Indian thought comes from existential condition. Things are that way; we simply have to learn. The process of *samsara*, of wandering on, is a gradual understanding, a seeing of the truth [*vidya*].

The ancient Hebrew idea of sin is wholly different from the Indian idea of karma. Sin cannot occur just through ignorance though ignorance is always involved. The story of Adam and Eve, in the book of Genesis, is a story of people knowingly doing what was wrong though they were not aware in advance of the consequences of their sin. It is not a story of ignorance, but of an ill will, which freely chooses what it knows is wrong. The Hebrew vision of salvation is free from karman. Of course there are consequences to sin, but the wrong of sin is clearly not merely a matter of the returning evil upon the sinner. Once the sin is forgiven, the one-time sinner is free from guilt. The material consequences [*karman*] are not important, providing there is a loving state of repentance;

self-forgiveness and loving God and obeying Him. The western understanding of two levels of reality comes from this attitude: the natural and the supernatural. Of course Adam and Eve live out karma on the natural level; but the truest reality is their fall and salvation on the supernatural level. This supernatural level is ethical, loving and spiritual.

The doctrine of original sin and the notion of *avidyā* both have underlying existential elements. We commit sin, or we carry out blind acts, because we are as we are. Both have a sense that human nature is somehow fallen: in the Indian view there is a fall from knowledge, because of the involvement of the Purusha with the Prakṛti; in the Hebrew view there is a fall from grace because of selfishness and pride.

> 9 And the Lord God brought forth of the ground all manner of trees, fair to behold, and pleasant to eat of: the tree of life also it the midst of paradise: and the tree of knowledge of good and evil.
>
> 10 And a river went out of the place of pleasure to water paradise. which from thence it divided into four heads …
>
> 15 And the Lord God took man, and put him into the paradise of pleasure, to dress it, and to keep it.
>
> 16 And he commanded him, saying: Of every tree of paradise thou shalt eat:

17 But of the tree of knowledge of good and evil, thou shalt not eat. For in what day soever thou shalt eat of it, thou shalt die the death.

18 And the Lord God said: It is not good for man to be alone; let us make him a help like unto himself.

19 And the Lord God having formed out of the ground all the beasts of the earth, and all the fowls of the air, brought them to Adam to see what he would call them: for whatsoever Adam called any living creature the same is its name.

20 And Adam called all the beasts by their names, and all the fowls of the air, and all the cattle of the field: but for Adam there was not found a helper like him-self.

21 Then the Lord God cast a deep sleep upon Adam: and when he was fast asleep, he took one of his ribs, and filled up flesh for it.

22 And the Lord God built the rib which he took from Adam into a woman: and brought her to Adam.

23 And Adam said: This now is bone of my bones, and flesh of my flesh; she shall be called woman, because she was taken out of man.

24 Wherefore a man shall leave father and mother, and shall cleave to his wife: and they shall be two in one flesh.

25 And they were both naked, to wit, Adam and his wife: and were not ashamed.

CHAPTER 3

1 Now the serpent was more subtle than any of the beasts of the earth which the Lord God had made. And he said to the woman: Why hath God commanded you, that you should not eat of every tree of paradise?

2 And the woman answered him, *saying*: Of the fruit of the trees that are in paradise we do eat:

3 But of the fruit of the tree which is in the midst of paradise, God hath commanded us that we should not eat; and that we should not touch it, lest perhaps we die.

4 And the serpent said to the woman: No, you shall not die the death.

5 For God doth know that in what day soever you shall eat thereof, your eyes shall be opened: and you shall be as Gods, knowing good and evil.

6 And the woman saw that the tree was good to eat, and fair to the eyes, and delightful to behold: and she took of the fruit thereof, and did eat, and gave to her husband who did eat.

The Hebrew vision, enshrined in the mythology of Adam and Eve, is a vision of punishment and reward; but it is also a vision of true responsibility, of love and of forgiveness. Man is made in the image and likeness of God: revenge is utterly forbidden. The animals are given to man for his use. There is no sense of wrong in the act of killing an animal in order to eat.

The serpent appears in both Christian and Hindu mythologies. It represents the pure power of cosmic energy; and also the energy of our own personalities. If this power controls man, it is evil; if it is used for a higher purpose it is good. Man, in the Christian vision is made in the image and likeness of God: in the Hindu view the detached consciousness of man either really is God, or is in some way divine.

The higher level of the aspiration of the Pandava kings illustrates the Indian consciousness of levels of spirituality above that level of obeying the laws of the material universe. The Bhagavad Gita calls men to turn away from 'action' — that is good deeds to reduce bad karman. The term *karman* can, incidentally, refer either to evil due to actions, or equally to the goods actions (deeds of sacrifice or of virtue) carried out to avoid that evil. In the Gita the lord Krishna calls all men to turn to love. Arjun will carry out his duty but purely as an expression of love.

The compendium that is the Mahabharata shows every level of the evolution of human ethics and consciousness. The appearance of Krishna and the stories of Shiva, in the epic, represent the birth of a personal God in the Indian consciousness. The supreme deity is celebrated as a loving personal Being, who calls men to release from the process of *samsara*; and whose grace aids them to achieve this; not so much through intellectual study, but through love. The Vedic rituals, which were originated to purge karma, were replaced by simpler ceremonies of respect and adoration, to be carried out as steps to personal union with the divine. God is seen as compassionate and as desiring, as it were, to speed the release of souls. The idea of divine grace is really an overt doctrine of the supernatural; and karma is o'erleaped. These new religions were more peaceful. The dharma of the soldier was accepted, but the code of revenge faded. Humility replaced pride. Religion emphasised the inner private life; and the public sense of shame, which belonged to the old warrior religions, was surpassed by a sense of inadequacy before the Deity.

The stories of the apparitions of the Deity were important in teaching the new religion; and the reactions of the saints and heroes to these apparitions inculcated the attitudes of the new spirituality.

CHAPTER 7

SAMKHYA

It is said that the hunting bow was the earliest technical invention of man, the hunter. But the wheel was the greatest mechanical innovation of man, the settled farmer. It is small wonder that it became an early image of spiritual power. It can be seen in the form of the Dharma wheel in Buddhist sculpture; it appears in the architecture of the Christian west as the principle light of the great cathedrals, illustrating how the many emanate from the One. Sometimes there are several concentric rims, supported by sets of spokes, which increase in number to form a mathematical series, as they span outwards.

In India the symbol of the *samkhya* wheel, carved in stone on temples and on statues, can have various numbers of spokes; and even three concentric rims. But if we take the classic *samkhya* system of Ishvarakrishna as our model system, we might imagine simply a hub, a rim and twenty-three spokes. These items together represent the twenty-five entities [*tattva*] of the Samkhya system. The hub of the wheel is the Purusha [*purusa*], or consciousness, and its rim is Prakirti [*prakṛti*], or objectivity. These two self-existent causes, these permanent entities [*tattva*], the hub and the rim, support the spokes that are subtended between them. The twenty-three spokes symbolise the various levels of beings that come to exist, as consciousness meets the unconscious.

In earlier Samkhya systems the hub is a many, rather than a one. The original Samkhya thinkers saw a host of purushas, or souls, endlessly wandering through space and time. These purushas in no way form the notion of a God, after the ideal of the Hebrew, or, indeed, the later, Hindu, theistic systems. As each Purusha, encountering the Prakirti, creates its own world, in their turn these worlds, these myriad sets of spokes, combine and coalesce, and create the common universe.

The Samkhya systems of metaphysics always include an enumeration of entities. It is this enumeration that is the cosmological basis of many later Indian philosophies. Thinkers all accept the existence of some kind of self and of some quasi-material substrate. They then enumerate the beings evolving from the interaction of these two primary sources. There are various versions of the enumeration of entities that flow from these sources; and there is a dispute between earlier and later teachers as to whether the Self is many or one.

The word *samkhya*, derived from the root *sam*, meaning 'together', can be rendered in English as 'enumeration'. There were, in ancient India, systems of enumeration of the principles of all of the sciences: mathematics, medicine, architecture, music and astronomy. The Samkhya was originally not a school of philosophy but an ordered numbering of cosmic principles. The early Indian held that, at the root and heart of the cosmos, sets of numbers regulated all things. As with Pythagoras, Mathematics ruled the flux. The simple numbers, one to nine, for early Indian thinkers, were probably shapes; and the mathematical intervals between musical notes revealed to them that a number was a quality and an entity, as well as a quantity. The basis of these sets of numbers, which regulated the aspects of the cosmos studied by the individual sciences, was the diatonic scale of Indian music. Later the quantitative relationships between sounds even regulated the construction of temples, with spaces and solids, heights, widths and depths similarly interrelating.

It is thus that the metaphysical system, which we know as the classical Samkhya, presents an architectonic arrangement of 25 cosmic elements.

The Cosmic One

The 'enumeration' [*samkhya*] begins, as we have seen, with a duality, in which the totality of things depends on two kinds of being: *purusa*– conscious being, and *prakṛti* – objective being, or Nature. The original Samkhya system taught, not one single purusha, but a myriad of individually conscious souls – *purusa* or *jīva*. These *jīva* were wholly separate from one another, and self-existent and permanent, having neither beginning, nor end. The original Samkhya did not envisage one, Supreme Being; and it had no concept of a personal God. But the system saw Nature, the *prakṛti*, as one; and, as uncreated, Prakṛti was existent in herself [*sat*].

Early versions of the Samkhya metaphysic are found in the Chandogya Upanishad [VI. 2-5]; where the primordial being [*sat*] is manifested in the threefold way as fire (red), water (white) and food (black); and these qualities are correlatives of speech, breath and mind.

The legendary author of the system is Kapila. Kapila is thought, or is believed, to have lived in the seventh century BC. Many earlier

Samkhya systems have been either wholly lost, or remain only in fragments.

The first complete Samkhya document that we possess is the Samkhya-karika of Iśvarakṛṣṇa. It was written during the third century AD. The exact dates of Iśvarakṛṣṇa are not known.

By Isvarakrishna's time, the vision of the ultimate Being was widespread. The yogis of the philosophical schools, or ashrama, taught the Supreme Being, Brahman. The puranas spoke of Brahma, the waking and conscious creator. Many devotees of religion worshipped the One in temples, as the personality of the Godhead; who is Brahman, Shiva and Vishnu (Krishna). The Vedas, as well as the Upanishads, had also originally included the idea of a Supreme Being, beyond the pantheon of individual gods.

For Ishvarakrishna, however, the only cosmic One was the Prakṛti. He had no concept of a God, personal or otherwise. He taught that there is a myriad of jivas, or conscious souls, all existing as wholly separate from a One that is Prakṛti. Consciousness is fragmented entirely. There is no Purusha; just an endless number of purushas.

The meaning of *prakṛti* is 'making' or 'placing before'. It then means: nature, character and constitution; and: cause, origin and source. In the Samkhya system it designates the original primary substance. This primary substance is the basis of our minds and bodies. It is not to be in any way equated with 'matter' as understood in western thought. It has a readiness to form the material world; but also it can become our minds and the subtle elements of our imaginative consciousness, when it has been moulded by that consciousness.

These elements lie in between the extremes of the matter and spirit of the western conception. When her association, or apparent association, with Purusha disturbs her gunas, Prakṛti is ready to produce all of the forms that we see in the visible world; as well as our means of seeing them. Thus the concept of *prakṛti* includes aspects of both Matter and Form, (and of Potentcy and Act of Existence), as conceived in classical Greek philosophy. Then again, Prakṛti is not to be fully equated with either one of these ideas.

The three-fold Misery

But the whole purpose of the Karika is the enquiry as to how we can be released from misery; from the triad of pain – threefold because there are three gunas – that is our experience of Nature.

> 1 From torment by three-fold misery arises the enquiry into the means of terminating it; if it be said that it is fruitless, the means being known by perception, no [we reply], since in them there is not certainty of finality.
>
> 2 The scriptural means of terminating misery is also like the perceptible; it is verily linked with impurity, destruction, and surpassability; different therefrom and superior thereto is that means derived from the discriminative knowledge of the evolved, the unevolved, and the knower.

There are three ways to knowledge according to Ishvarakrishna: perception, scriptural tradition and reasoning. The perceptual means of terminating misery are the material, causal methods that temporarily put an end to the pain that we experience, at one particular moment: medicine, for physical pain; and diversions of a material kind, clothes, entertainment food and the like, for mental pain. These, unfortunately, can never absolutely and entirely remove all pain. They can only remove individual pains. And we are tranquil only until the next grief arrives.

The religious rites laid down in the Vedas again only remove the individual *kārma* that the sacrificer has acquired during the period covered by the sacrifice. Because of our inattention, however, attendance at rituals can cause demerit, and thus subsequent further pain. It is difficult to enact the rites with sufficient perfection. Thus the only remaining palliative is detachment; brought about by philosophical contemplation; leading to an understanding of the entire cosmic process.

In detail, this philosophical knowledge is the awareness, first of all, that the Purusha has not been evolved from other beings. It simply exists as itself and of itself. And he does not further evolve any other beings. Then, secondly, we must be aware and that the Prakṛti, equally, has not evolved from another being. Yet she can evolve further beings. Thirdly, we must attain the philosophical knowledge that there are those elements, which are evolved and yet can also evolve further beings; and fourthly we must know that there those things, which have evolved, but which can evolve nothing further.

iii. Primal nature [*Prakṛti*] is not an evolute; the seven, beginning with the Great One [i.e. *mahat*, the intellect] are both evolvents and evolutes; the sixteen [i.e. the five organs of sense, the five of action, the mind, and the five gross elements] are only evolutes; the spirit is neither evolvent nor evolute.

The argument of the Karika is entirely philosophical: it is in no way an appeal to belief. The Purusha is simply each one's self-awareness. It does not need to have its existence proved. If someone thinks that the Purusha is the product of something else, it is up to him to prove that; because it does not appear to be so. Again the Prakṛti is a given. Her three gunas are equally unproven; but to Indians the existence of the variety of things, including the embodied consciousness of each one of us, is proof enough. The remaining evolutes are attained as the result of reasoning about our experience. This reasoning, based on experience, has made the Samkhya the Indian philosophical system most attractive to philosophers throughout the world. It remains entirely Indian, however, being based on the ontology of the three gunas and having release – *moksa* – as its only aim. How do we know that there is any such thing as 'release'? Well the guru meditating on his own self-awareness begins to see that he could exist, as self-aware, without being aware of any particular object. Sometimes he enters into a strong state of self-awareness where perception of material objects fades and they do not seem important. He finds this state of self-awareness blissful. He then thinks he would like to exist solely in this state of self-awareness. Thus *moksa* becomes a possibility. But then in matters of consciousness possibility and actuality are not clearly distinct. He then knows he will achieve *moksa* somehow one day.

It is important that the Samkhya Karika first of all establishes existence of Prakṛti, in its manifestation as matter. We see things, which we regard as being made of matter, but we cannot directly experience the existence of the generality of matter. The existence of matter, however, can be known as certain, for the following reasons.

1. The individual, limited and finite things depend on something more enduring and pervasive than themselves.
2. All individual things possess common elements and thus have a common origin.
3. The division of cause and effect are manifest in the universe; and yet every being can be seen as an effect; therefore no individual being is the first cause.
4. An effect and a cause are different and so the universe, the collection of beings we see, is not its own cause.
5. There is an obvious unity in the universe, which suggests a single cause. ['Universe', from Latin, means 'turned to one' - 'many' is understood].
6. There is evolution in the universe – beings are formed from other beings by a gradual process. Evolution implies a principle, which cannot be equated with any one of its stages. It is something superior to its products, though it dwells in each stage in a different manner.

Radhakrishnan sums up these arguments by referring to the distinction, which was made by Descartes, between 'eminent' and 'formal' causes.

The ultimate cause, Prakṛti, must contain, eminently, all reality; but individual beings are not actually existent in the ultimate cause. Equally the formal or immediate causes of individual beings are not actually existent in Prakṛti.

The Samkhya teachers say that this ultimate cause, Prakṛti, is unevolved or unmanifest [*avyatka*]. The twenty-three fundamental principles, which are derived from that ultimate cause, are manifest [*vyatka*]. And from these twenty-three, all the things that we see are further derived.

Through perception and through our feelings we experience the gross world, the intellect and the subtle senses and so forth. From these principles we reason to *prakṛti*.

The Mind

One of these principles is *manas*, the mind, which receives all physical sensations. Mediaeval Western philosophers reasoned to the *sensus communis*. They held that the individual sets of sensations, received by the different senses, could not separately produce the idea we have of one whole object; possessing different qualities of sound, colour, resistance, taste and so forth. There must be a common receptor in the human person, which recreates the external object from the various sensations. This receptor they called the *sensus communis*. Since they held that sensation was entirely physical, they located the 'Common Sense' in the brain. Indian thinkers also, by an identical process of reasoning, consider that we can know *manas*. Thus far two principles of the Samkhya, *manas* and the unmanifest *prakṛti*, can be arrived at logically.

Manas is made of subtle matter. However patent of thought subtle matter may be, it can never be conscious. However helpful in linking the jivas to Prakṛti and in enabling the jivas to witness the objective world, subtle matter remains entirely an aspect of Prakṛti; and it is never, in itself, capable of consciousness. Thus the fact of consciousness requires the Purusha as witness of the world.

> *(a)* Because all composite objects are for another's use, because there must be absence of the three attributes and other properties, *(b)* because there must be control, *(c)* because there must someone to experience and *(d)* because there is a tendency towards 'isolation' or final beatitude, therefore, the spirit must be there.

We frequently experience that we dream of objects that are not physically present. For Indian philosophy the phenomenon of our dreaming is an indication of the existence of subtle matter. The existence of the Purusha, along with the fact of sensation as a mental repetition of the world of material objects, is a proof that there must be a subtler element of energy, which can appear as any object that is required. To the Samkhya, electrical activity in the brain, as we conventionally understand electricity, could not fully explain sensation. The tanmatras – the five subtle elements – are required; along with the experiencing Purusha.

The Gunas

The Unmanifest, *prakṛti*, has three qualities: the gunas. These may be seen as three different kinds of energy. In the realm of the unmanifest, just as in the realm of particle physics, object and quality are not distinguished. Energy can be seen as a quality that objects possess, or as that of which objects are made or, indeed as the object itself. Quality and quantity are likewise not to be separated. Subtle vibration and movement [*śabda*] are what the Unmanifest is said to be made of, to possess, or, if you will, to be. As hearing was, in Indian thought considered the subtlest and truest of the senses, sound [*śabda*] was thought to be basis of *prakṛti*. The gunas, or three qualities [*guna*], are thus three groupings of vibrations: heavy and slow [*tamas*], medium [*rajas*] and fast and light [*sattva*]. They correspond to the ways of playing notes on the scale of the *raga*. The following citation of the Samkhya refers to qualitative and ontological aspects of the gunas, which appear in nature as we experience it; and therefore must be attributed to Prakṛti. That the spirit does not possess these gunas is clearly affirmed.

> 1. Knowledge of objects beyond the senses comes from inference based on analogy; what knowledge is obscure and not attainable even thereby is gained by valid testimony.
>
> 2. Non-perception may be because of extreme distance, extreme proximity, injury to the organs, non-steadiness of mind, subtlety, veiling, suppression, and blending with what is similar.
>
> 3. The non-perception of that [i.e. Primal Nature] is due to its subtlety, not to its non-existence, since it is perceived in its effects; the great one [*mahat* — i.e. the intellect] and the rest are its effects, which are both like and unlike their cause — Nature...

> 4. The manifest is 'with the three attributes' [*guna*], 'undistinguishable', [or 'non-separative'], 'objective', 'common', 'insentient' and 'productive'. So also is Nature. The spirit is the reverse, and yet also [in some respects] similar.
>
> 5. 'With the three attributes'- That is to say, the manifest has three attributes of pleasure, pain, and delusion. By this assertion are set aside those theories that attribute pleasure and pain to the spirit.
>
> 6. 'Undistinguishable', just as Nature cannot be distinguished from itself, so also the Great Principle [*buddhi*], being connate with Nature, cannot be distinguished from Nature....

The *kārikā* on the Karika is by Vacaspati Mishra. Vācaspati Miśra was a later Samkhya teacher who lived in the ninth century AD. His Tattva-kaumudī was a commentary on the Karika of Ishvarakrishna; taking cognisance of the metaphysical arguments of Buddhists and of the later Advaitins. Vascapati's commentary on Verse xi of the Karika, clearly asserts that the three gunas are not to be attributed to the Purusha. They are totally one with Prakṛti; and they thus belong to the perceived object rather than to the perceiving subject.

Nature, as manifested, is indistinguishable from the three gunas and from all their effects. But to realise the existence of Nature (or matter) herself, we need a process of reasoning. To modern people it is a simple step — only a subtle, and perverse, modern thinker would say that we do not actually experience the universe as a totality and therefore cannot be sure of its existence as a totality. For the Samkhya on the other hand the existence of the Purusha is also self-evident. One only needs to sense the existence of one's self as an existent independent of any objective impressions that one may be at that moment receiving. In classes of philosophy on the topic, I ask everyone to attempt to do this. But not everybody can. Perhaps you have to be an introvert to sense yourself, not only independently of what objects you are perceiving, but also independently of moods and feelings you are at that moment experiencing. For many people consciousness is adjectival rather than substantive!

Purusha

The human person, that we experience being in this life, is a combination of body and soul. When the Purusha, at conception, becomes involved with the subtle, or sattvic part of matter, she acquires qualities of that subtle matter, which she sees at first as qualities of herself. At the same moment she acquires a living, material body. She is thus no longer pure consciousness, but sees herself as having moods and feelings, and possessing a physical body. This body is very much perceived as a part of what we might call her 'empirical self'. Not only are her senses and limbs part of her, but even her clothes and spectacles. Ultimately she, the Self, is entirely different from the material world of which her body is a part. She is different from the subtlest of matter. But her perception is reduced to a single point of view. She is constricted by one pair of eyes. But she does understand, in her contact with the world, that there are different kinds of things; some pairs of things are alike and some pairs of things are unalike. Thus she has a principle of enlightenment. This principle of enlightenment is *mahat* — the great one —, or 'seeing' in the mental sense. The 'knowableness' of the universe is *mahat*; it is an organising principle; it has a recognisable and predictable form. For each individual jiva, *mahat* is intellect [*buddhi*]. As soon as she 'sees', she has to become aware of a subjective point of view. Thinking that this viewpoint is right and superior to some other points of view, she immediately develops a sense of self, which is individual, and thus needy and demanding. This is *ahamkara*. One could say that *ahamkara* is an attitude born of the involvement of the Purusha with matter and that *buddhi* is an attitude of the jiva, which is automatic once her focus is narrowed. All this, however, is involved with the creation of an organ, which is physical and actual, however subtle aspects of its matter may be. This is *manas*, the common sense. The common sense is an organ linking the *jīva* to the physical body. It is created at the parental conception, when each soul enters its body. The soul functions thus, in the imprisoned state of its wandering [*samsara*], through *manas*; *manas* collects all the information from the senses and enables the jiva to think in a material way.

But we have to gradually try not to do this and prepare ourselves, through meditation, for our release into the bliss of our own pure consciousness.

The Tattva-kaumudi of Vacaspati Mishra refuted Buddhist and Advaita systems of philosophy. Many of Mahayana Buddhist philosophies attributed the universe, and the objects within it, to our ideas. These ideas are the cause of our pain. But Vacaspati Mishra clearly asserts the objectivity of the gunas. When our consciousness unites itself to them it is bound to be unhappy, because of their objectively unstable nature. The Advaitins held that the Prakṛti was an imaginary imposition upon the one, sole Purusha; and, thus, ultimately not different [*advaita*] from Him. Vacaspati Mishra thus taught a realm of the gunas which existed separately from God and was as real as God, though not independent of Him. Vacaspati Mishra was a *dvaita* thinker; and *dvaita* means 'dual'.

Emptiness

The 'emptiness' [*śūnyatā*] philosophies, and 'emptiness' methods of meditation, were being developed, in India, during the centuries around the birth of Christ. There had always been schools of thought, in India, teaching that matter is not real, or, indeed, that all is an illusion. The *śūnyatā* schools of Buddhism taught that the flow of impressions was the only reality, that this flow of impressions required no cause and was dependent on no knowable substance. The Advaita Vedanta taught that the Self of Brahman was the only reality; and that the universe was ultimately given separate, objective reality by our ignorance, or false idea [*vijñāna*]. By emphasising that the gunas are not to be attributed to the spirit, Vacaspati Mishra opposes thinkers who seem to reject the reality of Nature; a reality, he claims, that has a clear basis, external to the perceiving self.

> Some people have held that it is idea [*vijñāna*] alone that constitutes pleasure, pain, and delusion, and that there exists nothing besides this idea that could possess these [pleasure, etc.,] as its attributes. In opposition to this view it is asserted that the

manifest is '*objective*', '*objective*' here stands for 'what can be apprehended.' That is, it is exterior to the idea. - And because it is 'objective,' therefore, '*common*' - i.e., apprehended simultaneously by several persons. If it were nothing more or less than the idea, then in that case, - in as much as ideas, being in the form of 'functions,' belong specially to particular individuals, - all that is 'manifest' would have to belong specially to particular individuals. That is to say, as a matter of fact, the idea of one person is not apprehended by another, the cognition of another person being always uncognisable. In the case of [manifest substance such as] the glance of a dancing girl, it is found that many persons continue to stare at it at the same time. This could not be the cause if it were otherwise [i.e., if the glance were a mere idea].

The Dancer

Although Vacaspati Mishra emphasises the objectivity of Prakṛti, 'the dancer'; the Karika holds that this evolution is twofold: both subjective [*bhāva*] and objective [*linga*]. In so far as the evolution depends on the Prakṛti and her gunas, it is objective. In so far as the evolution depends on *ahamkara*, or sense of self, as the Purusha, by means of Prakṛti, imagines he is associated with Prakṛti, it is subjective. The image of many eyes seeing the dancer emphasises the original Samkhya idea of a multiplicity of purushas, or individual consciousnesses, all witnessing an objective event.

The dual aspect of reality, as *bhāva* and *linga*, appears again in the ideas of modern physics.

Shamkara [*śaṁkarācārya*] lived during the eighth century AD, according to some. But others give his dates as a thousand years earlier. He was born in Kerala and he travelled all over India and died in Kashmir. He had denounced caste and meaningless ritual. He had taught both the love and the understanding of God. He had rejected the Buddhist doctrine of emptiness. Shamkara's *advaita* view saw reality as simply one — 'non-dual'. If we could truly see things as they are, we would reject the divided [*dvaita*] view of things and of ourselves as being entities separate from God. We would then finally become God; and the separate objects, that we imagine we see, would disappear.

An event, in nuclear physics, does not take place if it is not observed. Many scientists are happy to understand this phenomenon in terms of measurements and formulae, which have no ontological import, or imaginative significance. However, Neils Bohr [1885-1962], the Danish nuclear physicist, proposed what has become known as the 'Copenhagen interpretation'. This offers a deliberate philosophical understanding of the data; and paints an imaginative picture of a microscopic world, different from our commonsense view of things. In *The Ghost in the Atom*, P. C. W. Davies and J. R. Brown set out at length (but condensed here) Bohr's position: 'Before the days of quantum mechanics, most Western scientists assumed that the world about us enjoys an independent existence. [...] This picture of the world is compelling because it is the one which most readily squares with our common-sense understanding of nature. [...] But it is precisely this common-sense view of reality that Bohr challenged with the philosophy underscoring the Copenhagen interpretation [since] it is meaningless to ascribe a complete set of attributes to some quantum object prior to an act of measurement being performed on it.'

Erwin Schrödinger [1887-1961] was a nuclear physicist in the same Copenhagen group; and he was a philosopher, who offered a new understanding of the Presocratic philosophers of ancient Greece, and who wrote about the ethical problems posed by scientific discoveries. He proposed an imaginary experiment in which a hammer was connected to a geiger counter; so that if, in the nuclear measuring apparatus, one atom decayed within an hour, then the hammer would fall. If, on the other hand, an atom did not decay, the hammer would stay in place. Now only the average behaviour of the atom can be known. That is the principle of indeterminacy. Schrödinger went on to imagine that a flask of lethal poison was placed under the hammer, in a sealed, airtight box; and a cat was also shut in that container. The cat, left in there for about an hour, would be in a sort of 'living-dead' state until the box was opened. When the box was opened, the event would become an event, as it was observed. The cat would be then instantly either living or dead; and the atom in the experiment would instantly have either decayed, or not decayed! This illustration is known as 'Schrödinger's cat'.

It is thus that the gunas of Prakṛti do not form the objects in the world that we see; unless those gunas are stirred by the presence of the Witness, Purusha!

As to whether there is a need for a further substantial being that might support Prakṛti, this would create the need for an infinite regress of such beings; thus Prakṛti must be its own self-supporting substance, says Vacaspati Mishra.

Ishvarakrishna did not believe in One God. He argues that there is ultimately a plurality of souls [*jīva*], rather than one Purusha; because there are different kinds of men and creatures. Vacaspati Mishra uses this fact to prove that individual souls exist separately from one another and are not the same as God, rather than to prove that there is no God.

> xviii. The plurality of spirits certainly follows from the distributive nature of the incidence of birth and death and of the endowment of the instruments of cognition and action, from bodies engaging in action, not all at the same time, and also from differences in the proportion of the three constituents.
>
> Some persons abounding in the *sattva* attribute represent aggregates of that attribute – e.g., the deities and saints; others abound in the *rajas* attribute, – such as men; others again in the *tamas* attribute, – such as beasts. This 'diversity' or 'differentiation' due to the distribution of the attributes in the various entities, could not be explained if the spirit were one and the same in all. On the hypothesis of plurality, however, there is no difficulty.
>
> xix. And from that contrast [the contrast that has been explained in Karika xi], it follows that the spirit is

> 'witness', and has 'isolation', 'neutrality', and is the 'seer', and 'inactive'.

Vacaspati Mishra explains, in his adumbration of the Karika, that the characters of 'sentient' and 'non-objective' follow from the characteristics of the Purusha as 'witness' and 'seer'. He says that it is impossible for the Prakṛti, which is objective, to be sentient; and again that no object can be shown to another insentient object. In the Samkhya system 'sentient' and 'object' are opposites. The Purusha, in himself, is entirely devoid of the three gunas. The Purusha does not thus essentially possess the sensation mechanism. He is only sentient in that he witnesses sensation. The Prakṛti that possesses the sentient mechanism is none the less, insentient without Purusha.

> Further, from *the absence of the three attributes* in the spirit follows its isolation – by which is meant the final and absolute removal of the three kinds of pain; and this property, as belonging to the spirit, is a necessary deduction from the fact of the spirit being by its very nature without the three attributes, and hence without pleasure, pain, or delusion.
>
> From the absence of the attributes, again, follows *neutrality;* since this latter property is such as cannot belong either to the happy and satisfied, nor to the sad and grumbling. It is only one who is devoid of both pleasure and pain who can be called *neutral* – also called *udāsina* [indifferent]. Lastly,

> the *inactivity* of the spirit follows from its being 'distinguishable' and 'non-productive'.

To say that the spirit is indifferent [*udāsina*] is to say that it is beyond the opposites of suffering and earthly happiness. We might translate *udāsina*, in this context, as 'bliss'; understanding 'bliss' as wholly beyond both pain and it's opposite, happiness.

Ontological Evolute

In the Karika itself, Ishvarakrishna continues to describe the nature of Purusha and his relationship with Prakṛti. The word *linga* means: mark, sign or token. In logic *linga* means: premise, inference; and thus: reason. The word that Ishvarakrishna uses for a thing derived from another thing is also *linga*. Whether in this case the word should be translated 'evolute' I leave the reader to judge.

> xx. Thus from this union, the insentient 'evolute' appears as if 'sentient'; and similarly, from the activity really belonging to the attributes [*guna*], the spirit, which is neutral, appears as if it were active.
>
> The word 'evolute' [*linga*] here stands for everything from the Great Principle down to the primary elements to be described later on. The cause of the mistake is said to be the 'union', i.e., proximity, of the spirit with the 'evolute.'
>
> xxi. For the perception of Nature by the spirit and for the isolation spirit, there is the union of both, –

> like that of the halt and the blind; and from this union proceeds evolution.
>
> '*For the isolation of the spirit*' – The spirit, while in union with the 'enjoyable' Nature, believes the three kinds of pain – the constituents of Nature – to be his own; and from this [self-imposed bond] he seeks liberation, isolation; this isolation is dependent upon due discrimination between spirit and the three attributes; this discrimination is not possible without the Nature … thus it is that for his own isolation the spirit needs Nature.
>
> '*From this union proceeds evolution.*' The said 'union' [of spirit with Nature] cannot by itself suffice either for 'enjoyment' or 'isolation' if the Great Principle and the rest be not there; hence the *union* itself brings about the evolution for the sake of 'enjoyment' and 'isolation'.

The epistemology of Ishvarakrishna is based on the relationship between Purusha and Prakṛti, as is his ontology. The ordinary, conscious soul, or *jīva*, united to Nature, through the illusion that Nature is her own nature, can only know Nature, indirectly, as its senses perceive a variety of material objects. The senses that the jivas acquire do not perceive Nature as such. But through reasoning the jiva can attain to the Prakṛti. It is through the detached, philosophical awareness of Nature, as One, as Prakṛti, that the jiva then advances towards release. Both in the ontological evolution of Nature, and in the epistemological release from Nature, intelligibility [*mahat*] is required. The road to freedom [*moksa*] reverses the process of evolution. A final change in knowledge (epistemology) is also a change in being (ontology).

This inference is based on *sāmānyatodṛsta*, which might be translated, 'the collection of perceptions' – that is the understanding of what is common to perceptions; and thus what underlies them – i.e., Nature and the three gunas.

This type of encounter with individual beings [*gignoskein*] and then the quest for a common account [*logos*] also lies at the heart of early Greek philosophy with the teachings of Heraclitus, just as in the Samkhya. The doctrine of the analogy of being — that we can understand Being, because individual beings are 'not unalike' [*analogos*] – is fully developed in the metaphysics of Aristotle. (But Aristotle did not reason from the assembly of the whole, in the conscious way of Ishvarakrishna. He rather reasoned from individual caused beings to an original, uncaused Cause.)

> v. Perception [*dṛsta*] is the ascertainment of objects [which are in contact with sense-organs]; inference [*anumāna*], which follows on the knowledge of the characteristic mark [*linga* i.e. the middle term] and that which bears the mark [*liṇgin* i.e. the major and minor terms] is said to be of three kinds; as for valid testimony [*aptavacana*], it is incontrovertible knowledge derived from verbal statement.
>
> vi. Knowledge of objects beyond the senses comes from inference based on analogy [*sāmānyatodṛsta*];

> what knowledge is not obscure and not attainable even thereby is gained by valid testimony [*aptagama*].
>
> vii. Non-perception may be because of extreme distance, extreme proximity, injury to the organs, non-steadiness of mind, subtlety, veiling, and blending with what is similar.
>
> viii. The non-perception of that [i.e. Primal Nature] is due to its subtlety, not to its non-existence, since it is perceived in its effects; the great one [*mahat* – the intellect] and the rest are its effects, which are both like and unlike their cause – Nature.

Perception – *dṛsta* – could be rendered – 'obviousness'. Because of the subtlety of her being, Prakṛti has a certain separateness of existence to the ordinary person, who can see the everyday world of objects. Yet, that Prakṛti, of which these objects are made, is only perceptible by the seer [*ṛsi*], who possesses a subtler and more sattvic consciousness. The term *sāmānyatodṛsta* might be translated as 'presented as bound together'. That *sāmānyatodṛsta* is the basis of the syllogism. Once we see that an object has a certain substance we can then know things about it that we do not immediately perceive. These things can often later be proved by further observation. An idea like the Universe can never be empirically seen in its entirety. Yet we can all understand the term. Empiricists thoroughly fail to explain this. And also maybe we do not need yogis!

Analogy

The Western scholastic doctrine of the analogy of being might be considered here. We may reason from one item to another provided they are partly the same as well as partly different; and provided the similarity is the principle, which lies at the root of the being of both items. Ishvarakrishna shows his respect for the revelations of the seers and indeed for the testimony of the scriptures; but the aim of the Karika is to attain contentment and release through the detachment of rational understanding. However, one wonders whether, without the testimony of mystical vision, men could have arrived at the Samkhya system in its totality.

Perhaps aspects have been first revealed by visionaries, and then, once arrived at, further established by reason. Certainly, the three gunas seem so obvious to Indians that, so far, I have not seen any proof of them. A pupil from Gujarat told me that, although in her family there is no knowledge of the Samkhya, the idea of the gunas is still used, among her family and friends, to describe the different temperaments that people have.

Causality

The nature of causality is fundamental to the age long debate between the different schools of Indian philosophy. In fact it may be doctrines of causality that characterise and distinguish those schools of thought as individual systems.

A most important dispute in Indian metaphysics is whether the effect exists within the cause, before it is actually caused. The doctrine of *satkāryavāda* – meaning the 'teaching' [*vāda*] of the 'sufficient cause' – is at the basis of both the Samkhya and the Advaita Vedanta systems. As we shall see later, the Advaita, or non-dual philosophy, holds that Brahman is the sole reality, in which all things inhere. The things that we see are thus 'non-different' [*abheda*] from Brahman, who is thus their sole real cause. All things exist in Brahman and are his effects. Thus the effects exist in the cause: the effects are 'non-different' from the cause. Thus there is only One Being. This is the meaning of the name of the school, non-dual [*advaita*].

The Samkhya also hold the same doctrine [*satkāryavāda*] with regard to Prakṛti and its effects. All things are the manifestation of its gunas. All things inhere in the Prakṛti. The Prakṛti is the cause of all worldy beings through the stirring of its gunas – its inner qualities. Individual things, in reality are no more than these gunas. The doctrine holds that things come to be from the gunas; and are thus manifest to our experience. In so far as all things are effects, these effects already exist in the cause.

The Samkhya philosophy, however, is not a non-dual philosophy; these effects could not take place through the causality of Prakṛti alone. The Samkhya system teaches the duality of Prakṛti and Purusha.

Cause and Effect

> ix. The effect is existent; [1] because what is 'non-existent' cannot be produced; [2] because there is a definite relation of the cause with the effect; [3] because

> all is not possible; [4] because the efficient can do only that for which it is efficient; [5] because effect is of the same essence as the cause.

A second and different translation will help to further elucidate the doctrine of the pre-existence of the effect in the cause. This translation is inclined to interpret the doctrine slightly in the direction of Aristotelian philosophy in order to make it comprehensible to the Western mind.

> The effect [*kārya*] exists or resides [*satkārya*] in the cause in a potential state or condition prior to the operation of cause for the following reasons: [a] something cannot arise from nothing; [b] any effect requires a material basis [*upadāna*]; [c] anything cannot arise from just everything; [d] something can only produce what it is capable of producing; and [e] the very nature or essence of the cause is nondifferent from the effect.

For Aristotle the Effect existed, potentially, but not actually, in the Cause. The pot exists potentially in the clay; and potentially in the fact that there is a potter. The Efficient Cause, the potter, needs to act so that change can take place. Once change has taken place, new beings, the Effects, exist. Obviously the Effects are different from their Causes. The Form of the pot takes over and 'subsumes' the form of clay; and the old, raw clay no longer exists. Thus there can be real change.

Clearly to the Advaita School, change is an illusion; and only real being is the unchanging Brahman. However, the Nyāya School of

Indian philosophy, like the Aristotelian schools of ancient Greece and mediaeval Europe, believed in the absolute reality of change. The Nyāyas taught that the cause is different from the effect. Their doctrine is called *bheda* [different]. This doctrine was based partly on their atomic view of matter; and partly on their view that the whole is more than the parts. Assemblies of atoms form wholes, which an efficient cause can change into different wholes. They considered that the effect was a new and different being. Even though the material cause and resultant effect might be made of the same atoms, the different arrangement of those atoms in the effect, brought about by the agent, constituted a different being. They disagreed with the Samkhya for whom the clay and the pot were only different from the point of view of the individual observer. The atoms of the Nyāya system are not as all creative and productive of forms, as is the Prakṛti of the Samkhya system. They do not contain all forms in such a powerful sense. They depend on the intelligent agency of the loving God, Ishvara, who orders the universe for the enlightenment of souls, to become the objects that souls need.

The Nyāya sees the necessity of an intelligent cause of the universe, as does the metaphysic of Aristotle. Both these systems of philosophy believe in the unqualified reality of the visible world that we experience.

With the Samkhya system, however, there is no all-creative and intelligent potter. The outwardly observable qualities, which things manifest, in the universe that we can see, must come from the inner qualities of Prakṛti. These inner qualities are the three gunas. The Purusha does not mould the gunas, as the potter kneads clay. The Purusha remains detached; He does not affect the gunas in a causal way. The gunas are merely influenced by the Purusha, as in loving admiration they imitate him. They reflect him, as a piece of crystal can reflect a rose. Cause and Effect are within the realm of Prakṛti. Cause and effect, in the Samkhya, are different arrangements of the same being. The jar is really the clay of which it is made; but there is a practical difference in that the clay cannot hold water. That is a difference seen from our point of view, which, as practical, is karmic. And *kārma*, our ability to act, is ultimately an illusion. Thus there is no personal efficient cause, because our karmic intentions and acts are part of Prakṛti. Thus ultimately there is no potter, as well as no Potter! Prakṛti is the sole source of material and of subtle Being; and, given the attraction of the Purusha, the source of all the forms that Being can take.

Dualism

But the Samkhya system is a dual system. Ultimately it sees two forms of reality: the Purusha and the Prakṛti. Within the domain of the Prakṛti, however, it does not envisage a further duality of cause and effect. And the Advaita Vedanta envisages no kind of duality at all. Brahman is the only Being.

The Samkhya and the Advaita term for cause is [*svabhāva*] – self-being. This *svabhāva* means: being its own origin, or source. The word is often translated as 'cause', in the sense that it supports all other beings. It could be called 'the ultimate substance'.

The balance of the three gunas produces all existents within Prakṛti. The balance is ever changing, as things in the world around alter; and new beings emerge and grow, while other beings wither and die.

xv. Because of the finite nature of specific objects, because of homogeneity, because of evolution being due to the efficiency of the cause, because of separation between cause and its product, because of the merging of the whole world [of effects], - there is the Unmanifest as the cause.

xvi. There is the unmanifest as the cause gone before; it operates through the three attributes, by blending and modification, like water, on account of the difference arising from the predominance of one or the other of the attributes.

' By modification like water'; - we all know how the water falling from the clouds, though naturally of itself having one taste, becomes sweet, sour, saline, bitter, pungent, and hot, according as it comes into contact with different modifications of earth and becomes transformed into the juices of fruits such as coconut, palm, wood-apples, and so forth; in the same manner [owing to the blending and the mutual suppression of the attributes], the attributes of Nature come to be predominant one by one and thereby bring about various modifications in the state of various products.

The image of water, used by Vacaspati Mishra, is redolent of mankind's earliest metaphysical speculations. We are reminded both of the Eleatic philosophers of Greece and of the Dao De

Ching of China. Water, is a primal image of the cosmic energy, which endlessly assumes myriad temporary forms and yet always remains itself. We see this idea beautifully illustrated by the cloud formations of later Taoist painter-sages. In the Samkhya world-view, this cosmic energy always has the three qualities, the gunas. These gunas, or qualities of energy, become by their blending, one thing and then another. The gunas are general: the finite objects of the world are specific. The notion of specificity is important. Of all the evolutes, only the material objects, which are made of gross matter, are specific. That means to say that the five elements of gross matter [*mahabhūtas*] only appear as individual concrete objects. The subtle being [*tanmātras*] of the senses remains generalised; but can take any temporary forms that the self wishes, in dreaming sleep, from that immense store of generalised potentiality.

On its own, the subtle hearing is the pure ether [*akaśa*]; or space and time. In deep meditation we simply can sometimes hear sound itself; rather than the sounds of individual things. In deep meditation, again, the seeing of the eye can be absorbed in itself; which is an experience of elemental redness. Redness, in Indian thought, is the primary source of all colour; and, indeed, of Form. In eastern metaphysics, it has often been believed that the subtle elements are an empirical experience for the sage, who has vision. The 'chi' of Chinese ontology will occasionally reveal it's very self in a flash of lightning; though of course all things are made of the chi, in one way or another. The Matter and Form of Aristotelian ontology, by contrast, are never the objects of perception, or of any kind of insight. They are attained purely by reason. For the Samkhya thinker, and indeed for the thinkers of many Indian systems of metaphysics, the gunas are almost an empirical experience, as is the Self; yet Prakṛti is attained by reason.

This mobile balance of gunas operates on every level of existence. It operates on the infinitesimal level of the finest atoms and then on the level of elements and molecules. It operates on the level of cells and microbes and then on the level of plants and animals. It operates on the level of the weather and of the entire cosmos. It operates in the individual human soul and on the social order of family and society. Just as, in the modern scientific view, a large crystal, displays in its outward and large form, the elemental shape of its fundamental molecule; so, in the Samkhya vision, does the changing universe reveal the blending and unblending of the gunas. And the crystal is, in ancient Indian science, a most noble and sattvic stone.

Guna means, literally, a strand of thread. It then comes to mean 'fold'; and from that meaning comes the derived meaning 'number'. In Indian mathematical science it means a multiplier. From the sense that a strand is subordinate to a thread, or, indeed, a fold is subordinate to a piece of cloth, *guna* comes to mean: a secondary element, a subordinate part, or a quality.

At the Upanayana ceremony, a Brahmin boy is given the sacred thread, which has three differently coloured strands, and he thereby accepts the rights and duties of his position. The sacred thread is the perfect image of Prakṛti. As the thread is no more than its strands, so Prakṛti is really no more than its gunas. The gunas are not qualities in the sense of additions or modifications, like the folds in a piece of folded cloth, they are Prakṛti's inner, or essential qualities, which make her herself. More than they she is not. Yet no guna can be conceived as existing on its own – thus the gunas are qualities not substances. Prakṛti is an ultimate substance. Prakṛti contains within herself the eminent causes of all material beings.

The Bhagavad-Gītā. Chapter 14

5. The three modes (*guna*): goodness (*sattva*), passion (*rajas*), and dullness (*tamas*) born of nature (Prakṛti) bind down in the body, O Mighty – armed (Arjuna), the imperishable dweller in the body.

6. Of these, goodness (*sattva*) being pure, causes illumination and health. It binds, O blameless one, by attachment to happiness and by attachment to knowledge.

7. Passion (*rajas*), know thou, is of the nature of attraction, springing from craving and attachment. It binds fast, O Son of Kunti (Arjuna) the embodied one by attachment to action.

8. But dullness (*tamas*), know thou, is born of ignorance and deludes all embodied beings. It blinds, O Bharata (Arjuna), by negligence, indolence and sleep.

9. Goodness attaches one to happiness, passion to action, O Bharata (Arjuna), but dullness, veiling wisdom, attaches to negligence.

10. Goodness prevails, overpowering passion and dullness, O Bharata (Arjuna). Passion prevails, overpowering goodness and dullness and even so dullness prevails overpowering goodness and passion.

11. When the light of knowledge streams forth in all gates of the body, then it may be known that goodness has increased.

12. Greed, activity, the undertaking of actions, unrest and craving – these spring up, O Best of the Bharatas (Arjuna), when rajas (passion) increases.

13. Unillumination, inactivity, negligence, and mere delusion – these arise, O Joy of the Kurus (Arjuna), when dullness increases.

The noblest of the three gunas is *sattva*. The basic meaning of *sattva* is 'existence', or 'being'. Now, in Indian thought Being is a positive concept; because, it is not Nothing. And so, in Indian philosophy, as in ancient Greek philosophy, Being is of necessity good. Thus *sattva*, the best aspect of Prakṛti, comes to mean 'goodness' and 'perfection'. However, sattva is never actually conscious. That vital, witnessing element, on which we build our self-awareness [*ahamkara*], is the Purusha. But sattva is the 'clear' guna that makes Nature ready for consciousness. It is the balanced and balancing guna. By being clear, a being is truly itself: by being balanced, a being is good and perfect.

Thus there are further, derived significances of *sattva*: whole, integral and pure, nature and essence. Perhaps 'clear' is one of the most important of the many meanings of *sattva*. Sattva is the crystal of Being, wherein Purusha can see Himself. (And did not Aristotle speak of the Prime Moved [*primum mobile*] as not being causally influenced in the sense of material causality, or force, but being drawn towards the Prime Mover [*primum movens*], or God, by love; and thus turning the entire universe?)

Sattva is the contemplative guna.

The second of the three gunas is *rajas*. According to the Rig-Veda, the cosmic sky has three divisions. The first is Svar, the sphere of light. The second is Rajas, the dim or coloured sky, and the third is Tamas, the darkness, or the space beyond ether. Rajas in Sanskrit can mean: the element air and that which is obscure, dusty, rusted, or polluted. In the Samkhya system, rajas is mobile, like the dust in the wind, gyrating here and then there; neither clear and suspended like sattva, nor dark and static like tamas. Its activeness is a sort of pollution; as takes place when dust is sprinkled on the surface of limpid water, causing motion.

Rajas is the active guna.

The meaning of *tamas* is 'darkness' or 'gloom'. It is the name for hell; and for a particular division of hell. It is the obscuration of the sun or the moon in eclipses. It is mental darkness, ignorance, illusion and error. In the Samkhya system it is the guna of heaviness, ignorance, dullness, sleep and illusion. But it is also the guna of solidity and without it no material thing could be.

Tamas is the static and solid guna.

Stones and rock are heavy with the principle of tamas; while in animals the rajastic principle causes mobility and the experience of pain. Again within the order of animals an increase in tamas results in the tortoise, and an increase in rajas gives the cheetah his rapid movement. If there is a further increase of sattva on the rajas of the animal; the monkey evolves: and then, if there is a different balance again, with more sattva still, and a little more tamas; man appears.

The society of man is composed of individuals of different physical make up and of different temperaments. Given that the balance of the gunas on the essential and, as it were, biological level gives a man his human nature; accidental adjustments in the mix of the gunas then give each man his individual temperament. The predominance of sattva in that temperament produces the man who thinks and prays. The predominance of rajas produces the politician, the soldier and the man of action. The predominance of tamas produces the businessman or the farmer – more tamas again and, perhaps, some more sattva produces the labourer. Thus there is an ontological basis in Indian philosophy for a caste system. This doctrine of distinct castes of men provoked a reaction in the teachings of Buddha; and in the practise of devotion [*bakti-yoga*] amongst the Hindus – of union with the Lord God. Most Indian thinkers avoided extremes of caste discrimination. With Buddha, the purest wish for enlightenment can overcome all difficulties of background and temperament. With the Krishna religion, the pure love of the personal God [*bakti-yoga*] had the same simple effect. With Ishvarakrishna, perhaps, whatever advantages the sattvic man might have, through his intellectual cognition of the truth; prayer, meditation and reflection, in the tamasic man, could overcome the cultural ignorance and intransigence of temperament.

From the point of view of the experiencing consciousness three gunas are experienced as pleasure [*sattva*], pain [*rajas*] and delusion [*tamas*].

> xii The attributes are of the nature of pleasure, pain, and delusion; they serve the purpose of illumination, action, and restraint; and they are mutually subjugative, and supporting, and productive, and co-operative.

> xiii The *sattva* attribute is held to be buoyant and illuminating; the *rajas* attribute exciting and mobile; and the *tamas* attribute sluggish and enveloping. Their functioning is for a single purpose, like that of a lamp.

The Rose and the Crystal

But what is it that stirs Prakṛti and guides the production of these existents? The stirring of the gunas, of themselves according to the Samkhya theory, is not sufficient explanation.

Unless there is another agency factor in the cosmos the gunas would blend evenly and exist forever without change. The world, as we perceive it, could not happen. There could be no individual consciousness as we experience it, or individual objects for consciousness to witness.

The other entity in the Samkhya system, the partner, or indeed, husband of Prakṛti, is *purusa*: the Witness. In Sanskrit, *purusa* means: male, or human being. In grammar it means the 'person' [of the verb etc.]; and in anatomy it means 'the pupil of the eye'. It then means that which makes a man what he is; his soul or spirit, or his essence. The word '*purusa*' is derived from the Sanskrit root *pri*: meaning to enjoy, or delight. In the Samkhya philosophy *purusa* is: the witness, the enjoyer or the consciousness of the universe.

In the vision of Plato and Aristotle, the creation of the universe by God is not an act of material causation. The world simply loves God and desires to order itself in a way that imitates him. In the Samkhya vision Prakṛti is said, by meeting Purusha, to awake from a sleep of dullness, ignorance and sadness. Purusha becomes reflected in Prakṛti through her clearest, or sattvic part. This accidental meeting stirs her gunas and the universe comes to be; though not through an act of ontological, or scientific causality. It is rather a chance conversation that has an unexpected influence. The traditional image of this relationship, in Indian poetry, is that of a rose reflected in a crystal. The rose does not alter the crystal; nor the crystal the rose.

Just as, during the Bengal night, the full moon, in all his radiance, is reflected in the forest pool, so Purusha sees himself reflected in the sattva of Prakṛti. And just as, when the moon is reflected in the forest pool, the wind on the water gives the appearance that his face is troubled; or again the reeds at the water's edge seems to trammel his visage; so does Purusha think, 'I have a mind and a body; I perceive things'. At that same moment Prakṛti thinks she is conscious.

Ego

Prakṛti, thinking she is one with Purusha and believing she is conscious, is *mahat* [the Great One]; the one and the same principle by which the universe both exists, in its conceived fullness; and, indeed, by which it is understood. The intellect [*buddhi*] is conceived and born from this principle. The principle that the universe is understandable [*mahat*] becomes in us, the principle of our knowing — *buddhi*, the intellect.

> xxii. From *Prakṛti* [primordial matter, Nature] issues *mahat* [*buddhi*, the Great Principle]; from this issues *ahamkara* [I-principle]; from which proceed the five elementary substances.
>
> The 'set of sixteen' is made up of the eleven sense organs, to be described later on, and the five primary elements. Out of these sixteen, from the five primary elements proceed respectively the five elementary substances - *ākāśa* [ether], earth, water, air, and fire.
>
> xxiii. Intellect is determinative. Virtue, wisdom, non-attachment, and the possession of lordly powers constitute its *sattvika* form [i.e., form when the constituent *sattva,* goodness, predominates]; the reverse of these is its *tāmasa* form [i.e., of its nature, when *tamas,* darkness, preponderates].

> Now 'determination' consists in the notion that 'this should be done,' and it belongs to, and forms the characteristic function of, *buddhi* [the 'Great Principle', will], which acquires sentience from its proximity to the sentient faculty of the spirit; and '*buddhi*' is regarded as not different from the said 'determination' ... this also constitutes the 'definition' ... of *buddhi,* in as much as it distinguishes it from all like and unlike things.

> xxiv. Individuation is conceit in the ego. Therefrom, creation proceeds in two ways, as the eleven-fold aggregate and as the five-fold subtle elements.

> xxv. The 'set of eleven' abounding in the *sattva* attribute, evolves out of the '*vaikṛta*' form of the 'I-principle'; the set of rudimentary substances from the '*bhūtādi*' form; and both of them from the '*taijasa*' form of the 'I-principle'.

As *buddhi* is born the man becomes aware of himself as *ahamkara* – 'I am'. As soon as he thinks, 'I am', he immediately thinks, 'I see' and thus develops his senses. This 'I' considers his senses different from the objects that they perceive; because 'I' tries to identify with the Purusha, rather than with Prakṛti. So the five subtle senses devolve from this act of will; and then from the sensible qualities of things perceived, the five elements are devolved, or organised from the gunas In order to fully apprehend the objects he perceives, he evolves the subtle body, and the central sense, or *manas*. As Purusha, reflected through *buddhi*, imagines his selfhood – [*ahamkara* or cause of self] – he thinks: 'I perceive this. I think this. I think that this X is in such and such a category.' Thus he imagines that, not only can he make judgements, but also that he can casually alter the world. But he cannot. The five activities [*karmendriya*] – walking, eating and the like – which evolve at the same time as the five subtle senses, or sense capacities [*buddhīndriya*], belong to the dimension of Prakṛti, which has been stirred, and altered somewhat, by the presence of the Purusha. Though the self identifies with these activities — Purusha thinks that the Purusha acts. But in his real self the Purusha never acts.

The subtle senses together form the subtle body, which passes from one gross body to another, during reincarnations [*samsara*]. But this subtle body will also disappear by merging with Nature, whose modification it is, when the Purusha becomes free. In reality, those subtle senses, the five tanmatras, appear only on the face of *buddhi*, as it were: just as the ripples made by the wind on a pool at night, move not the moon, but only the moon's reflection.

Primal Nature

> lix. As a dancer desists from dancing, having exhibited herself to the audience, so does Primal Nature desist, having exhibited herself to the spirit.

> lx. Generous Nature, endowed with attributes, brings about by manifold means, without benefit to herself, the good of the spirit, who is devoid of attributes, and confers no benefit in return.

lxi. It is my belief that there is not any other being more bashful than Primal Nature, who because of the realisation 'I have been seen' never again comes into the view of the spirit.

lxii. Of a certainty, therefore, not any spirit is bound or liberated, not does any migrate; it is Primal Nature, abiding in manifold forms, that is bound, is liberated, and migrates.

Verily no spirit is bound; nor does any migrate;
nor is any emancipated. Nature alone, having
many vehicles, is bound, migrates, and is released.
Bondage, migration and release are ascribed to
the spirit, in the manner as defeat and victory are
attributed to the king, though actually occurring
to his soldiers, because it is the servants that take
part in the undertaking, the effects of which - grief
or profit - accrue to the king. In the same manner,
experience and emancipation, though really
belonging to Nature, are attributed to the spirit, on
account of the non-discrimination of spirit from
Nature, as has been already explained....

lxiii. Nature by herself binds herself by means of seven forms and by means of one form she causes deliverance for the benefit of the spirit.

'*Nature binds herself by means of seven forms*'; i.e.,
by virtue and other dispositions [all properties of

> the will] except wisdom. For of the benefit of the spirit in the shape of experience and final release, she releases herself by herself, '*by means of one form*', i.e., by wisdom - by discrimination. That is to say, she does not again bring about the experience or emancipation of that same spirit.
>
> lxiv. Thus, from the repeated study of the truth, there results that wisdom, 'I do not exist, naught is mine, I am not,' which leaves no residue to be known, is pure, being free from ignorance, and is absolute.
>
> ... '*I am not*' merely precludes all action from the spirit; ... And since there is no action of the spirit, there arises the idea of 'not-I'; I here stands for active agency in general ...
>
> Or we may interpret the three forms in another way. The sentence, 'I am not,' means that 'I am the spirit, *not productive*' and because non-productive, 'I have no action' — 'Not I'; and since without action, 'I can have no possessions', hence, 'naught is mine.'

The seven forms of evolution, which bind, are virtue, vice, error, dispassion, passion, power and weakness. The reader, by now, used to the triadic logic of Indian thought, will understand that virtue as well as vice, and dispassion as well as passion, are all equally due to erroneous knowledge. Virtue is very much a matter of cognition and ego. Rabindranath Tagore recounted how his father forbade him to read an American book of ethics and morality; saying that such self-conscious awareness of virtue was wicked.

And so the Purusha, finding himself reflected in Prakṛti and identifying himself with Buddhi, thinks, in his reflection, that he has *kārma* – that, as it were, he is a moon caught in the reeds of the earthly pool. He can imagine, seeing his own reflection troubled by the wavelets of the pond, that he is suffering. But it is not so. He has no causal relationship with Prakṛti; nor, indeed, with any entity in the material world, or in the subtle realm.

The Elements

The mathematical arrangement of principles, or kinds of entity, in the Samkhya system is helpful and most interesting. This traditional enumeration gives a dyad, a tryad and four pentads. There is undoubtedly a reflection of ancient musical forms. The Samkhya, like most Indian schools, considered sound to be the primary *tanmātra*. The primary awareness of self, and bare consciousness, is thought of as hearing undifferentiated cosmic sound. From this cosmic sound comes all creation. — Krishna is frequently portrayed as playing a flute; and Shiva as dancing.

Enumerations relating to the basic principles [*tattvas*]

The set of 25

First and foremost, of course, is the set of 25 that encompasses the basic principles of the system, namely:

[1] pure consciousness - *purusa*
[2] primordial materiality - *mūlaprakṛti*
[3] intellect - *buddhi* or *mahat*
[4] egoity - *ahamkara*
[5] mind – *manas* [both a sense capacity and an action capacity]

The five sense capacities - *buddhindriyas*
[6] hearing – *ṣrotra*
[7] touching - *tvac*
[8] seeing - *cakśus*
[9] tasting - *rasana*
[10] smelling - *ghrāna*

The five action capacities – *karmendryas*
[11] speaking - *vac*
[12] grasping/apprehending – *pāṇi*
[14] excreting - *pāyu*
[13] walking/motion - *pada*
[15] procreating - *upastha*;

The five subtle elements - *tanmatras*
[16] sound- *śabda*
[17] contact – *sparṣa*
[18] form - *rūpa*
[19] taste - *rasa*
[20] smell - *gandha*;

The five gross elements - *mahabhutas*

[21] space/ether - *akaśa*

[22] wind/air - *vāyu*

[23] fire - *tejas*

[24] water - *ap*

[25] earth - *pṛthivī*

According to Samkhya philosophy, among these twenty-five principles, only the first two are independent existents, namely, pure consciousness [purusa] and primordial materiality [mulaprakṛti]. In other words, only items [1] and [2] exist in some sense as 'distinct' or 'separate' from one another. The two are described in Samkhya philosophy as being ungenerated, outside of ordinary space and time, stable, simple, unsupported, nonmergent [or nondissolvable], without parts, and independent. The relation between them is one of simple copresence. Pure consciousness is inherently inactive, but primordial materiality is inherently generative in the sense that it is capable of generating a set of discrete or manifest subdivisions when activated by the catalytic presence of pure consciousness. Items [3] through [25] make up the various subdivisions of primordial materiality and are, thus, internal to primordial materiality ...

Common Sense

The notion of a central sense, *manas*, is common to many systems of Indian philosophy. Since the material objects that we perceive relate to all our senses, it must be presumed that there is a central, or common sense, which receives impressions from the several different senses and puts them together. This is the equivalent of the *sensus communis* of St Thomas Aquinas [1224-1274] and other mediaeval western thinkers. Those thinkers, however, held a simple dualist view of matter and spirit. The *sensus communis* was, for them in the organ of the brain; and entirely material. For the Samkhya there is a range of Being between the very heaviest matter and the clearest entity ready for consciousness; because of the three gunas. Manas must be sattvic, but it must also have parts; because it is connected to the different senses and faculties of bodily activity. It is, of course wholly different from the Purusha, which is the pure and only spirit in the Samkhya system.

Manas, and the cognitive faculties, require a support; and a medium between itself and the gross body. This must be the subtle body [*linga ṣarīra*], made of the subtle elements [*tanmātra*]; and combining with the gross elements [*mahabhūta*], to form the senses. The subtle body is said to be 'specific', unlike the subtle elements of which it is made. It is, like the material things of the world that we see, an individual object. The necessities of manas and the *linga ṣarīra* are arrived at purely by reason, in the Samkhya view; which does not depend on the evidence of seers and mediums, just as it does not depend on the testimony of scripture.

> xli. Just as a picture does not exist without a substrate, or a shadow without a post or the like, so too the cognitive apparatus [*linga*: intellect, etc.], does not subsist supportless, without what is specific [i.e., a subtle body].

The term '*linga*' here stands for the will, the I-principle, and the rudimentary elements, because they are the means of knowing and these cannot subsist without a substrate...

xlii. Formed for the sake of the spirit's purpose the subtle body acts like a dramatic actor, on account of the connection of 'causes and effects' and by union with the all-embracing power of Nature.

'*Formed for the spirit's purpose*', the subtle body acts like a *dramatic actor,* on account of its connection with the '*causes*' in the shape of virtue, vice, etc., - and '*effects*' in the shape of the taking up of different kinds of physical bodies, the latter being the effects of virtue, etc. That is to say, just as a dramatic actor, playing different parts, acts like Paraśurāma or Yudhiśṭhira or Vatsarāja, so does the subtle body, occupying various physical bodies, act like a man or a brute or a tree.

xliv. By virtue is obtained ascent to higher planes, by vice, descent to the lower; from wisdom results the highest good, and bondage from the reverse.

xlv. From dispassion results 'mergence into Nature'; from attachment which abounds in the *rajas* attribute, transmigration; from power, non-impediment; and from the reverse, the contrary.

When a person is reborn, some of their characteristics are the result of effort in a previous life; but there are incidental characteristics due to the nature of the parents and the body newly taken. Ishvarakrishna and Vacaspati Mishra recognised a third source of characteristics; Nature herself.

l. The nine forms of contentment have been held to be the following: Four internal, named [1]

> Nature [*Prakṛti*], [2] means [*upadāna*], [3] time [*kāla*], and [4] luck [*bhāgyā*]; and five external due to the abstinence from objects.

The *contentment* called 'Nature' consists in that feeling of satisfaction which the disciple has on being told that 'discriminative wisdom is only a modification of Nature and, as such, would come to every one in the natural course of events, and there is no need of having recourse to the practice of meditation, etc. So, my child, remain as you are! ...'

Balance

The means [*upadāna*] indicates any programme of specialised activities, that members of an ashram, a temple community, or, indeed, of a family at home might undertake in order to advance their spirituality. The finest, or most sattvic, of the five vital airs, which animate the organs of the body is *upadāna*. Prescription in modern Indian medicine is aimed at balancing these airs or winds [*vāyu*]. The force in each one of us that tends to lift ideas and thoughts is *upadāna*; and, indeed, *upadāna* can raise the operations of the body and the emotions onto a spiritual, or sattvic plain. These airs are collectively known as *praṇa*. The specialised breathing exercises that lead to that desirable balance of airs, or energies, are *praṇamayāna*. The *āsana*, or physical positions of yogic exertion, also bring about this equilibrium; emphasising the primacy and dominance of *upadāna vāyu*. But equally, Ishvarakrishna taught the study of the Samkhya philosophy would bring about that same desirable balance. It is a feeling of relaxation, freedom and joy. I have found that the study of Indian philosophy can have exactly the same effect as the practice of the asanas. Further, when I have missed the regular practice of the asanas, I have sometimes found that the study of Indian philosophy has kept my body supple in the meantime.

Things are good because of their sattvic part, and situations are good because they lead to an increase of the sattvic element in the things and people involved. Goodness is not a subjective quality but an external reality which individual consciousnesses merely recognise. We thus exist to improve. That is the nature of our own being. The Samkhya is therefore not propounding an ethic that cannot be logically derived from the world that we perceive. It does not simply say because such and such is the case, therefore we must do so and so. It seeks rather to speed our progress away from tamas and rajas towards sattva, by pointing out that our yearning for this journey is the truest part of our very selves.

To those who seek perfection, the fact that any course of development, or yoga, follows a natural sequence and that ripeness comes in due course, should be a consolation.

And, in any case, people arrive at contentment and detachment for no particular reason [*bhāgya*]. And they may have no knowledge of yoga, philosophy, psychology, or, indeed, any religion at all. It is a very Indian attitude that this should be a source of contentment to the follower of yoga. To the follower of eastern systems of spirituality (or, indeed, any spirituality), who regards enlightenment as an achievement, or philosophy as a qualification of some kind, and therefore a matter of competition, *bhāgya* can be a cause of deep despair and great frustration.

The five external forms of contentment arise from abstinence from the five objects of sense: sound, contact, form, taste and odour.

The Jaina system, the earlier Samkhya system and other systems conceived of no single, infinite deity, but a myriad, perhaps even an infinite number of individual purushas. The purushas had not only the eternity of existence unceasing; but they had the opposite, counterbalancing infinity of existence without beginning. While reflected in Prakṛti, each Purusha would form *buddhi* and thus become a *jīva*. As a jiva it would perform the long wandering pilgrimage of *samsara*. It would enter a body at conception and use its newly found senses to perceive. It would thus form an ego or a self-identity – *ahamkara*. At the death of that body the Purusha is bereft of the perception and thought, to which he has become very accustomed. He loses his self-identity, which he has formed a habit of obtaining through a body. He thus seeks another incarnation. Throughout all these incarnations *buddhi* remains the same. Because of his association with the sattvic part of Prakṛti *buddhi* contains the modifications. These modifications, samskaras, are the causal traces of the impressions made by thought and sensations. They are the memory of the jiva, the memory of previous incarnations. The samskaras [*samskāra*] can be positive or negative: they can cause the soul to strive after higher incarnations or remain for a time on a lower level. Ultimately each Purusha must reach the goal of his quest; which is the paradoxical realisation that his quest is futile. He does not need the limiting experience of perception. In the Purusha himself, is wisdom beyond knowledge of a conceptual kind; and, realising this, he is free. He is radiant and sublime and his total contentment is in the bliss of his own being. He no longer needs to consider any object because it his own being that is truly satisfying and beautiful.

The full moon at its zenith in the clear night sky; tranquil and radiant amid the myriad stars; floating free of the mountains and the forest and of the activities of the denizens of earth, unaffected by anything below; neither blind nor seeing, neither laughing nor weeping, nor happy nor sad, yet somehow utterly magnificent and beautiful; has long been the image of the Purusha in the Indian consciousness.

CHAPTER 8

PURVA MIMAMSA
Jaimini

In the novel of Jane Austen, *Sense and Sensibility*, the affable and upright character Sir John Middleton exclaims: 'Company, company, where would we be without company?'

Man is a cooperative species. Men achieve most things by working together rather than in isolation. The crucial means of living together and working together are the greetings and expressions of mutual friendship. Perhaps Sir John Middleton, using the word 'company', is thinking of the round of social entertainment; but we could further add to his dictum, and include all engagements, whether for the purpose of pleasure or for business. If human cooperation depends on civilised 'company' in Jane Austen's sense, we might well ask, where would company be without ritual? Ritual initiates and closes the meetings, which are companionship; and ritual expresses love as well as respect. The word, 'ritual', derived from the Latin *ritus*, means something prescribed or lain down. But rarely has this prescription been the deliberate act of one individual person. So many of our social gestures, formal and informal, have grown up with time. They have simply come to be. Ritual movements are simply actions among hosts of others; and greetings are simply words used, not to describe, but rather to greet.

The meaning of *karman* is 'action', but *karman* further means: work, special duty and then religious act. Jaimini uses the word *karman* to describe ritual and thus he equates ritual, in the first instance, with all actions — cooking, planting and reaping. Then he gives the word 'action' higher and nobler values. Perhaps everything that a human being does with deliberation is, if he is honest, sacred.

Human cooperation is impossible without ritual. In the morning we not only say 'good morning' to the family but at the same time we also say 'good morning' to the Morning. For the early Aryan, as for many modern Hindus, the morning *pūjā* and the *agnihotra* sacrifice are as necessary as the spring sowing, or the autumn reaping; or as waking and sleeping.

Jaimini wrote the Mimamsa Sutra about 400 BC. It is a text of investigation [*Mimamsa*]. Jaimini's School of thought is known as the Pūrva Mimamsa, as opposed to the later orthodox schools of Shamkara, Ramanuja and Madhva, which are collectively called Uttāra Mimamsa. 'Earlier' [*pūrva*] also means 'basic,' and 'later' [*uttāra*] again means 'further, more developed'.

The Mimamsa Sūtra begins with idea of *dharma*, the basis of the Vedic vision of man's place in the scheme of things. A Hindu student once told me that Dharma is 'the good way to go'. In a sense the word *dharma* can mean 'action', but often with a force of intelligent purpose, as following a progressive and improving course. Thus *dharma* also means duty. Duty depends on Nature, in the physical sense, and also upon social situation. Each individual personality has his own Dharma; which regards his health, his place in the family and his social position. Dharma is not an empirically given entity, it is revealed over time: just as the very idea of the course of time itself is not revealed in one moment.

The idea that Dharma is understood as the result of lengthy observation, and exchanges of experience with others, reveals an important aspect of Jaimini's philosophy. All is revealed empirically, but not instantly; rather, everything appears gradually. Observation requires memory and report. And Jaimini's method is not to prove, but simply to describe.

> 1.1. The idea of Dharma does not arise from sense-perception, because the latter is limited to the present, while the idea of Dharma goes beyond the present …
>
> Dharma is indeed linked up with action, for we often say that a person does his Dharma, and that implies action …

According to Jaimini the subject of the Vedas is action [*karman*] and the world of action — the physical universe. In order to obtain paradise, we need to understand nature and action. The Vedas are part of a living oral tradition of interpretation. It is important for Jaimini that the Vedas are not entirely reliable in themselves, as they are read in each era. They are not simply the eternal word. Jaimini is recording an oral tradition of investigation and guidance. And it is thus that he is a philosopher, rather than a theologian. Indeed, the Vedas, for Jaimini, are a conflicting product of Nature; the Nature that produces everything and is founded on the three interacting Gunas. From the point of view of our observing minds the interacting Gunas produce different levels of subtlety. The sattvic guna furnishes the possibility of higher ideals. Western materialistic philosophies always fail to give any account of why we need to be ethical, and thus of why we want to be philosophical at all. Thus Jaimini finds a universe that includes the reality of our ideals; but a universe where the existence of a creator God is not a necessity.

> 1.2. The subject matter of the Vedas is action; and they would be meaningless if we interpret them in any other light; hence they are said to be non-eternal. They are not eternal because they give expression to conflicting opinions ... The Vedas are really an expression of the Gunas or the attributes of Nature; and that is so because the *Gunas* are the most important part of nature, — for it is chiefly in this form that Nature appears to us, when we look at it from a distance (or in a broad perspective). The Gunas are said to be born of Nature or *Prakṛti* in the same sense in which a child is born; for there is a natural desire to have something which will last for some time (and that is why *Prakṛti* creates Gunas and lives through them).

The Sūtra then explains that action [*karman*] is the basis of all life. It then distinguishes between the life forces acting within a human being [*karman*] and his deliberate and intended actions [*dharma*]. All actions and events are Karman. There is no opposite of Karman. Thus there is no fundamental difference between cause and effect; each is simply an event. But the intelligent and intended actions of men [*dharma*] have an opposite. When we act unintelligently — that opposite is *adharma*. Above all, the actions of the sacrifice should be deliberate and intelligent, to bring about purification and improvement. The Dharma appears in the Veda as a series of injunctions [*codanā*]. Another meaning of *codanā* is 'impulse of the heart'; thus there is a subtext to all Indian thought of regulation that is very positive; because Dharma is also self-fulfilment. To happily live our Dharma is what we truly desire.

> 1.1.1. The duty [*dharma*] is an object distinguished by a command.

The relationship between the ideas of Karma and Dharma is interesting. One could say that it is the relationship between efficient and final causality. Dharma is a kind of causality, which becomes more significant when we consider the social dimension. Here we have the basis of the distinction between Nature and Nurture. What is purely the product of the interaction of entities is Nature [*prakṛti*]: what is the product of intentional action [*dharma*] is that which creates society. And then again society creates Dharma.

> 1.3. Dharma is founded on the word of the Vedas, which is the highest word …
>
> There is an immutable law of action at work within all forms of life, according to which all must act. For instance, we see things growing in size, but without apparent action; but there is sound, motion, or vibration within them unperceived …
>
> The action of a healthy body, performed spontaneously or in the ordinary course of Nature, is obviously the

> result of impulse; and that is not the idea of Dharma as given in the sacred books; and it would be an incorrect application of the rules laid down by them to think that it is so.
>
> (The idea of intention is important; for) in making expiation by means of sacrifice, the most important thing is intention, because it is closely connected with sacrifice.

It is important not to assume and incorporate the overt idea of free will into the notion of deliberate action [*dharma*]. Like most Indian systems of philosophy Jaimini's conception is entirely knowledge based — intentionality implies merely that the action is thoughtful, that the thinking intelligence [*citta*] is involved. As soon as the mind knows something it acts. The word *citta* has a fullness. Our intelligence is necessarily ethical. It is not merely a biological calculator.

Also it is of the nature of mind [*manas*] in most Indian systems that it can only think of one thing at a time.

> 2.4. Even though we can perform only one action at a time, certain actions, such as censure, effort, complete acquisition of knowledge, and speech are more important than others; and the most important place is given to intellect [*citta*], because it is the effective cause of action. That is so (because it is the function of intellect to decide, and) we can proceed to action only when there is an order or decision to that effect ...

> If there were no impulse to action, a person would not be able to act at all, with the result that the laws of action would be proved to be untrue. But we find that there is an order from within, calling upon us to act; and, as this order is constantly repeated, there is a corresponding repetition in the text to express the idea of this law. Before we act, however, we find that there is an order to act on the one hand, and a prohibition against it on the other; and when in the end we act or do not act, it means that there is a balance of judgement on that side.

It is vital, not only for the understanding of the Mimamsa and Indian philosophy, but also for the understanding of all religion, that the command to virtuously act comes from within and not from without. Gurus and counsellors, priests and parents are useful in helping us to see what is right; that is, what we actually think is right; and in giving us courage and support in doing what is right; but they cannot command us to think, or to act.

'The balance of judgement' is not a balance between two actions, but a balance between acting and not acting, in the first instance, and again between acting and not acting in the second instance. In Aristotelian philosophy the balance is similar and the same concept of dual choice is found. However, Aristotle considers there to be a faculty of will, which separately operates, after the faculty of intellect has grasped the situation and apprehended the desirable object. In Indian philosophy will and desire are usually one [*iccha*]. The object is apprehended as desirable because of the particular balance of its Gunas. In the human consciousness the particular equilibrium of these external *guna* lead to the inner balance of *rasa*. The *rasa* are the feelings we experience within ourselves, as we observe different objects. Each object exists and has its special nature because of the Gunas within it. Each object observed creates the special Rasas within each one of us. As different individuals we see objects differently. The relationship between Guna and Rasa bridges the gap between subject and object, between 'ought' and 'is' — and thereby hangs a tale.

The vision of Jaimini is of the essence of all Indian Philosophy.

> In certain actions, especially those which we regard as religious, or of a virtuous character, the impulse to action, as we have often heard, is of an irresistible character; and the explanation of it can easily be understood.

What a positive perception of ourselves that when we read holy scripture, we run to the Good! The result of action is for the soul, and yet the soul exists for action — that is the good action, which is Dharma. Jaimini does not prove the existence of the soul. He believed in a plurality of permanent, individual selves; but he did not believe in God.

> 3.1. The result, however, is for the sake of *purusa* or the individual soul; and the soul too is for the sake of action; and all these are connected together by means of purpose. This is a universal law, applicable in all circumstances; for if there be no purpose, there

> can be no action. The result of action follows action: were it otherwise, we should be able to get the result of action without action; and a person is moved to action because of the effect or result he expects to produce. The purpose and qualities of a person become one in action, for that is the law of action.
>
> A person can engage in only one action at a time, and there is good reason for saying so. This is a characteristic of all for it is a universal law. But all action is performed for the sake of something else, and this should be accepted, even as the sacred books tell us.

Desire is crucial in the instigation of intelligent action; but then action clearly flows from desire, as desire flows from sensation and cognition. Again we must say that there is not, for Jaimini, a clearly separate faculty, in the human personality, like the free will of western philosophy and theology.

> 3.5. When we hear the name of sweetmeats or cakes, a desire arises within us, and the cause of the desire is the name itself. We may hear only one man sing the praise of the cake; or it may be all, because all are associated with it; or only the singers of its praise may desire to have it, — having been drawn to it from what they have heard. All these desires are associated with knowledge, and so should be grouped together.

The translator (N.V. Thadani) in his footnotes — and perhaps in his interpretation — has likened the Purva Mimamsa to the Bhagavad-

Gita, where we are told by Krishna that we must not act for the reason of desiring fruits of action [*karmaphalahetur*]. The Gītā has a message of personal devotion and loving service of God. It combines many doctrines including the austere way of doing the good thing for its own sake. We may not desire anything. Especially we must not desire virtuousness. The desire of virtuousness is still desire; and desire must be extinguished. This doctrine is redolent of Buddhism and other traditions of renunciation. But the classically religious aim of Jaimini's thrust is not the extinction of desire, but the attainment of happiness. To desire happiness is the essence of virtue. To desire virtue is not the same as desiring happiness. Desiring to be virtuous, or indeed desiring to extinguish desire, is too self-reflexive. Goodness is right desire. The Mimamsa is a humanistic, as well as a religious view.

The phenomenon of purification applies to things as well as to men and so Dharma is the improvement of the universe as a whole; and the purification of a man is a part of the natural scheme of things. Purification for the early Hindu is a cosmic reality, as is growth, or fulfilment.

> 4.3. The highest aim of action is not only to purify the actor, but also the material objects used in connection with it; and if we study the Vedas properly, we shall find, as a result, that this is the explanation of their real meaning.

> 4.2. Purpose, action and result are all connected together like the limbs of the body ... Atreya says that there can be no action without result; and if the result

> is not known, it should be inferred … This result is brought about by skill in action, and is not connected with the origin of purpose (or desire); and there is always an impelling force which brings about the union of action with result, and the connection between them is important.

Jaimini regards this process of action and result as unprecedented and not to be understood [*apūrva*]. Later Mimamsakas, however, attempted to give more developed and philosophical explanations of the power of actions to produce fruits over a long period of time.

Knowledge

Jaimini offers three means of knowing [*pramana*]. These are perception [*pratyakśa*], inference [*anumāna*] and authoritative testimony [*śabda*].

It is not Jaimini's temper to probe the realms of metaphysics; but rather simply to say what is. His realism brings into play our awareness of wholes and our sense of the meaning of processes, as recognisable wholes. It is thus that he is aware of final causality. A process is not just an accidentally connected chain of events; a process can be itself an event, which causes the micro-processes within it to take place. Such a process is the life of a plant.

> 3.5. When we use the word 'whole', it means in every case the whole of what is produced; and it is greater than different things of which it is made. When we divide the whole into its parts, the last in the series can

> have but one purpose to serve; and the same is the case with a sacrifice or an offering properly and intelligently made.

Cosmic order [*ṛta*] is basic to the world's existence and to the possibility of Dharma. This order is revealed by the sequence of time. We enjoy ordering things because thereby we link our Dharma to the Dharma of the world and achieve a sense of peace; indeed, classification is the Dharma of the scholar.

> 6.4. When ideas and objects are scattered about, their arrangement in some scientific manner is a source of comfort; — like an asylum; and the idea of a law of Time arises from the existence of both (things and their orderly arrangement).

Interpretation

The poems of the Rig Veda were chanted a thousand years before the epoch in which Jaimini lived; and brahmins had taken meticulous care not to stray from the original words. Later, however, by the time of Jaimini, not only had the meanings of many words been lost, but beliefs had also shifted.

The Purva Mimamsa gives rules for the interpretation of the ancient text. We apply these rules when the surface meaning makes no sense or does not fit the text.

1. To analyse individual syllable meanings to find the true sense.
2. To study the verbal root.

3. To consider the manner in which the verse should be chanted [*krama*].

4. To consider the proximity of words over against intended verbal connections.

5. To consider whether we should take a common meaning, or whether we should consider an unusual meaning.

6. To consider whether the text is using the 'disguise' [*linga*] of metaphor.

7. To compare the problematic passage in question with the principal and well-understood passages in the rest of the text.

Once the 'disguise' has been revealed the newly understood sense will fit perfectly into the sentence.

Guiding principles are:

1. The text must be treated as a whole.
2. We must be guided by common sense and instinct.
3. A word must fit its context.
4. We should first study under the guidance of a competent teacher.

7.3. It is in this manner that we can understand the idea of the purification of the sacrificer through *Soma* (or the function of the mind). We cannot say that we get the meaning from its original or uninflected form, for we get it by means of division into parts; and we can understand it by seeing through its 'disguise'.

How the parts of *soma* give rise to a hidden meaning is obscure. The root *so* is connected to *sāya*, meaning 'evening'. There is possibly an image of the rise of the full moon after sunset. Moon is associated with mind, because both are changeable. Again, according to an obscure way of counting letters, Agni, the god of fire, represents the intellect [*citta*], or the stable part of the mind [*manas*], as it contemplates the more permanent forms of reality.

> 2.3. When we see through this 'disguise' [*linga*] we find that *Agni* (the god of fire) means 'intelligence'; and if we interpret the word according to this rule, we find that it refers to a fundamental concept of philosophy. It is in this manner that we ascribe the meaning 'intelligence' to *Agni*, as a result of which we get the idea *Dharma* or the law of life.
>
> But different books follow different plans; and we are told that we can achieve the highest end by refraining from action.
>
> But the Vedas repeatedly tell us that it is only by means of action that we can succeed in achieving results; and in order to understand this properly, what has been said in respect of *Agni*, should be extended to the other gods as well. The text has two meanings, which are consistent in themselves throughout, and the reference to action in this manner is intentional.

It is only through intelligence that we can see the permanent and all pervading law of Dharma. Again it is just not a matter of mindlessly reading an infallible text. To achieve a sound interpretation, training under a teacher is a necessity — a sound understanding of the text can only occur under the auspices of a cultural tradition. For the Hindu, tradition is as important as text.

Intelligence, by observing events, forms the idea of time. Observation is a process, just as the realties that we observe are processes. Observation is not a series of single, unrelated mental acts to which is then added another arbitrary mental act, which then somehow synthesises these unrelated acts into an artificial whole. How could that additional mental act not be another isolated event? How could it relate things, if things are not already related to one another? For Indian philosophy the laws governing mind are not different from the laws governing matter. The idea of time simply comes from observing Change and observing Change is not different from watching things change.

> The idea of Time arises from something that makes its appearance ... we can also get it from the meaning of the word immeasurable.
>
> Similarly, we get the idea of Change from Nature, or *Prakṛti*, which is subject to Time and takes place from moment to moment; and this fact of the interaction of Change and Time becomes apparent from what we see of things that remain (after others have disappeared); and we can see this even in a period of two days, according to a universal rule. According to this, Time and Change occur simultaneously.

> Anything that is essentially good (mixed with clarified butter), and associated with both intellect and the mind (*Agni* and *Soma*) is above change. But all that arises from the mind is like *Prakṛti*, — (subject to change); and this corresponds to the changes of the moon from the new to the full moon.

Finally we have a deep insight into the essence of ritual. Purification is raising a substance from a changeable state to a more permanent condition. The example of the clarification of butter by heating is that clarified butter is less likely to decay. Also the butter becomes translucent. Thus the purification of mind takes place when mind is altered from the unstable state of arbitrary passion and spontaneous activity, which does not order things, to a stable condition, which sees the permanence of things — this is a metamorphosis to intellect [*citta*]. Just as from time to time, at sunset, the full moon rises and is equal to the sun.

Just as Jaimini does not accept God, he seems also not to accept gods. For him the notion of a god furnishes an instance of 'disguise' [*linga*], of one thing standing in for another.

> A god represents an aspect of Nature, or Prakṛti; but if the word has two meanings, there is an implication that there is something in respect of the whole text which has not been properly expressed, and something needs to be taken from the one to the other side.

The Purva Mimamsa classically illustrates the Indian attitude to written text.

1. The hymns are handed down by an oral tradition [*śruti*] of exact chanting.
2. The hymn is received by the heart as well as apprehended by the intellect.
3. The experience of hearing the chant purifies the soul. The individual word meaning and the affective tones of the song are aspects of the sound [*śabda*] as a whole. This whole metamorphoses our being, leading to *moksa*.
4. There is no original, or ur-text.
5. Thus earlier, later and regional variations of the Mahabharata are equally valid.
6. There is no sense of earlier and later interpretations. The true enquirer, reading the text, or hearing the chant, according to Jaimini's injunctions, arrives at absolute truth.
7. The written texts exist for the purposes of study, to aid memory and to take the hymns to other regions. The written is not superior to the recited.

It is only recently that western scholars have abandoned the notion of a perfectly correct, original text of any classical writer — the ur-text. During the nineteenth century Shakespeare scholars still sought to arrive at an original perfect text of a play. Their vision was inspired by a simple notion of biblical inspiration. The aim of Christian, Protestant scholarship was to re-establish the original and perfect word of God. For Catholicism the interpretation of the Church has been a crucial factor in each age; for Catholics the versions of the Bible currently provided and interpreted by the

Church are the word of God. Now that we know that the notion of a perfect ur-text of any work is unreal, some have reacted to produce crazy theories; for example that Shakespeare did not write *Macbeth*, but that each individual reader, or listener, writes the play. We need not consider such notions. We need only recognise that, more than two thousand years ago, Jaimini took a balanced view of texts and scholarship.

Śabara

The earliest surviving commentary on the Purva Mimamsa is the Bhasya of Śabara, who lived during the first century before Christ. The tenor of Jaimini's work is pragmatic; the task being to enable the reader to realise and understand the Dharma. Ideas of Dharma, Nature, Action, Time and so forth are clearly presented to the reader's philosophical observation; there are possibilities of discussion, but none of dispute. Such is the analytic nature of concepts.

Taking a simple realist position, Jaimini has no interest in exploring the philosophical avenues that fascinate other thinkers.

The Bhasya of Śabara, however, does just this. The text firstly contemplates the permanent self. The injunctions of the Vedas, he says, would be without meaning if there were no permanent individual self to obey and then to receive rewards. Śabara clearly distinguishes the self [*purusa*] from the understanding [*buddhi*] and the senses [*indrya*]. He speaks of a permanent cogniser known only to itself.

Jaimini tends to simply state his view rather than to establish truth by argument.

> 1.1.5. The relation of the word with its denotation is inborn — instruction is the means of knowing it (*dharma*) — infallible regarding all that is imperceptible; it is a valid means of knowledge, as it is independent, according to Bādarāyaṇa.

The commentary of Śabara moves towards a philosophical elucidation.

> '*Autpattika*' ('inborn'), — what we mean by this is 'constant'. It is existence (presence) that is figuratively spoken of as 'origin'. What is meant is that the relation between a word and its meaning is *inseparable*. — It becomes the *means of knowing Dharma* in the shape of *Agnihotra* and such acts, which aren't known by means of sense-perception and such other means of knowledge. — 'How so?' — Because there is 'instruction'; 'instruction' stands for the speaking of a particular set of words.

Jaimini often quoted the Brahma Sūtra of Bādarāyaṇa, who was his earlier contemporary.

Śabara presents, here in his commentary, a more developed system of logic. He offers the four main Pramāṇas: perception, inference, comparison [*upamāna*] and tradition [*śabda*]. Under the heading of 'comparison' he develops further specialised concepts of inference.

Arthapatti, 'presumption,' also consists in the presuming of something not seen, on the ground that a fact already perceived or heard would not be possible without that presumption; for instance, it is found that, Devadatta who is alive is not in the house, and this *non-existence in the house* leads to presumption that he is somewhere outside the house [as without this, the aforesaid fact of his being alive and not in the house could not be explained].

Abhāva, 'Negation ', 'Non-apprehension', stands for the non-existence (non-operation) of the (five) means of cognition (described above); and it is what brings about the cognition that 'it does not exist' in regard to things not in contact with senses.

The Bhasya distinguishes two kinds of inference: (1) where an invariable relation obtains between objects that we perceive [*pratyakṣātodṛṣṭa*], as with smoke and fire; (2) where the relationship cannot be directly perceived, but is grasped in the abstract [*sāmānyatodṛṣṭa*], as with the sun's motion. Vātsyāyana, the Nyāyika, agreed with this distinction.

Regarding the ultimate origin of all speech the Bhasya of Śabara agrees with the Grammarian, Bhartṛhari, that the word is eternal. The vocal efforts of the speaker only manifest that word. Bhartṛhari was the greatest Indian grammarian of classical times. He was an Advaitin. Modern scholars have approximately dated his life as between 450 and 510 AD. He was the exponent of the philosophical development of grammar. His seminal work, Vākyapadīya, was also called the Trikandasī, or 'Three Chapters'. For Bhartṛhari, the spoken word is a manifestation of the universal, or the eternal word, which is in turn a manifestation of *śabda-brahman*. Brahman, or *śabda-brahman*, is God as eternal word. Because of our ultimate blindness [*avidyā*], an important notion for Bhartṛhari, we cannot recognise the eternal word as Brahman Himself.

For Śabara and the Mimamsakas the physical word has its own independent reality. The sound of the word is produced by the physical effort of utterance, but under the guidance of the intellect of the producer, it becomes a manifestation of the universal, which is eternal.

> If the word were only *manifested* (and not *produced*, by the utterance), then the sound heard would always be the same, whether it were uttered by many or fewer persons. From this we conclude that some portion of the word is *produced* by each of the speakers, … the word is *manifested* (not *produced*) by human effort; that is to say, if, before being pronounced, the word was not manifest, it becomes manifested by the effort (of pronouncing). Thus it is found that the fact of the word being 'seen after effort' is equally compatible with both views.
>
> Whenever the word '*go*' ('cow') is uttered, there is a notion of all cows simultaneously. From this it

> follows that the word denotes the class. And it is not possible to *create* the relation of a word to a class; because, in creating the relation, the creator would have to lay down the relation by pointing to the class; ... If, however the word '*go*' is eternal, it is the same word that is uttered many times and has previously been heard also many times, as applied to other individual cows; and thus by a process of positive and negative concomitance the word comes to be recognised as denoting the particular class. For this reason also the word must be eternal.

There seems here to be a very close connection between the universal and the sound essence referring to it. Although Śabara does not believe in a God, who named things, names are not made up by individual men. The relationships between word we hear and the 'inner' word we intuit; and again between the 'inner' word and the universal are established in the nature of things. The universal in Indian thought is in any case a sound energy form. In much Indian thought the abstract is, in a subtle way, concrete.

Though Śabara dwells on the metaphysics of karma, his response is a simple acceptance, based on the necessity of the ethical nature of reality.

> there is such a thing as *apūrva*, — because action is enjoined — in such injunctions as 'Desirous of Heaven, one should sacrifice'. Otherwise, — if there were no such thing as *apūrva*, such an injunction

> would be meaningless, as the act of sacrifice itself is perishable, so that if the sacrifice were to perish without bringing into existence something else, then the cause having ceased to exist, the result (in the shape of heaven) could never come about. — From this it follows that the sacrifice does bring into existence something (some force or potency which continues to exist or operate till such a time as the result is actually brought about).

Again in the earlier Indian vision the universe itself somehow delivers the fruits of action — thus there is a mystery as to how cause or action, and fruits or effect, are linked. What is the nature of a substrate that must provide an underlying continuum, such that a cause can have so belated an effect? The answer is not easily supplied. Just so in modern biological science we have to accept the evolution of species; although the process of evolution cannot be wholly observed, because it takes place over eons of time and only happens once.

Free will and the schools of Mimamsa

Prabhakara lived, according to one tradition, from 650 to 720 AD. There is a tradition that Prabhakara was a pupil of Kumarila. But the style of Prabharkara's commentary [*bṛhatī*] on the Bhasya of Śabara might indicate that he wrote before Kumarila. Prabhakara was a grammarian and a philosopher of the Mimamsa; but in effect he started is own school. His followers set out his view of voluntary action as:

> The consciousness of something to be done [*kāryatājñāna*], or the feeling of the sense of duty; the desire to do it [*cikīrṣā*]; which implies the consciousness that it can be done [*kṛtisādhyatājñāna*]; the volition [*pravṛtti*]; the motor reaction [*ceṣṭā*]; and the act [*kriyā*].

The crucial concept here is that of 'volition'. However, the Sanskrit Dictionary of Monier-Monier Williams does not give 'volition' as one of the meanings of *pravṛtti*. This dictionary gives: moving onwards, advance and progress; as basic meanings of *pravṛtti*; then: activity, exertion, and efficacy; as further meanings; and then, the full philosophical sense: 'defined as consisting of the wish to act, knowledge of the means, and accomplishment of the object'. The Mimamsakas do not contrast *pravṛtti* with any word directly meaning, 'determined', in the modern sense, as western philosophy often does. Karma and dharma are softer and subtler ideas. My conscious, well-intended and ethical actions are Dharma. Radhakrishnan, however, states:

> In the Vedic sacrifices, the injunction by its verbal power [*śābdībhāvanā*] tends to produce action in the agent towards this end indicated in the injunction The Mimamsa assumes human freedom, otherwise human individuals could not be responsible for their acts.
>
> The law of karma, when rightly understood, is not inconsistent with freedom.

The modern western philosopher has a clear concept of causal determination and an equally clear concept of free will. He then sometimes states that free will is an impossibility. However, he recognises that, in order to be happy and mentally healthy, we need to, at least, imagine that we are free. Thus mental health and happiness are, sadly, based on a delusion! This philosophy also recognises that in order to regulate society and prevent crime we have to condemn and punish some negative actions and we have to treat other negative actions as forms of illness. But really these actions are all the same — they are all unfree. Thus man is condemned, in much modern western thought, to illusion and dishonesty.

However, the clear idea that I have of freedom seems to me to be its own justification. It makes sense of life, which is thus fundamentally positive and honest.

Prabhakara is thought to have lived in the seventh century AD. Kumarila probably lived a little later. Prabhakara wrote a second order commentary [*bṛhatī*] on the Mimamsa Bhasya of Śabara. Prabhakara disagreed with Kumarila over the certainty of perception and other issues, but does not, in fact, mention Kumarila. From the differences between them, however, two distinct schools of followers developed within the Mimamsa.

Pārthasārathi Miśra probably lived in the tenth century AD. He wrote Śāstradīpikā – 'A light on the Shastra' – a commentary on the Purva Mimamsa of Jaimini; and Nyāyaratnākara –'The Abode of Jewels of Logic'. He had many interesting views especially that the universal and the individual were not distinct. We perceive them as one.

Both Prabhakara and Pārthasārathi Miśra were non-theists.

The Eternal Cosmos

The Mimamsakas never believed that the entire universe was periodically absorbed into God and then reborn again. There is one beginningless and everlasting Cosmos. The process of works and effects continues for eternity; like seeds and plants, which then become seeds again. The souls equally have no beginning, having existed eternally, and they will last forever into the future.

CHAPTER 9

KUMARILA BHATTA

Kumārila Bhatta

The foremost commentator on the Purva Mimamsa of Jaimini was Kumārila Bhatta, who lived just after Prabhakara. He is said to have been born in Assam during the eighth century AD. He was a reformer and the greatest exponent of the school. Little is known about his life, but there is a legend that he was a Buddhist at some time in his youth. He is one of the greatest Indian philosophers.

The Purva Mimamsa School of thought, in stark contrast to the Samkhya and other Indian philosophies, emphasised the exact performance of the rituals laid down in the Vedas. The School likewise emphasised the code of Manu, and its perfect interpretation, as a guide to life. Originally the Mimamsa had no special theistic emphasis; or necessarily any belief in God at all. The aim of existence was simply Moksa. Moksa was attained through ritual; and through ritual's right minded and perfect performance. The source of all knowledge was Shruti [*śruti*] — revealed texts. It was thus that the school laid great emphasis on grammar and on logic, as the means of understanding the meaning of revealed texts and the laws and the rubrics of ritual prescription. Kumarila organised many temples to admit only the three higher castes. Only members of these higher castes, he thought, had sufficient education and wealth to understand and carry out all the minutia of brahmin religion. Kumarila was a strong opponent of Jainism and Buddhism and he took part in many public debates with the teachers of those faiths.

The rigidity of Mimamsa attitudes to worship during the eighth century AD must be contrasted with the growth of Bakti amongst all classes, who responded to the rich emotional fulfilment offered by the personalities of God — Vishnu and Shiva; and who turned from the aridity of philosophical ways and the sterility of ritual.

Kumarila Bhatta insisted on the orthodoxy of Vedic ritual and on the supremacy of the priest, as the chief enactor of that ritual. His development of the Mimamsa, however, is to introduce a strong theistic emphasis. But he remains a true Mimamsaka in that his God is not the author of the Vedas.

His Ślokavārttika is a commentary both on the Mimamsa Sūtra of Jaimini and on the Bhasya of Śabara. The Ślokavārttika treats the opening of the first chapter of Jaimini's work; and Kumarila's later writings, the Tantravārttika and the Tupṭīkā, cover the later chapters.

The Ślokavārttika begins:

> 1.1. Reverence to Him who wears the crescent moon, — Him who is embodied in pure consciousness, Him whose three eyes are the three Vedas. And who is the source from which all prosperity flows.

It is clearly a dedication to Shiva. The capital *h* for 'Him' is a trope of translation; but other theistic statements in the writings of Kumarila justify this interpretation. Throughout the ages since, some Mimamsakas have kept to the non-theistic purity of Jaimini. Pārthasārati Miśra in his commentary, Nyāyaratnākara, interpreted the dedication as applying to the reader: 'to him [small *h*] who has been purified by the sacrifice.'

The Ślokavārttika commences with a strong Vedic influence; and the statement that the knowledge of the Vedas is as important as the acknowledgement of God.

> 1.9. My greed is great for the gem of Vedic knowledge, when shinning with additional lustre in the light of the Mimamsa Sūtra.
>
> 1.10. For the most part Mimamsa has, in this world, been made Atheistic; and this effort of mine is made to turn it to the theistic path.
>
> 1.11. 'Henceforth (proceeds) enquiry into (the nature of) Dharma' — such is the first aphorism, propounded with a view to explain that the purpose of the Mimamsa Sūtra is the (desire to know the nature of the) object called 'Dharma'.
>
> 1.12. For, who would begin (the study of) any science, or any action, while its purpose remained unexplained?

This is a touching and informative affirmation of the greatness of Jaimini, illustrated by observing the clarity of his starting point — the mark of the greatest minds.

There follows an argument [*adhikaraṇa*] regarding the interpretation of the injunction at the beginning of the Bhasya of Śabara: that after completing his study of the Veda the student should bathe. The student obeyed the injunction not to bathe during a period of studying the written text of the Veda. The injunction: 'and so bathe,' can be interpreted in two ways; depending on whether the conjunction 'and so' is *atha*, or *atah*. The first has a propitious and possibly more remote sense; so that the bath is not immediate but subsequent on being further instructed by the teacher. The student then bathes, indicating the closure of the process, and leaves the teacher's house. If we accept the word *atha*, the injunction is in accord with the Mimamsaka orthodoxy; namely that a teacher of the Mimamsaka tradition is totally necessary to the successful reading of the text. The objector [*pūrvapaksa*], takes the second reading — *atah*; namely that the student bathes immediately after putting the text aside and goes without consulting the teacher further. For the objector the authority of the teacher is less. Although there is circularity in the orthodox Mimamsaka statement, the objector's position is perhaps one of self-contradiction, if he intends to go about teaching students. The setting out of the common sense, or realist point of view is often circular, but the objection of the sceptic is, equally often, self-defeating. The difference between the presence, and the absence, of a diacritical inscribed on a leaf; or between the presence, and absence, of a slight breath in the chant, is part of the problem. For Kumarila the authority of the teacher is supreme.

Interpretation

Kumarila considers, in a manner similar to that of the opening of the Bhasya of Śabara, the problems of universal and specific interpretation.

> 1.47-49. Where Vedic sentences and those of Jaimini contradict one another, in their direct signification, there this ('Specification') has its use: the Sutra has to be interpreted by means of 'supplying the ellipsis', etc, whereas the Vedic sentence has to be taken in its direct signification.

> 1.49. When Vedic sentences contradict one another, then may secondary implications be applied to them also.

> 1.49-50. 'Just as the Vedic sentence is the means of the right notion of Duty [*dharma*], so is also Jaimini's assertion our means of ascertaining the meaning of the Veda ...'

Dharma

The Ślokavārttika now begins a long argument as between two contestants [*adhikaraṇa*]. The opposition asserts the non-authoritative nature of Dharma. The Sūtra and the Bhasya both assert that Dharma is authoritative. The case of the opposition to the authority of Dharma is that Dharma is not known by the senses. But this is also Kumarila's argument. It is precisely because the Dharma is not known through the senses that it is authoritative. What is known through the senses cannot be relied upon. It follows equally that the Dharma cannot be known by inference because, firstly, inference depends on sensation; and, secondly, inference depends upon the comprehension of a middle term. There is no middle term that can mediate between the sensible world and Dharma. But further the idea of Dharma can neither come from memory, nor from the word. The view that the Vedas record the vision of seers is firmly rejected by the Mimamsakas. They considered yogic insight to be unreliable. The view of the Grammarians that the Vedas are the product of the eternal Word is equally not accepted. The use of the word [*śabda*] depends on the observation of a trustworthy person; and indeed on the trustworthiness of his memory [*smṛti*].

> 2.16. And in order to establish the incapacity (of all other means of knowledge), there is a mention of the 'Senses' …

> 2.17. Though inference has its applicability to objects enunciated above (the past etc), yet without the comprehension of relation, Inference itself is not possible.

> 2.18. In the case of Duty, however, there is no comprehension of the relation of any mark with either the generic of the specific (forms of Duty) — by which it could have been amenable to inference.

> 2.19. 'But the 'Word' [*śabda*] too cannot function, without a comprehension of relation.' Yes, (that is the

> case with) the *term*; but Duty is denoted not by the *term*, but by a *sentence* …
>
> 2.22. 'It is always an object perceived by means of knowledge, that is got at by the Word; and like 'memory' [*smṛti*], no authority can belong to it by itself.'

The arguments of those opposed to the Dharma, however, do not defeat the later Mimamsaka, after Jaimini, because thinkers like Kumārila Bhatta accept the injunctions [*codanā*] of the Veda as self-evident rather than as proved by a process of argumentation. The Vedic injunction is *per se* authoritative. The rejection of its dependence on some fallible means of knowledge helps the Mimamsaka to give the form of the Dharma as it really is. The Dharma is self-causing. Again Hume has claimed that the moralists proceed from 'is' to 'ought' in way that has no logical justification. But the Dharma simply exists as an underived obligation. The 'ought' contains its own special 'is' within itself. Roads and signposts are metaphors for the spiritual progression. But no one person made the road; and the rocks and trees that we recognise were not actually set up as signposts.

The Indian idea of God is often simply that of a supreme spirit. He is not always the full creator and dissolver of the universe. For Kumarila Bhatta, God is not the author of the Vedas. There was no way men could ever receive communication from such a Being; or if they could, God might exaggerate to display his splendour. Thus there would be no additional validation of the Veda in saying that God was their author.

5.16.61. In the same manner the Veda that would proceed from Him would only be doubtful, and hence could not be admitted as a sure proof of His existence (and creative power). And as for that (Veda) which is eternal, how could it make mention (of facts and processes with reference to the creation of livings beings, &c.)?

5.16.62. For, if the Veda existed before objects (created), then there could be no connection between this Veda and the objects created. Therefore the passages (occurring in the Veda) (which appear to describe the process of creation) must be interpreted as praising up something else (*i.e.*, some injunctions of the sacrifices, &c.)

Verse 61 furnishes an example of the 'application of secondary implications' (Ślokavārttika 1.49 above) in the interpretation of Veda.

The injunctions [*vidhi*] of the Veda enjoin Dharma, which is happiness. What leads to pain, or 'non-goods' [*anartha*], is *adharma.* We carry out the actions enjoined because they are enjoined, and because they lead to happiness itself, rather than merely leading to fleeting happy moments. The general injunctions [*vidhi*] lead to particular instructions [*codanā*]. These *codanā* include the prescriptions for the rituals; which are not immediately obvious as being acts of virtue. It is thus that the Veda does not enjoin virtue for its own sake, according to the Mimamsa. It is to be noted that the Advaita thinkers do not consider ritual to be the highest way to release. The text of the Bhagavad Gita enjoins detached virtue (virtue for the sake of virtue). This the Mimamsakas do not accept.

Actions enjoined by the Vedas are *nitya:* actions forbidden are *naimittika.* If we do not obey the injunctions we commit sin [*pratyavāya*]. There are, of course optional activities, which we carryout for specific ends, every day. They are *kāmya.* While they are not forbidden, too much attention to *kāmya* makes us selfish. It is thus that ultimately our individual natural good is non-meritorious. Equally indeed, the natural good of the society of which we are members, is non-meritorious. However, though the aim of the Vedas is not primarily the benefit of society, we may be sure that the honesty and the high mindedness that the Vedas enjoin are always socially beneficial.

There is a difference between the vision of Kumarila and that of Bhartṛhari, the grammarian. For Kumarila the authority of the injunction is not that of the eternal word [*śabda*]. Men, to record what they remember, use words; these words are thus the result of perception. But our knowledge of the Dharma is pure and infallible. We know that some actions are wrong. Here we have to recognise the fundamental difference between the realism of Kumarila and radicalism of the Advaita Vedanta.

The Nyayikas rejected the view that the Vedas were without personal authorship. Firstly, they said, the authors are named, and secondly the sentences of the Vedas are like any other sentences. But, for the Mimamsa, the Vedas are a series of injunctions. These injunctions simply exist. As soon as we read them, or hear them, we know that we have to obey them. The poets have written the injunctions down and priests have preached them; but neither priest, nor poet, has devised the injunctions.

Our actions are can be meritorious or non-meritorious. Non-meritorious actions can be indifferent, or harmful to the progress of our spirits. The results of this merit, or the results of this harm to our spirits, can be long delayed — thus there must be some spiritual force at work. Perhaps the benefit or harm will affect us in a later incarnation.

According to Kumarila Bhatta there is the unseen power [*apūrva*], which exists in all the actions that we perform. The Sanskrit *apūrva* means: unprecedented, extraordinary, not having existed before. This power, Kumarila says, does not exist in the agent prior to his carrying out the action. After the action has been carried out, its fruit may be manifest much later, by this power [*apūrva*]; even beyond the lifespan of the agent.

The doctrine of *apūrva* was much criticised by other schools. Uddyotakara, the Nyayika [sixth century AD], who wrote the Nyāyavārttika, was born in what is now the state of Haryana, in North India. He defended and revived the Nyaya philosophy. He denied the eternality of such a power as *apūrva*, which, he said, would mean that there was no such thing as death. He also argued that if *apūrva* were one, then the destiny of all would be the same; if the power were many, then how was it manifest in individuals and how did it become hidden. Shamkara criticised the doctrine on the grounds that *apūrva* is not a spiritual force; and virtue must be desired for its own sake and not for the sake of its fruit. For the Mimamsakas, however, the *apūrva* is an absolute, like evolution for modern biologists; though we cannot witness the totality of evolution we still accept it as a real, existent force.

The doctrine of *apūrva* gives a strange metaphysical reality to the ethical dimension; but I do not think that thereby the doctrine is unethical. It is not erroneous to give the ethical dimension some existential solidarity. We know that it is wrong to steal. We know that this truth is more real than any philosophical explanation of its ground.

Knowledge

All Mimamsakas reject the seeing of the yogis. Material objects cannot be perceived at a distance; contact with the senses is a necessity; and the claim that the yogi develops his senses to an extreme degree, so that he can see into a spiritual dimension, is bogus, because the senses cannot fundamentally change. In any case when the yogi says he has seen something that is then past; and therefore is a matter of memory. Thus what the yogi tells you cannot be infallibly known, by him or by you, because memory is fallible.

Kumarila taught that there were six means of knowing [*pramana*]:

Perception - *pratyakśa*
Inference - *anumāna*
Testimony - *śabda*
Comparison - *upamāna*
Implication - *arthapatti*
Non-apprehension - *anupalabdhi*

pratyakśa

For the Mimamsakas perception is always of the individual. Perception [*pratyakśa*] is *saksat pratītih* — *saksat*: 'directly, with the eyes'; *pratītih*: 'approaching, clearly understood'. They accept the distinction of indeterminate and determinate perception. Pārthasārathi argues that on first contact we grasp an object devoid of all relations. Then determinate perception apprehends the relationship between the object and its qualities; and this again depends on the previous apprehension of those qualities. When we name an object we remember the class to which that object belongs.

Kumarila, however, believes we can apprehend the class without the name. Prabhakara allows and emphasises the function of memory in determinate perception.

anumāna

Inference is clearly accepted by the Mimamsa. Kumarila frequently points out that the Buddhist arguments against certain knowledge are themselves inferences; and yet the Buddhist philosophers deny inference.

śabda

Testimony [*śabda*] is accepted as a *pramana*. Testimony depends on memory [*smṛti*]; and memory can be influenced by human will; or, indeed, lack of will, where concentration is lost. The Vedas, however, cannot depend on human testimony, which is ultimately fallible. How then can testimony [*śabda*] be a *pramana*? Well there is not really a clash between logic and brain functioning. When memory is valid its testimony is absolutely true. When memory fades, its evidence is not sound. In the first instance, when someone says that he remembers something, we may need to look at further means of corroboration. But when total corroboration is achieved we know that that testimony is valid; and thus it is an example of the *pramana* of *śabda*.

Some philosophers have been confused over the relationship between the fallibility of the human mind and the infallibility of logic — the Mimamsas not.

upamāna

Comparison [*upamāna*] is also accepted as a separate means of knowing.

> 5.7.1-2. 'Being asked by the town-people, 'like what is a *gavaya*?' if the forester says that 'a *gavaya* is just like a cow'— then we have what is commonly known as 'Analogy'. According to the view of Śabara however, this is nothing apart from 'Verbal testimony'; and hence 'Analogy' is explained in a different manner.

arthapatti

According to the dictionary, *arthapatti* means: inference from circumstances, the disjunctive hypothetical syllogism. Kumarila does not allow this Pramāṇa. The word *arthapatti* is made up from *artha*, meaning: purpose, cause, thing, object of the senses; and possibly from *pata*, meaning: fall and flight. Jhā translates *arthapatti* as 'presumption'. One might think this 'presumption' a perfect method of establishing the remote and unseen causal process that is Dharma. It is thus that Kant has established the synthetic *a priori* and indeed, moral and aesthetic necessities. However, Kumarila does not agree. Vedic injunctions are known to be true provided that they are not contradicted by other means. They do not need to be established by *arthapatti*, which Kumarila considers a tenuous means. Prabhakara, however, accepted *arthapatti*.

anupalabdhi

Kumarila accepted non-apprehension [*anupalabdhi*] as a form of knowledge. Through non-apprehension we obtain either its non-existence in a location, or its absolute non-existence [*abhāva*].

> 5.3.40. … If it be asked— 'How do you (Mimamsakas) apply cognisability to Negation (which is a non-entity)?'— (we reply), that we hold Negation to be a real entity.

Prabhakara opposed Kumarila — and, indeed, Jean-Paul Sartre [1905-1980], the French philosopher — in the matter of absence. Prabhakara took a view similar to that of the Nyayika; that there is no perception of absence. When the pot is not in the room; there is simply a perception of the room, as it is, without the pot. We perceive the substratum [*tanmātradhī*] of the pot's being in the room, without the pot.

Prabhakara thus rejects non-apprehension [*anupalabdhi*] as a separate means of cognition. It is merely an inference to a negative qualification of the room.

Kumarila's doctrine of *svatahpramana* means that any valid act of knowing has its own validity and confidence. Knowledge [*jñāna*] is a 'success' word like 'winning'; it is not a 'tentative' word like 'trying'. Thus he disagrees with the Nyaya view that perception theoretically needs to be supported by an infinity of further perceptions.

The objective and realistic basis of Kumarila's epistemology requires that in order to understand knowledge we need to study valid instances of knowing. The sceptic bases his conceits on instances of error, and not on instances of knowing. If, because of a jaundiced eye, we judge silver to be gold; there still exists a background condition of a gold colour, and in this sense our cognition still has validity. Further perceptions may correct the impression; but three or four cognitions will normally establish the truth.

The mystery of knowing is that we can know our own fallibility. To say, 'I know I can be wrong' is almost a contradiction. And yet it is true. The need for correction is the pragmatic vision of the realist. Kumarila's vision does not stray into a coherence theory of truth, in which our ideas support one another from within and then somehow reach to the outside world. For Kumarila we live in the outside world and, normally, we know it.

Act and Potency

The soul, in contact with manas, which is in turn in contact with the senses and these in contact with the object, grasps the form of the object. Thus Kumarila did not hold a correspondence theory of knowledge. Correspondence theories of knowledge are mechanistic. They hold that there is some correspondence between the idea in the mind and the object that the idea corresponds to. But the idea and its object are finally two separate entities that never quite come together. Many people find the correspondence theory unsatisfactory. They desire a more perfect model of knowledge.

It is thus that Kumarila Bhatta, among many others, considered that objects must be members of a class, whose form can be grasped. That form is one though its instances are many. Whether we see that form as residing in our minds, or as residing in or on the object, that form is one.

This is an aspect of the One and the Many. In a sense the theory of forms is mysterious, but it is more satisfactory than the correspondence theory, when deeply reflected upon.

> 5.13.15. Inasmuch as the Individuals themselves are different from one another, they can never be cognised by a single Idea; because (being many and diverse) they cannot have (any notion of *single* commonality for) their object ...
>
> 5.13.17. For these reasons you must also admit of the *Class*, which is apart from the Individuals and their capabilities, and yet embraces all Individuals, and pervades through each of them.
>
> 5.13.18. Thus then, for us, there is a distinct object of the Idea of a single commonality; and it is a natural

> property of the Individuals. As such, it maybe named either 'Sāmānya', or 'akrti', or 'Jāti', or 'Shakti'.

The word *sāmānya* means: common, similar or normal. Whereas the word *akrti* means: form, shape and configuration. The term *jāti* stands for: class, species, family, clan and race. Finally *shakti* means: power, strength, energy, potency, efficacy and meaning. The idea of the word *shakti* is more the original energy behind things [*potencia*], whereas the idea of the other three words is what is common to a group and what shape [*actus*], in a sense, designates that group. We can never, however, separate the potentiality [*potencia*] of a thing from its real existence [*actus*].

The primal cosmic energy [*shakti*] forms all things, both material and subtle. Parts of the primal energy are sometimes still. Then things are formed. This stilling is ever happening. Then again things are ever dissolving back into energy. But it is false to say that things are really only energy; that only energy exists. Forms [*akrti*] are real as well. Perhaps the mistake of materialistic philosophy is to say that only matter exists. Matter, as we experience it, is always formed in some way or other. The highest form we experience is that of the human mind. We are conscious of our minds and we love them, as we consciously experience and love all things.

Vedic Injunctions

Kumarila's attitude to Vedic injunctions mirrors his realism regarding the perception of objects. Injunctions are to be obeyed. 'Thou shalt not …' is not a description. We immediately perceive its truth. Injunctions are written down by the poets but not written by them. The 'Atheist' here, in Jhā's translation, is not the denier of God, but rather the denier of the Divine, or of the realm of perfect ethics, or whatever.

> 2.154. The Atheist in denying the authority of the Veda, lands himself on the (absurdity of) setting aside the authenticity of a directly perceptible fact. Because when a conception has arisen (and the self-evident authority of such a perception has already been proved), any assumption towards its denial could only be needless and far-fetched.
>
> 2.155. The absence of human agency, with regard to the Veda, having been proved, it lies upon the Atheists to point any difference between the Vedic conceptions and the perceptions due to faultless cognitions.
>
> 2. 242-43. For the comprehension of Dharma and Adharma, there is no other means save the fact of their being enjoined and prohibited (respectively). Hence the introduction of an inferential argument in this connection is not proper...

Were the basis of morality utilitarian we would do things that are obviously wrong, for immediate good reasons. We might even transgress the most sacred relationship, that of Swami and Guru, for some good reason, bringing advantage to someone; and this would be absurd. Hume taught that Nature, for our own benefit, has implanted in us a horror of certain actions. On a practical level, human psychology is such that human beings require barriers in order to remain sane and to live together: on the ontological level, each action has a quasi-infinite number of consequences; and thus a calculation of painful and pleasurable effects is impossible.

Finally our intuition tells us that pain and sinfulness are not one and the same.

> 244-245. And again one who, though with qualms of conscience, has intercourse with his preceptor's wife, would be incurring a great Dharma; because thereby he would be conferring a great benefit of happiness to the woman.

> 2.245-246. And further, how can one, who would (in the matter of Dharma and Adharma) rely solely upon Reasoning, independently of any prohibitions or otherwise (scriptural), have any qualms of conscience, when he finds that his action does not give pain to any person?

> 2.246-247. And further, he who would ascertain (the character of) Adharma independently of Scriptural prohibitions would land himself on 'Mutual Dependency' — inasmuch as he would be attributing *sinfulness* (Adharma) to *pain*, and *pain* again to *sinfulness*.

Kumarila taught that an act of knowledge has four elements:

1. The knower – *jñātā*
2. The object of knowledge – *jñeya*
3. The instrument of knowledge – *jñānakāraṇa*
4. The result, or the object's being cognised – *jñātatā*.

When philosophers worry about cognition, it is because they tend to split apart things that are, of their nature, one. If I start thinking of my cognition of 'x' as something other than 'x', I am in serious epistemological trouble. I am also in ontological trouble too. This is for the simple reason that there is no such thing as 'a cognition'. Cognition is really only the object's being cognised — its cognisedness [*prakaṭatā*]. The cognition is inferred from the relationship between the knower and the known. The cognition is not seen directly, otherwise you would need an infinity of cognitions of cognitions. If we look into ourselves as we cognise, we are aware of a relation between ourselves, as knowers, and that which we know. This 'looking in' is *mānasapratyakśa* — as it were, 'presence before the eyes of the mind'.

Cognition is pure event; it is not an existent with a momentary time span. It is thus not a cause of further perception; as are the senses. The existence of the senses, however, is continuous; and thus they are substances with causal power. The senses are themselves objects, which can be perceived.

4.55. Not even for a moment does the cognition continue to exist; nor is it ever produced as doubtful (or incorrect); and as such, it can never *subsequently* operate towards the apprehension of objects, like the Senses, etc.

4.56. Therefore the only operation of Cognition, with regard to the objects, consists in its *being produced*; that alone is Right Notion (Pramā); and the condition itself as accompanied by this Right Notion is the Means (of Right Notion: Pramana).

4.57. This 'being produced' too has been explained by the author of the Bhāsya, as identical with (with the cognition itself) …

4.60. The means of right notion may be (1) either the sense, or (2) the contact of the sense with the object, or (3) the contact of the mind with the senses, or (4) the connection of the mind with the Soul, or (5) all these, collectively …

4.62. The contact of the sense with the object is not with the whole of it; and hence there is no chance of the perception of all objects by means of a single Sense-organ, for those that hold the character of Pramana to belong to the senses; …

Were we to take the contact of the object with the sense as the whole of perception, we would then be tempted to deny sense perception. Thus the Buddhist argument is elaborated:

> 4.63. Because they do not hold the relation of the sense to consist in *mere contact*; and they deny such a relation simply with a view to avoid the absurdity of the sense of *Touch*, which is a means (of a particular class of perception), giving rise to the cognition of *colour*.
>
> 4.64. Just as in the accomplishment of the Pramana, the only cause is the fixed relation of the Sense and the Object, through their inborn amenability (to one another), so would it also be in the case of the Result.
>
> 4.65. Though the contact resides equally in both (the sense and the object), yet, it is only proper that it should be mentioned as residing in only one of the two. Or the Sense may be taken as the only uncommon substratum of the relation ...
>
> 4.68. Being the best means, on account of close proximity (co-substrateness), this (the contact of mind and Soul) is the only Means of Right Perception, and hence the true character of the Means of Right Notion, can belong to no other agency.
>
> 4.69. If such character of Means of Right Notion be attributed to all the agencies (noted in Kārika 60) taken collectively, there can be no objection to it. And for

one, to whom the Sense is the Means of Right Notion, the sameness of the object is clear.

We cannot take the contact between sense and object alone as the sole cause and substrate of the cognition; because objects are perceived by more than one sense and therefore the operation of the common sense [*manas*] is required. Further for an event of fully conscious knowledge [*jnā*] to occur, the soul [*jīva*] must be in contact with the central sense [*manas*]. Modern people understand that our minds are 'taking in' all sorts of events and objects without our being aware that this is happening. Indian philosophy would point out, nevertheless, that the value of such unconscious operations is that they somehow contribute towards the happy, conscious experience of cognition.

By 'their inborn amenability (to one another)' in Verse 4.64, Kumarila refers to the early Indian theory of sensation. Here the five subtle elements [*tanmātra*] operating in the five sense organs [*buddhīndrya*] respond to the five gross elements [*mahabhūta*] of which all material objects are made. For example, the subtle sound element [*śabda*] within the hearing system [*śrota*] responds to the vibrations in space [*akasa*]; and again the *tanmātra* of form and colour [*rūpa*] in the system of seeing [*cākśus*] responds to the very visible element of fire [*tejus*]. In the modern view of the physiology of seeing, specialised pigments in the retina respond to light from pigments on the surface of the object.

Kumarila regarded the cognition as *svatahprāmāṇa*. The term *svatahprāmāṇa* is made up from *sva* (in an adjectival form —*svatah*) and *pramana*. A *pramana* is a means of knowing. Thus we might say the cognition is 'in its own right', or authentic. The cognition is achieved instantly in perception [*pratyakśa*]. The object is seen directly [*saksat pratītih*]. This is the essential realist doctrine in all cultures — G. E. Moore, in his 'Refutation of Idealism', points out the utter obvious to which man-the-philosopher is so often blind; namely, that we are in no need of a special warrant to prove that we see what we see.

Kumarila was opposed to the idea that the cognition carried an interior certificate of correctness. That the cognition is 'self-luminous' [*svapakasa*] was the position of Prabhakara. Descartes frequently talked as if ideas mediated between the perceiving mind and the objects it perceived. When an idea is clear and distinct, he said, the perceiver knows that it 'truly represents' the object. In this way of describing things, an inner quality of the idea is the mark of its outer truth.

Kumarila, however, while undoubtedly taking a direct and realist position in the matter of perception, thought that cognition brought about a 'peculiarity' [*atiśaya*] in the object cognised. This peculiarity was a way of inference to the cognition, which was not directly known. Although this seems like a weakening of his position, it may be just a practical realisation that we see objects from a viewpoint. The Nyayikas and the Vaishesikas attacked this position, saying that being cognised was not a quality of the object, but a special relationship between the object and the cognition of it [*svarūpasambandha*]. The process, they said, is not like the cooking of rice where the uncooked rice [*taṇdula*] is changed into the cooked [*odana*].

For Prabhakara perception is new knowledge [*anubhūti*]. Knowledge, which relies on comparison with past experience and therefore depends on remembrance [*smṛti*], risks being erroneous. In itself the cognition is self-luminous [*svapakasa*] and true [*yathārtha*]. Error [*viparyaya*] is not false knowledge; error is the confusion [*akhyāti*] between what is seen and what is remembered. The literal meaning of *akhyāti* is: bad repute. The word for 'error' – *viparyaya* – means, literally, 'turned the other way'. Thus knowledge can be, as it were, turned the other way. But the notion of 'false knowledge' is a contradiction. Knowledge cannot be false.

Finally we might say that the self is not an object of perception; and yet it is directly known. This is the mystery of self-consciousness.

This argument [*adhikaraṇa*], which concludes with the reiteration of the 'precedence of sense perception', does not help in the establishment of Duty. This argument only establishes what is present at a time. Kumarila recognises that sense perception can apprehend a wider universal where the individual is undefined. But again the Dharma as enjoined in the Vedas is always defined. We can of course form a notion of Dharma; just as we can have a notion of 'function' in mathematics. But just as there is no true abstract definition of Function, because each function is individual, and such that a range of individuals can satisfy it as arguments, so there can be no abstract definition of Dharma.

Dharma and the Buddhists

The first phase of Buddhist philosophy [*abhidharma* — about the dharma] saw ultimate reality as energy, producing the effects that we experience and cognise, but which itself is beyond cognition and experience. This early phase did not deny causality because the incomprehensible energy caused our experiences; and the merits of our lives brought about our reincarnation. Again the teachings of the Buddha cause the release of men from reincarnation. This early phase, however, denied the reality of the object and therefore of the cognising subject, the ego, or self. The second phase was Madhyamika, or the Middle Way. Madhyamika denied the existence of the primal cosmic energy and of causality — reality was not Being [*sat*] but Emptiness [*śūnyatā*]. The world we perceive is neither existing nor non-existent, but empty [*śūnya*]. Emptiness is not a third between Being and not-Being. It is a denial of the difference; and thus a denial of metaphysics and all philosophy. There are no true causes or effects. Our experiences trail or seem to be connected with past impressions and could even lead to the experience of another life. A reincarnation, however, is again empty, merely appearing to drag past experiences in its wake. The realisation of *śūnyatā* is itself release [*moksa*]. The third phase of Buddhism was the Yogacara or idealistic phase. Yogacara probably means 'way of meditation'. The Yogacara School accepted mental life. If we see a patch of blue, they said, we see a patch of blue — but it does not necessarily correspond to anything. The denial of external reality then necessitates the denial of ourselves as well. And this again they said either is, or leads to, release.

All these doctrines are sceptical of the existence of matter and of the external world; and this requires a denial of sense perception. G. E. Moore, the common-sense philosopher, would agree: sense perception is a given in the first instance. Its denial would have to be elaborately proved. This denial never can be proved in fact. And in any case the Buddhists deny reasoning, which proof requires. What is given in sense perception is not a mental picture, but the real, solid, three-dimensional world. Thus Matter was held by the Mimamsa to be real and atomic in nature; as the Vaishesika School also held.

> 4.40-41. The Buddhas have urged that 'The eye and the ear naturally functioning without direct contact with the object, the 'contact ', that you have put into your definition, as the common factor in all Sense-perception, cannot be accepted to be so; and even if we grant the functioning of these by contact, there could (in the case of the Eye and the Ear) be no intercepted perception; nor could an object larger than the Sense-organ, be perceived, — as we find to be the case with skin, &c.'

Incidentally the Samkhya had a theory of sight wherein a ray from the eye made contact with the visible object. Kumarila was at pains to reject this Samkhya view because such a view would help the Buddhist argument.

Later in the Ślokavārttika, Kumarila appears to focus on the Yogacara school of Buddhism; speaking of the way of unsupportedness [*nirālambanavāda*].

> 5.3.5. 'Even if only the 'Idea' (or sensation) is accepted (to be a real entity), all this (that is ordinarily known as the 'External World') may be explained as '*Saṁvṛtti* Reality'; and as such it is useless for you to persist in holding the reality of the (external) object.'

> 5.3.6. But there can be no reality in 'Saṁvṛitti' (Falsity); and as such how can it be a form of reality? If it is a reality, how can it be 'Saṁvṛtti'? If it is false, how can it be real?
>
> 5.3.7. Nor can 'reality' belong, in common, to objects, false as well as real; because the two are contradictory; for certainly the character of the 'tree 'cannot belong in common to a *tree* as well as to a *lion*.

Here we have Kumarila, the realist. We are reminded of G. E. Moore in a tutorial, with raised eyebrow and glowering eye, banging on the table; 'Is this a table or isn't it?' — It misuses words to talk of 'false' and 'true' realities. The tree and the lion are not in the same family. Thus nothing is not another kind of being; and falsity is not another kind of truth; error is not another kind of knowledge; and wrong is not a slightly different kind of right.

Cognition

Prabhakara taught that every act of cognition was threefold [*tripuṭīsamvit*]. When we think, 'I know this' [*aham idam jānāmi*], there is firstly a presentation of the subject [*ahaṁvitti*], then of the object [*viṣayavitti*] and finally the conscious awareness [*svasaṁvitti*]. The cognitions are of the nature of light; and thus certain and self-illuminated [*svapakasa*]. The self is (amazingly), according to Prabhakara, not self-luminous. It requires cognition to become self-aware and thus when not cognising an object, as in deep sleep, the self is not conscious. The cognition is cognised as a cognition but not as an object. It is thus known by inference. When we apprehend an object, we know that we have a cognition. Prabhakara realised that he was opposing Śabara's observation that in the apprehension of objects we perceive objects and not cognitions. And here it is Śabara who expresses the true realist view.

Kumarila certainly held the view that the existence of a cognition, as such, can only be known through inference; but a cognition is a modification of the self, an aspect of the self's awareness. The cognition, however, possesses neither self-awareness, nor substantiality. It is not a third factor of knowledge.

For Prabhakara cognition grasps the form of the object and cannot be false. We know that our cognitions are true, he says, because we are impelled to act on them. Our consciousness of our cognitions is its own confirmation. No external corroboration is required.

Prabhakara's view is of course hugely mistaken. Our thoughts do not possess a tick or a cross, which marks them as true or false. In the first place we have no warrant to deny that we perceive the objects of this world; so we need not look for a separate warrant to guarantee our perceptions. Our confidence is, of course, corroborated by the coherence of our experience — but this is not a 'coherence theory' of truth. Truth is in the original, valid perception.

> 5.3.17-18. The denial of the external object is of two kinds: one is based upon an examination of the object itself, and another is based upon reasoning. Of these, that which is based upon a consideration of the object may be laid aside for the present; that which is based

> upon reasoning, and as such is the root (of the theory), is what is here examined.

The denial of reason presents an obviously contradictory situation. When the Mimamsaka deals with the denial of reason, he simply avoids the path of self-contradiction. The assertion of the validity of cognition is seen as a dialogue between two people, rather than a description of one person puzzling about his own mental states. Thus we are positively on the realist path.

> 5.3.36. If the cognition, of the Subject and Predicate, as belonging to the speaker and the hearer, were without corresponding realities, then both of them would stand self-contradicted.

Further, when we try to prove such a position as this by argument, we find that there is no such universal as 'devoid of support' [*nirālambada*]; and no concrete instance of such a negative. Thus the second proposition of the Buddhist's syllogism, i.e. giving the general rule and offering the concrete instance, is missing.

> 5.3.49. If you seek to prove *the fact of being devoid of a substratum* [*nirālambada*], as Universal, — then you are open to the faults of having your *predicate unrecognised*, and that of the *absence of the instance*.

It may also be noted that Kumarila did not accept the total universal Being as a valid cognition; and equally for that reason again he held that *nirālambada*, as a universal, must be rejected.

Finally the Buddhist argument is rejected by common sense.

> 5.3.74. And your conclusion at this point is also contradicted (and hence rejected) by facts known to all persons (who always recognise objects apart from their cognitions).

Yogacara Buddhism distinguished between two kinds of ideas. On the one hand it recognised ideas that were purely fanciful, or relative, and, on the other hand, ideas that were absolute.

> 5.3.88-89. For us, dream cognition would certainly be falsified by the perception of a waking cognition contradicting it; while for you, what would constitute the difference (between the reality of waking-cognition and that of dream-consciousness, both of which are held by you to be equally false)?

Dreams have a substantial basis. The dream cognition is a perception not of the external elements [*mahabhūta*] that make up material objects, but of the subtle elements [*tanmātra*] operating in the five sense organs [*buddhīndrya*]. In the modern view when we dream that we hear a sound, some sound receptors deeper in our brain are operational. Far from being empty, ideas have a basis in the concrete world. There is no such thing as 'pure imagination'. Finally, we have cognitions of such things as atoms, on the one hand, or, on the other hand the idea of Nature herself, who is the general cause of everything. We arrive at our idea of Nature because we have contact with her constituent elements, which are concrete.

5.3.113-114. Even such objects as are never perceived (such as the Samkhya 'Prakṛti'), are found to be comprehended by cognitions; and the origin of these cognitions lies in (its constituent elements) the earth, &c.

Negative Statements

When we understand something we truly recognise its elements. Sometimes, however, we make mistakes. Perhaps we think that a shell is a piece of silver. The fact that things can sometimes be cognised in error, instead of truly, does not undermine the validity of cognition in itself. There must be something truly cognised, in order that we can recognise other cognitions as erroneous. Here Kumarila is close to the Nyayika for whom error lies in the hasty judgement, when we are unclear of what our impression actually is. But we do nevertheless really see what we see. But Kumarila's view of negation also follows the Nyaya. He sees absence itself as concrete, rather than as the result of a judgement that something is missing from a concrete situation.

If a cognition were devoid of a substratum, then it would be false. Negative statements have to be accepted in order to describe real situations. They can be premises leading to a positive conclusion.

The disjunctive syllogism can have a particular negation as its middle term:

Rupa is either here or at home.
Rupa is not here.
Therefore she is at home.

Thus a negation is epistemologically positive. But as far as ontology is concerned it is surely negative.

> 5.3.117-119. Therefore it is only that (cognition), which comprehends an object otherwise than in the form it exists in, that can be said to be 'devoid of substratum'; and that Cognition which has 'negation' for its object is, in fact, one that has a real substratum; because this 'negation' too is not an independent entity by itself; for it is not so comprehended. For you, however, both of these ('absence of substratum' and 'negation as substratum') together with their causes can never be ascertained.

Therefore, 'This is not a jar' has a real substratum; the cognition has for its content the absence of any quality of being a jar in the object considered.

For the Buddhist each cognition cognises itself; thus, for him, there is no problem of a substratum for negative cognitions. But the Ślokavārttika sees this as a loss and not a gain. Since the Buddhist does not accept causation, further understanding of the activity of cognition is not possible. But there is a much more important difficulty. Cognitions are distinguished by the diversity of the forms of the objects that minds cognise. Our cognition of a triangle is distinct from our cognition of a square. But *qua* cognition, the two cognitions are identical; it is the two shapes that are different. Cognition as such has just one form.

> 5.4.111-112. If the cognition in the first be assumed to have only one form, then all other conceptions in connection therewith cannot but be of the same form. And it is for this reason that the difference between the *cognition of the jar* and the *cognition of that (cognition)* is not fully established. It is only in the conception of the form of the cognising cognition that there can be any accumulation of forms …

But the cognition of the cognition and the cognition of the cognition of the cognition, and so on forever, do not have different forms and therefore are not distinct. They thus have no separate existences; and thus the whole infinite series is, in reality, non-existent.

> 5.4.116. Therefore Cognition by itself being only one, it is established that the difference in the conceptions is due to the diversity among objects of cognition; and as such what business have we to postulate another form (for the cognition itself)?

The Syllogism

Kumarila and Prabhakara give the syllogism as only having three members.

The statement of the case [*pratijñā* and *nigamana*].

1. The major premise, stating the general rule and giving the practical instance [*udhāharā*].
2. The minor premise [*hetu* and *upanaya*].

The hill is on fire.
Whenever there is smoke there is fire.
There is smoke on the hill.

This is of course the same fivefold Indian syllogism. The statement of the case and the conclusion are combined in the first line; and the reason and the approach to the situation are combined in the third.

The Mimamsakas thought that the order of the premises did not matter.

Inference, according to Kumarila, depends on the recognition of the relationship between the Major and Minor terms; here the major is 'fire' and the minor is 'the hill'. The middle term is 'smoke'.

The Buddhist doctrine of momentariness, where each experience is a '*dhamma* arising' (the Pali word and Buddhist sense) and has no relationship to any other *dhamma*, would imply that there is no such thing as inference. The doctrine of inference is interwoven with the doctrine of causality; or, rather, the fact of inference and the fact of causality are so entwined. It is all, for Kumarila, the fullness of realism.

The Buddhist claims that the *sāmānya*, or class, on which the inference depends, is itself the product of inference. Thus, says Kumarila, the Buddhist cannot accept inference.

There is a hint that the Buddhist must recognise the relationship (of containment) between the terms of the syllogism in order to then deny that relationship.

> 5.5.166. The recognition of the relationship of the Major and Minor Terms ought surely to be looked for (in all cases of inference). But, prior to the action of Inference, the Buddha can have no idea of it.

If the Middle Term 'smoke' were a mere impression [*vāsanā*], it could not contain the other ideas; and so the conclusion also could not be logically arrived at. The impression also would be solitary — isolated from other objects and experiences.

> 5.5.167. Nor is a knowledge of the Middle Term possible, through mere impression (Vāsanā); for (in that case) the cognition of the Major and Minor terms too would be arrived at in the same manner, and not through the three-membered argument (in the form of inferential syllogism) ...

> 5.5.169. One, to whom the cognition of the Major and Minor terms arises from a Middle Term, which is cognised by Sense-perception,— for such a one, there is nothing more to be desired.

> 5.5.170. Even in a case where the cognition of the Major and Minor Terms is due to an inferred Middle Term,— the first Middle Term must be one that has been cognised by Sense-perception.

Clearly here Kumarila sees perception as a whole grasping of the object within the complexity of its basic relationships; and not merely as a physical sensation. Perception is an intelligent act; recognising its object as coming under a universal idea, and thus being connected to other ideas.

The Buddhist refutation of sensation is as follows: to say, 'I see the mountain,' is an inference derived from a physical sensation. This inference, they say, goes wholly beyond what is given, as all inferences must. The Buddhist does not deny the event of sensation; but each sensation is, as it were, mere impression [*vāsanā*].

The Mimamsakas hold that the inference from fire to smoke is of a specific character [*dṛṣṭasvalakśana*], whereas the inference to the burning capacity of fire is unspecific [*adṛṣṭasvalakśana*]. This is a most interesting distinction. If we often notice the concomitance of smoke and fire, we are aware of an empirical structure that gives a visible sign of itself. But if we have a scientific, or rational, understanding of things, we grasp the potency of fire. We grasp its, as it might be, hidden, nature; literally: 'the unseen sign of itself' [*adṛṣṭasvalakśana*].

John Stuart Mill, the proponent of empiricism, is unclear both about the difference between an accidental structure observed and the inductive recognition of a coherent structure leading to valid expectations of future events; and again unclear about the further difference between inductive structures and the unchanging and necessary principles of the universe.

The soul is not only necessitated by the Vedas but is apparent to itself — being the 'I' — being consciousness. Again the 'I' is clearly discernible from the body. The soul for the Mimamsa has a perishable and an imperishable aspect. The perishable aspect is its contact with manas and the senses. Kumarila takes the Vedic sense of 'consciousness' which is extinguished at death to be consciousness through the senses [*samvid*]. The meaning of the Sanskrit *samvid* is: consciousness, intellect, knowledge, but also; perception, feeling and guilt.

Contact between the Soul and manas produces cognitions, which are fleeting. The fact of cognition does not alter the perduring nature of the soul. Once the cognition has gone the soul reverts to its pure and imperishable substance; though it has the capacity to take on the cognition, the cognition is never its real nature. Equally manas will die with body; and no contact with the soul can ever change the atomic nature of manas. Manas is entirely perishable.

> 5.18.147. The Soul, by Itself, is imperishable. And perishability belongs to (its connection with) the senses, &c., together with the capabilities of (of *Dharma* and *Adharma*). And the 'absence of consciousness' (mentioned in the passage 'there is no consciousness after death' refers to the Material Senses, &c. (The meaning being that after death, the Soul ceases to have any cognition through the material sense-organs and body, &c.)

For the Mimamsakas, as for the Nyayikas, there is no need for a subtle body, or indeed a series of ever-subtler bodies, because, of its nature, the soul can interact with the most refined energies [*sattva*] of matter. Indian philosophy has not been particularly concerned with the gap between soul and body. For the West matter and spirit have recently become wholly opposed categories; whereas for Indians they are the poles at either end of the spectrum of being. The form [*akrti*] of the material object is what is cognised by the soul, via the material impression made on the senses.

Western thought has increasingly been dominated by the principle of sufficient reason. Indian philosophy has always been contemplative and experiential as much as rational. Conscious souls are a given and matter is a given; therefore there can be no deep cosmic and ontological inconsistency between them. The inconsistency resides in our own failure to understand!

> 5.18.100. 'On tearing open the Body, we can see the colour, &c., of the interior of the Body, but not Pleasures, &c. Therefore, like the Mind, and the Will, these (Pleasure, &c.), too cannot be regarded as properties of the Body.
>
> 5.18.101. 'Pleasure, &c., being properties must have a substrate, like taste, &c., and that which is the substrate of these (Pleasure, &c.,) is the Soul.'
>
> 5.18.107. The arguments of other theorists (for proving the existence of the Soul) being thus rejected, the *Bhasya* proceeds to show that the Soul is itself directly cognisable by the notion of 'I'.

> 5.18.130. The idea of '*My Soul*', indicating difference (between the *soul* and the 'I'), must be explained as being due to the difference (from the soul) of 'cognition', which is a state of the soul (and hence often spoken of as such).

> 5.18.131. Of the word 'My' (i.e., 'I') the direct denotation can be none other than the 'Soul'; therefore the notion of difference (expressed in 'My Soul') must be due to the aforesaid cause, and the difference is due to the difference of 'Cognition,' (and therefore the expression 'My soul' cannot be taken to point to any other *soul* than the one expressed by the 'I' in the word 'My').

The soul is the Person and the doer of actions — the enjoyer. The Person is the underlying substrate of the experiences of happiness and unhappiness. Remembrance of the action has no part in the enjoyment of the fruits of the action in a later existence; but intelligence is a permanent aspect of the soul. Cognition is the application of intelligence to material things. Cognition of objects can only take place through the sense organs. These cognitions occur in the changeable aspect of the soul; though they depend on the intelligence of the permanent aspect.

Because the soul apprehends changes in various parts of the body, it cannot be atomic. It is one and all pervading [*vibhū*]. The Mimamsa does not accept the view of the Advaitin, that soul [*ātman*] is ultimately Brahman. The Advaitin analogy of the sun lighting many objects and appearing, itself, to have different qualities, is not the situation for the Mimamsaka. Along with the Samkhya and the

Nyaya, the Mimamsa doctrine considers that a plurality of selves is necessary to account for the variety of experiences. The doctrine further considers that the diverse qualities of different souls do not merely belong to their having different bodies. Each soul is unique, possessing its own quality of *dharma* and *adharma*.

Ideas, fleeting and unsupported, cannot be the soul. The soul cannot be replaced by a myriad of ideas trailing past connexions, and each a bit of consciousness in itself, as the Buddhists hold. We discern in the self a permanent substantial aspect [*dravya*], which can be the object of cognition and an aspect of consciousness [*bodha*], which is the cognising subject.

At *moksa* what is released? Well the soul, pure in itself, does not need past cognitions. In this sense it is the true Person. The person we know and possess in this life is, so to speak, a version of the Person. It matters not that we forget, later, the actions that bring about fruits that we enjoy in paradise.

> 5.18.21. 'If it be held that at the time of the performance of an action, and at the time of the appearance of pleasure, &c., the character of the Soul is transformed, then its eternality disappears.'
>
> 5.18.22. *Reply*: We do not deny the applicability of the epithet 'non-eternal' to the Soul; if 'non-eternality' mean only 'liability to modification'; as such liability does not necessarily imply destruction ...
>
> 5.18.26. According to my theory the Person (*i.e.*, the Soul), while passing through the different conditions

of pleasure, pain, &c., never, for once, relinquishes his character of an Intelligent substantial Entity.

For Prabhakara and his followers the soul is the unintelligible substrate of qualities such as knowledge, experience, pain and pleasure. It is not the direct object of self-perception. We remember past cognitions because of the permanent substrate [*āśraya*], common to past perception [*pūrvabhāva*], and present recollection [*smṛti*]. But we are not directly conscious of the soul itself — it is the agent [*kartā*] of cognition, but it is not itself the object of cognition. The self in manifested in all cognitions especially those that are not cognitions of a bodily nature. Being entirely distinct from cognition, it is eternal. On Prabhakara's view of the soul, there is no mystery in our being unconscious in deep sleep.

Pārthasārathi Miśra held to the opposite point of view; namely that the soul is both subject and object of perception. He thought that if the recognition of the self, albeit through inference, did not treat the self as an object, it would lead to cognition without an object, which is impossible. But, on the other hand, we can argue that the self, cognised by self-consciousness, remains of its nature of subject and never becomes object. Kumarila gives the example of a man walking, who is the agent of the walking but not the object of the walk.

The followers of Kumarila argued that we can become conscious of the jar without being conscious of self; sometimes, however, there is a distinct consciousness of the self, a second cognition, where the mind turns on itself and the subject is the object of itself.

They agreed with Prabhakara that we are never conscious of self [*ahaṁpratyaya*] without being conscious of an external object [*viṣayavitti*]. To make a clear distinction, in an epistemological sense, the self is the object of the self; but in an ontological sense the subject never becomes a true external object. Self-awareness is the product of a higher degree of life.

For Prabhakara the *ātman* is quite distinct from consciousness [*samvid*]. He is as anxious as Kumarila to stress individual responsibility and avoid any doctrine of Advaitism where consciousness is ultimately one and the ego is really the *ātman*; and *ātman* is Brahman.

From this difference between the two teachers, Kumarila and Prabhakara, developed the two principal schools of the Mimamsa, which have survived until the present day.

For Kumarila inner perceptions are similar to outer perceptions. Through the external senses *manas* is in contact with objects in the external world: through the internal senses *manas* is in contact with the feelings of the body and the emotions.

> 4.83. The mind being a Sense-organ, the idea of pleasure, etc., is also 'Sense-perception', because it is only when in contact with the mind, that the soul experiences them.

Prabhakara proved the atomic nature of manas. Causes can be intimately connected [*samavāyikāraṇa*] with the effect, or not intimately connected [*asamavāyikāraṇa*]. In the case of the cognition the intimate cause is the self. Yet the cognition is ephemeral and it is an effect; it is thus a quality, residing in the permanent substance of the self. But how can a temporary quality arise in permanent substance; for example, when I cognise myself as feeling tired? This must be due to contact with other substances; and primarily with the substance of *manas*. Now cognitions are many and various and thus *manas*, which is the primary contact of the self, must also be atomic.

If the knower were only an idea, as most, though not all, schools of Buddhism claim, selfhood would be momentary. Thus the forms of cognitions as past and present would be invalid. We can only think, 'I know now', because we have an idea of pastness. Without this sense of pastness, even the momentary awareness of a knowing self would not be possible. The series of ideas is not what we recognise as self and object, existing under the forms of past and present time.

> 5.18.120. The 'series' (of ideas) cannot be said to be the object of Recognition; because none of the two forms (past and present) can possibly belong to it. As the series did not cognise it in the past (as it did not exist at the time of the first cognition), nor does it cognise at the present moment, because of its non-objective (unreal) character.

Cleverly the Buddhist can argue, when we have a cognition of the *ātman* such that he is at once both subject and object, that the idea likewise can have this dual character; and therefore why need we infer a permanent cognising subject as separate from the object. And again, cleverly, is not the human soul, once cognised, both an idea and a substance?

5.4.67. 'But even you hold the 'Self' (Ātmā) to have the character of both cogniser and cognised.'

5.4.68-69. (Though the Self is really one, yet) being somehow or other, taken as diverse, in the shape of its diverse properties, — we attribute the character of the *cogniser* to (the Self in the character of) the Idea, and the character of the *cognised* to (the Self in the character of) substance and the rest. If it be urged that 'then, (even in your own theory) there is no absolute difference (between the cogniser and the cognised)', — (we reply) where have you found me accepting (or holding) such *absolute* difference? The fact of the word 'I' applying only to the Pratyagātman is based upon the extreme proximity (of the cognising 'I' with the cognised 'object').

The self-cognition of the *ātman*, grasped by perception [*pratyagātman*], is a unique case. Here the cognition and its object are entirely one, as the 'I' cognises itself, realising that it is doing so and, in the case of this philosophical discussion, reports this realisation to itself and to others. In order to make the distinction between the cognised and cognising 'I', a tinge of *manas*, is needed. In *moksa* the *ātman* will exist as pure self-consciousness, experiencing the bliss of her own being, without the cognitional process.

The western scepticism involving the separation of mind and object, soul and body, are clearly answered here along with Buddhist objections. Idea can grasp matter; and soul can grasp idea. We have never held an '*absolute* difference' between matter and spirit and between subject and object. Through the intuition of the 'I' [*pratyagātman*], we attain the realisation of the 'I' as substance, self and idea, i.e. as soul.

Prabhakara believed that *samsara* is always painful.

The last death of the body is the end of Dharma and *adharma*; and that is release. The soul takes this step of liberation when enough knowledge and merit have been accumulated. Pārthasārathi regarded release as not bliss, but merely as freedom from pain; because in the general view of the Mimamsakas the soul needs manas and sense-objects in order to be self-aware. Kumarila, however, was positive, regarding *moksa* as the *ātman* finally realising itself. (This is a position close to the Advaita, according to Radhakrishnan).

Matter and Universals

The Buddhists taught that universals are not real and only the individual item is apprehended. Both Kumarila and Pārthasārathi argued that when we perceive the individual thing we perceive the universal at the same time; and so the universal is equally the object of perception.

Pārthasārathi Miśra states that the universal is not absolutely and distinctly different from the individual. The two perceptions inhere in the same object; because they highlight different aspects of the same object. In the cognition 'This is a cow', we have a perception of 'this' [*iyambuddhi*], as well as a perception of 'cow' [*gobuddhi*]. But the distinction is not a contradiction like, 'This is silver' and, 'This is not silver'. There are not two separate cognitions, which inhere in the same object. The one cognition consists of 'this' and 'cow'. There is no real difference between the individual and universal.

The followers of Prabhakara, however, did not agree. They held that the universal is eternal and the individual is ephemeral; and thus that we perceive either the individual, or the universal in a single act of cognition. We cannot perceive difference and similarity at once. When we recognise the similarity between two objects we perceive the universal.

The difficulty with this view is that the gap between the individual and the universal is too wide. The act of recognition requires that, having recognised an animal as a cow, we can a moment later recognise the individual as the same individual; therefore we must have in the first instance recognised the individual as well as the 'cow'.

Kumarila, himself, held that recognition is of the individual as class member. There is one cognition of one object.

The question of universals and individuals is close to the question of the whole and its parts. Both questions stem from the problem of the One and the Many. On both questions Kumarila took a moderate stand. Our experience is that we perceive wholes, which are made of parts, but that, equally, we do not have to perceive all the parts to perceive the whole. Whether we regard an object as a whole, or whether we regard it as a collection of parts, depends on our point of view.

The section of Sūtra V treating of this matter is called Vanavāda – 'way of the forest'. In ancient times men had retired to the forest to reflect and study. These philosophers contemplated the One and the Many; and the adjoined mysteries of the whole and the part; and of the universal and the individual. It was about distinguishing the forest from the trees.

> 5.15.71-73. We have the idea of 'Forest' with reference to a *collection of trees*; — but we could not hold the idea of the *class* 'Cow' to belong to a *collection of cows*. Because the idea of the *class* 'Cow' is similar to that of the 'tree' (inasmuch as just as to each of the individual trees belongs the character of 'tree', so to each individual cow belongs the idea of the *class* 'Cow'). Nor can we assume the (idea of the *class* 'Cow' to belong to) a collection (of individual cows); because that idea of the *class* 'Cow' does not resemble that of the 'forest' in the point of the non-cognition of this latter apart (from the trees constituting it).

> 5.15.73-74. Nor can a conglomeration of the dewlap, &c., be the substrate of the idea of the *class* ('Cow'); because the operation of these (dewlap, &c.), ceases with the bringing about of the cognition of the individual (cow); whereas the idea of the *class* 'Cow' rests in the commonalty of (*i.e.*, the entity common to) these (individuals) Then, if you deny a *corporate whole* (apart from the constituent particles, — as held by the Buddha), the *Class* still remains untouched …

The forest is a collection of individual trees; but the universal 'cowness' [*gotva*] is not an enumeration of the features and qualities by which we recognise the cow. These individual features disappear as we recognise the animal; whereas we see the individual trees and their collectivity, the forest, at one and the same time.

The Buddhist thinkers can deny the recognition of the whole apart from the constituent particles. However, the idea of the class cannot be so easily put aside. The two issues are, for Kumarila, markedly different. On the argument of the whole and the parts Kumarila will not be drawn to any extreme.

> 5.15.76-77. Both difference and non-difference (of the *Whole* from the parts) have been affirmed and denied by some people. But between the two sets of arguments it has never been ascertained which is the stronger and which the weaker; Therefore it is best to take the middle course (*i.e.*, admit of both difference and non-difference partially).

The question is like a multi-coloured object of which it makes no sense to ask, 'Of what colour is it?'

For Kumarila the existence of material atoms was speculation. This speculation was not a foundation for doubting the reality of what we perceive.

> 5.5.183. The Mimāmsakas, again, do not necessarily admit the existence of atoms; and so on that ground you cannot postulate the falsity of a perceived entity.

5.5.184. One, who would deny the visible concrete whole, by means of invisible atoms, would also assert the absence of a hare, through its horns!

5.5.185. It is only when the existence of a concrete whole is established as a fact, that the existence of atoms is postulated, and that simply as a means for the accomplishment of the idea of the whole.

5.5.186. Therefore an object is to be accepted, just as it is always perceived, — be it either as a 'Sāmānya' or otherwise (specific entity).

Thus the firm realism of Kumarila Bhatta in the matter of whole objects, such as living things, leads to a clear recognition of universals as real entities. Yet 'universal' is a relative term. What is a universal from one point of view is an individual from another. Using the basic clades of the animal kingdom as exemplars, Kumarila uses the word 'form' [*akrti*] for class. It is the *akrti* that the soul grasps through manas. The class 'cow' is thus close to the individual and to the real. The relationship between the individual and the universal is *samavāya* — smoothly together woven. The term *sāmānya* means: equally, jointly, and together.

5.5.187. In comparison with the genus (Sāmānya) 'Being', the class 'cow,' comes to be accepted as a specific entity. Therefore one, who holds the specific entity to be amenable to Sense-perception, need not deny the existence of the 'Sāmānya' (Genus).

> 5.5.188. If it be urged that 'it is not *as a genus* ('Sāmānya') that a 'Sāmānya' is perceived by the Sense', — then (we reply) *Is* there any idea of any object perceived being a specific entity? (The fact is that) whatever a person comprehends can be spoken in both ways (i.e., as a *class* and as a specific entity).

It is important to recognise, however, that Kumarila does not hold the existence of universals as separate cosmic powers presiding over reality. They exist only in their individual instances. For the Mimamsaka there is no realm of divine ideals; man is uplifted by the injunctions of the Vedas alone.

The traditional treatment of the problem of universals in western philosophy can be simplified into a tripartite structure.

> The thought of Plato is that universals have their own existence in a realm of ideas ultimately stemming from the 'Idea of the Good'.

> The Nominalist tradition of the western Middle Ages was that universals are either things [*res*] or words [*voces*]; and that words are just things that group other things under headings.

> The Aristotelian tradition of moderate realism is that universals are real but exist in things, as their properties. The 'instantiation' of a property does not create another property; the one property exists in all things that possess it.

> Russell has considered universals to be objects collected under mathematical functions or under propositions; objects are grouped into classes, and these classes are ontologically no more than the objects they contain.

It is worthy of note that Frege undoubtedly considered concepts to be realities and that descriptive functions had a universal correspondence in reality. He may arguably have been an Aristotelian or even a Platonist.

It is also notable that there is a logical advantage in the Platonic thinking. The following syllogism seems correct to our intuitive understanding —

Birds have feathers.
Dodos are birds.
Therefore dodos have feathers.

But for the nominalist there is a difficulty here in that the second premise implies that dodos exist, and actually they don't exist any longer. For the Platonist, however, the idea of dodo exists in its own right.

In *Principia Mathematica*, Russell himself insisted that a Null Class – a class with 0 members – could still exist. This is an attempt to resolve the Nominalist problem. His immediate followers took the Null Class to have a basis of existence in the brains of thinkers or in sentences on paper. But this may not be fully satisfying from a philosophical point of view.

Dinnāga, the great Madhyamika logician [480-540 AD], was born near Kanchipuram, in Tamil Nadu. He taught that universals were *vikalpa*, meaning: having more than one aspect, or uncertain; and *kalpanā*, meaning: made, fashioned, composed, and thus, imaginary. His ontology did not allow the existence of universally consistent physical entities, such as the substances of Aristotle or the class [*akrti*] and genus [*sāmānya*] of Kumarila. According to Dinnāga and the Madhyamika, we merely observe 'Dhammas arising' and have no warrant to argue to anything else. These Dhammas appear to cluster and relate to one another in ways that suggest the existence of realities beyond themselves. Universals are examples of such creations of imagination.

As a logician Dinnāga proposed that we replace the class of 'cows' with the opposed class of 'non-cows'. However, the class of 'non-cows' is obviously a construction based on the 'class' of cows. The class of 'non-cows' is clearly not an independent reality — it is a construction over against the individual cow, which is the sole existent. It is called the *apoha*, meaning: denial, or exclusion. — And the *apoha* sets the limit [*nimitta*] by which the class 'cow' is defined. But the Madhyamika position is that the class of 'cow' is equally, again in modern terms, a construction. This construction is built as a result of our needs to find milk and our ability to recognise the dewlap, the udders and the other features we associate with what we call 'a cow'. To Bimal Krishna Matilal [1935-1991], this *apoha* gives a clear ontological advantage.

> To sum up: it must be admitted that the Buddhist substitute, *anyāpoha* (exclusion of the other) has a clear advantage over

> the Naiyāyikas' objective universal such as cowhood. Since exclusion is not construed as a separate reality, we need not raise the question of how it is related to what by its own nature excludes … It is more clearly an artificially-formed class without any illusion about any underlying common property (a positive one) to be shared by its members.

The advantage of which Matilal speaks is only an advantage if we assume that reality has the momentariness of our subjective experience. Here Matilal seems to be leaving go of his usual position of moderate realism. But perhaps he is just unfolding the position of Dinnāga.

However, it is easy for Kumarila to deliver the realist answer. If the Idea has no substance how can it be negated? Inference and negation are causal acts in the Mimamsa system, albeit causality of a special kind. Thus ideas, as causal agents, are substantial. The substantiality of things leads to the substantiality of ideas of things.

> 5.4.136. But as there is no other substance (than conception), even an 'Apoha' cannot be possible for you. Because for the Idealist, there is no such thing as a 'non-Idea' (or non-Conception) that could be said to be negatived (by the 'Apoha').

Again the notion of the *apoha* of 'cow' depends on the idea of 'cow'.

> 5.14.1. Those, who have assumed the Class ('Cow') to be *a negation of the absence of Cow*, — even these people have clearly, by the assertion of the negation of

> the absence of *Cow*, admitted of an entity in the shape of *'gotva'* (the *Class* 'Cow).

> 5.14.2. It has been proved before (by the Buddhas) that a *negation* is only another form of positive entity, which consists in the negation of 'Horse' &c.

Further the *apoha* cannot be derived from one or several individuals. The exact form of one individual, taken in abstract, does not apply to all other individual cows, because of individual differences; and therefore it cannot play the role of the universal.

> 5.14.3. The specific (abstract) form cannot be held to be such an object, because it is undefined (abstract and unqualified). Nor could it apply to the individual black cow, &c., because that would not be *common* (to all cows).

Being

Kumarila taught that we know, through perception and reason, the world of real objects. Where we understand how things work, that is the way things actually do work. He rejects the earlier Buddhist view that the relationships that obtain between the objects we see are unsupported [*nirālambanavāda*] by any rational foundation. He equally rejects the notion that the nature of reality is emptiness [*śūnyavāda*], rather than being or non-being. Again he rejects the Advaita view that all is Brahman.

Kumarila held that there were four categories of being [*bhāva*] and four categories of non-being [*abhāva*]. The categories of being were:

Substance – [*dravya*]
Quality – [*guna*]
Action – [*karman*]
Generality – [*sāmānya*]

He regarded force [*śakti*] and similarity [*sādṛśya*] as aspects of substance. He saw number [*samkhya*] as a quality; and inherence [*parantantratā*] as not a different category from the thing itself.

Prabhakara held the latter four to be additional categories.

Kumarila held that there were ten substances: earth, water, air, fire, *akasa*, self, mind, time, space and darkness. Prabhakara held to nine substances, not recognising darkness.

The Mimamsakas accepted neither the creation of matter, not its utter dissolution. Matter is, for them, in some way, eternal

Despite his dismissal of the thought processes of Madhyamika logicians like Dinnāga, Kumarila is in awe of the goodness of the Buddha himself. When I look at my statue of the Buddha and it brings peace into my heart and home, I am aware of that deeper good beyond the cognitional level. Faith is often the most direct root to this good. And it is perhaps faith that the Buddha teaches.

> 5.3.202. As a matter of fact, this denial of (the reality of the external) objects, — following on the assumption of such an 'Impression-theory', which is incorrect and devoid of reason, — was declared by the Buddha, with the sole object of alienating the affections (of men from such worldly objects); and somehow or other, some people (the so-called followers of the Buddha) fell into a mistake (and accepted it to its utmost extent, as the denial of all external substratum of cognitions).

Negation

Kumarila uses negation as a proof of Vedic injunction; namely that the lack of any material, human, or religious means of establishing the Vedas actually establishes them perfectly. This does not mean that negation has to be a positive force.

> 5.9.1-2. In the case of the object where the aforesaid five means of knowledge do not function towards the comprehension of the existence of that object, we have Negation as the sole means of cognition. The ascertainment of the non-contact (non-existence) of an object depends upon the validity of this (Negation) as a means of cognition.

Kumarila then defines the different types of negation.

> 5.9.2-4. The non-existence of curd in milk is called 'Prior Negation' (Prāgabhāva) (1); the non-existence in the curd is called 'Destruction' (Dhvaṇsa) (2); the

negation of the horse, &c., in the cow, and *vice versa* is known as 'Mutual Negation' (Anyonyābhāva) (3); the lower portions of the hare's head, being devoid of hardness and a supernumerary growth in the form of horns, is called 'Absolute Negation' (Atyantābhāva) (4).

5.9.5-6. If Negation were not accepted as a (distinct) means of cognition, then we would have the existence of curd in milk, of milk in curd, of the jar in a piece of cloth, of horns in the hare, of intelligence in the earth, &c., of shape in the Soul, of odour in water, of taste in fire, of form together with these two in the air, and of tangibility and these three in the Akasa).

We can only classify entities. Because we have just divided negations into different classes, negations must have some sort of being.

5.9.7-8. Nor again could we have any usage with regard to the differentiation of causes and effects, &c., if Negation were not classified into those different kinds, such as Prior Negation, &c. Nor again is such a classification possible with regard to a non-entity. Therefore Negation must be an entity. For what is the negation of an effect, other than the existence (continuance) of the cause.

At the end of this verse he seems to ground the negation of the effect (where an effect has not taken place) in the real being of the continual cause. Here there is a hint of moderation and simple realism, as in his treatment of error in cognition. There is a danger, however, in Kumarila's treatment of negation. He seems to step away from the pure realist position towards what we may call super-realism.

> 5.9.9. Or again, Negation must be an entity, like cow, &c., because it is capable of forming the object of the notions of collective affirmation and differentiation; and also, because it is an object of cognition.

His acceptance of negation as an entity seems to totally undermine his refutation of the *apoha* doctrine of Dinnāga; namely that the *apoha* does not have causal and inferential force, and also depends on the positive and real force of 'cow' for its existence.

Prabhakara clearly took the realist view of negation. A negative statement is just that. It does not have an ontological counterpart. Non-being is not a special kind of being. Prabhakara certainly takes Kumarila as saying the converse, namely that negation is an entity. Kumarila's acceptance of darkness as a substance may be an indication of his thinking in this matter. But, on the other hand, in his treatment of cognition, the metaphysical substrate of a negative cognition is purely the being in the real world that is the identical ground of the positive cognition.

Meaning

If we ask, 'What is the meaning of the Vedas?' there is an expectation of a fairly simple answer. This is the holist sense of meaning. Traditionally there have been three ways of regarding the Vedas; three ways of answering our question. Firstly the *aitīhāsika* theory regards the *saṁhita* as an historical record of heroes who later came to be regarded as gods. This is how it actually was [*itīhāsa*]. The *aitīhāsika* theory is repugnant to Vedic orthodoxy. The second view is the *ādhyātmika*, or *ātmavāda*, theory. This is the supremely spiritual and simple view that the sacred syllable [*aum*] is the whole and full meaning of the Vedas. The *aum* represents the absolute, the Vedas and the world. But the *aum* is a purely contemplative absorption. It does not provide any understanding in a cognitional sense. It does not even furnish an understanding of the three totalities of: absolute, Vedas and world. These have to be explained externally and verbally.

Thus a third position of compromise arose. The linguistic Advaitinism of Bhartṛhari accepted the *aum* as the final and full meaning of the Vedas, from which sound and knowledge cascaded. Thus understanding was achieved and philosophy made possible. The disciples of Prabhakara strongly supported this approach. They were followers of Shaivism. The Vaishnava religion with its devotional and theistic emphases, favoured the second [*ātmavāda*] theory.

Do words ultimately refer to individual objects or do they ultimately refer to qualities? Put another way, does realism mean particularism [*vyakti-śakti-vāda*] of meaning, or generalism of meaning [*jāti-śakti-vāda*]? Russell's class logic is clearly a case of meaning generalism. For Russell, words do not directly refer to objects and names are short forms of description. The description is made up of generic terms.

Early Indian theories of language held that nouns refer to the generic. They are 'class sounds' [*jāti-śabda*]. Kumarila held this generic view, for the injunctions were the classic use of the nominal term. The injunctions are law-like because they have no reference to any particular object; they refer to non-generics, used indefinitely. They are existential quantifications.

Another debate amongst Indian grammarians concerned the question of which sound event was the primary carrier of meaning. Was it the letter, the word, or the sentence? Here Kumarila follows the middle way.

> 24-26.111-112. It is true that it is not possible for the Sentence (as a whole, independently of the Words) to express any meaning; because, inasmuch as the cognition of its meaning is otherwise explained (as being based upon the meanings of Words), it is altogether unwarrantable to assume an independent denotive capacity in the Sentence (as a whole, apart from the words composing it).
>
> 24-26.112-113. It is extremely difficult even to assume the denotativeness of the Word to lie in its component Letters (though even this has been proved to be impossible) ...
>
> 24-26.136. (Being atomic themselves) the Sounds cannot produce any perceptible effects other than the atomic. Consequently, we could have cognitions only of the atomic factor of the Words (and we could never

have any perception of Words as they are ordinarily known).

The third debate in Indian philosophy of language was about the duration of the word. Is the word a momentary phenomenon, or is it eternal. Kumarila, because of his passion to avoid scepticism and to defend the reality of the Vedas, held to the eternality of the word.

> 6-23.3. When the word is momentary (as is held by the Buddha), then it is incapable of giving any sense. Consequently, if the comprehension of meanings from momentary words be sought to be established, by means of arguments, then the comprehension of the Veda would become groundless.

The notion that words are momentary is connected to the idea that the word refers to the individual and visible object. Were this the case the idea of Dharma would be incomprehensible. Meanings underlie reality. For example space [*akasa*] reveals itself when earth is removed as we dig a hole in the ground.

> 6-23.4. In the face of the groundlessness of these comprehensions (of the meanings of Words), we could have some refuge in the case of perceptible objects (which are amenable to the sense organs, and as such, are not totally dependent upon verbal expression). As for *Dharma*, however, depending as it does solely upon the Veda, it would lose its ground altogether.

> 6-23.5. And we should also reject the theory of an eternal usage being based upon objects having a

beginning (and as such necessarily perishable). In the case of the use of the jar, the idea of the (perishable) *individual jar* is a mistaken one, as it really pertains to the *class* 'jar' (which is eternal).

6-30-32. The Akasa too, being eternal, — when it happens to be covered up under the Earth or Water, — is rendered visible only by the removal of these (Earth and Water) by means of *digging* and *pumping*. And thus we see that here we have perception (of *Akasa*) only after effort. Consequently your reasoning — 'since it (word) is perceived only after an effort'— becomes doubtful.

The fifth element [*akasa*] is all pervasive; both in space and time. It is therefore eternal; and it is the substrate of all matter. Many Indian schools accepted *akasa* as a scientific fact. Some Buddhist schools though of *nirvāṇa* as a similar substrate of energy, similarly supporting the illusions (for the Buddhist) of world and self. Kumarila held that the ear itself is *akasa*, which is localised in the body. He noted that the Samkhya and the Vaishesika supported him in this view.

Prabhakara did not accept the distinction between sound and lettered sound [*dhvani*]. This distinction is widely held in Indian philosophy, and is notable in the Samkhya and other cosmological texts, as well as in the view of Kumarila. Prabhakara taught that all sound was lettered; and that letters and not words were the fundamental carriers of meaning. The potency of the word depended, he said, on the potency of the letters. A word has the power to mean something, whether we understand it or not. That is the eternality of the word. This view perhaps seems extreme; but if lettered, or meaningful, sound is a fundamental part of the universe then the authenticity of the Vedas can be comprehended, without referring to God or to some other source of inspiration.

In any case, as Kumarila would agree, true words respect the nature of things — the Vedas were not composed by men; merely taken down by poet and interpreted by priest.

Both Prabhakara and Kumarila deny the *sphoṭa*, holding that the 'eternal word' of Jaimini is the simple and sufficient explanation of meaning.

CHAPTER 10

THE PROOFS OF GOD'S EXISTENCE

The Six Systems

The Sanskrit word *dharśana* has a huge variety of meanings. The root of *dharśana* is *dṛiṣ* meaning, 'see'. Thus *dharśana* can mean: looking seeing, showing, teaching, observing and contemplating. Hindu philosophy is traditionally divided into six systems [*śaḍ dharśana*] — six ways of contemplating reality.

The six schools of Indian philosophy exist because of their differences on the ontological plane. Thinkers differ as to whether there is one supreme consciousness, or simply an innumerable host of conscious souls [*jīva*]. Again thinkers differ as to whether matter exists independently of consciousness, or whether matter flows from the supreme consciousness of God. And there again the schools vary in their solutions to the metaphysical question of causality.

In ethical matters, disputes between the schools concern the role of ritual in the process of spiritual release. The Mimamsaka insist that the action of ritual is necessary in order to obtain release from the endless process of reincarnation. The Samkhya and the Nyaya claim, oppositely, that ritual is harmful, and an impediment to salvation. These differences of response to metaphysical and ethical questions lead to, and reflect, different emphases on the relative importance of different areas of philosophy. The Samkhya contemplates the cosmology of ancient India and in that consideration sees how the one becomes the many. The Advaita Vedanta of Shamkara is a metaphysic of pure consciousness. Thus the writings of Shamkara are rich in the consideration of the four kinds of consciousness. Nevertheless the fourfold division of consciousness, that Shamkara affirms, is common to the six Hindu systems. Differences occur over and against an underlying sameness. Ashrams of the Samkhya and Nyaya are less ritualistic, but yet practice a certain amount of ritual; and the Mimamsaka studies logic and metaphysics as well as scripture and ritual interpretation.

During the seventh century BC, the six systems of Hindu philosophy developed.

1) Samkhya - Yoga
2) Nyaya - Vaishesika
3) Mimamsa
4) Advaita – Shamkara
5) Viśistadvaita – Ramanuja
6) Dvaita –Madhva

Upanishads

The Upanishads date from an earlier period. They open our minds to philosophy beyond philosophy.

In the Chandogya Upanishad, the old man points out to the boy the minute space at the heart of the Nyagrodha seed and says: *'tatt tvam asi'* – 'That thou art'. Shamkara held that this is a statement of the ultimate oneness of all things. Madhva held the very same sentence to be the statement of a dualism between 'that' and 'thou' — between God and the individual human soul. Thus developped the philosophies of non-dualism [*advaita*] and dualism [*dvaita*]. The Upanishad can be interpreted as yielding either reading. But it can also be contemplated as yielding neither.

The classic Hindu education was based upon five subjects: literature [*kāvya*], drama [*nātaka*], rhetoric [*alamkara*], logic [*tarka*] and grammar [*vyākaraṇa*]. Logic was the initiation into philosophy. The Nyaya philosophy, based as it is upon logic and emphasising the importance of logic as the foundation of philosophy, lies at the heart of Hindu thought. The other schools basically accept the Nyaya system of logic; though they do differ about the theory of knowledge and have different accounts about the means of knowing. Thus Nyaya logic may be said to be Hindu logic.

The Advaitin (Shamkara), however, does not accept the position of the Nyayika on erroneous perception. For Shamkara, and for some Buddhist schools, the mind always perceives a phenomenological object, whether true of false; for Gautama, the Nyayika, the mind always perceives the real but can set that real under the wrong heading.

The semi-legendary founder of the Nyaya School was Gautama [or Gotama] the *akṣapāda* [who meditated]. Nyāya Sūtra of Gautama and Nyāya Bhasya of Vātsyāyana were probably written between the second century AD and the fifth century AD.

The Nyaya philosophy is a knowledge-based system. Each soul has to avoid pain and achieve pleasure; but this achievement is purely a learning curve. There is not the strong sense of a good-will component in the soul, as in the Christian teaching, or as in the philosophy of Śrī Madhvācārya, the Hindu. The Nyayika does not believe in free will. Activity [*pravṛti*] causes birth [*janma*], which causes pain [*duḥkha*]. Activity itself is caused by aversion [*dveṣa*] — hate, implacability etc, by attachment [*rāga*] — lust and avarice, and by stupidity [*moha*] — suspicion, carelessness and misapprehension. These defects, in their turn, are caused by false knowledge [*mithyājñāna*]. True knowledge does not change our natures straightaway, but gradually, through the contemplation of the truth, the defects in our personalities are overcome. When this has been achieved, we stay in the body till we die, accumulating no more demerits; and then we are released by death from the process of reincarnation. For the Nyayika, study is the first means of release. But part of true study is reflection; and then again, in addition to study, yoga, or meditation, is needed. The Nyayika does not favour religion. He has a distinctly unorthodox view of the deities, as souls being stuck in a sort of heaven, from which they cannot be released. Religious ritual, the Nyayaika thought, would expand the lower self to a massive degree, rather than achieve the higher self. If we achieve religious action we could ultimately become a god, like Indra or Brahman, but that, in the Nyayika view, is not release [*moksa*] but a disaster.

As the belief in a benign and personal God increased, the Nyayikas taught that God arranged the experiences of souls so that their knowledge increased and they proceeded through transmigrations to release. No human effort is required, however; God does it all [*purusakāra*].

Udayana

The Nyaya was generally theistic. The use of the Unseen [*adṛṣṭārtha*] as an explanation of the visible world was usually regarded as unsatisfactory. A series of finite *adṛṣṭa* causes would necessarily be infinite and therefore impossible; just like a chain of observable material causes. The Nyāyakusumāñjali of Udayana is a statement of the Nyayika proofs of God's existence. The birthplace of Udayana is traditionally remembered as Kariyan, in the modern district of Samastipur, in Bihar. He was one of the greatest thinkers of the Nyaya School. He developed his ideas at a time when the school had become increasingly preoccupied with form and method, rather than with the teaching of a complete philosophy. He linked the Nyaya thought with the Vaiśeṣika School of realist metaphysics. Thus he looked forward to the later Navya-Nyāya, or New Nyaya School of the fourteenth century.

Udayana thought that the universe is highly structured. He had essentially a whole view. The components of the universe that are formed of atoms are not merely just atoms. Living bodies, molecules, atoms and subatomic particles, all possess equal reality — they equally exist. It is not true that electrons are, as it were, more real than wholes that are built of electrons. The mere existence of atoms and the force of karman cannot explain everything. The universe is too regular not to be planned.

Further there are two levels causation. There is the natural level of causation, but also the moral level. There is an obvious moral structure, whereby men increase in wisdom and virtue. Just as in natural causation all material levels are equally real — from the subatomic to the bio molecular — so on the level of human consciousness, the aspirations of men, and the hierarchy of values that they experience, constitute a totally different realm of being. This moral level is as real as the material level; though its being exists in the thoughts of conscious spirits. Material scientists who have such a yearning to know the truth, have a sort of unconscious consciousness of this moral level, though officially they are only interested in their study of the natural level of being.

Udayana believed the huge diversity of souls and the rich variety of individual experiences, necessitated the moral explanation that every kind of soul, in every kind of circumstances, would have to exist and then to find its way to the good. There is again a highly organised natural structure, which serves these ends. The form of this natural structure is too complex and perfect to be explained by the random interaction of the atoms. There must be a personal lord [*īśvara*] who has wisdom [*jñāna*] and desire [*icchā*]; and who can make volitional effort [*prayatna*]. There must be a God who watches over all and who bestows the fruits of *karman* [*karmaphalapradanirodaḥ*].

Kant thought that the fact that prudent and virtuous conduct on the whole profited, although not in every case, was an indirect indication of the existence of a beneficent creator God.

For Udayana liberation [*moksa*] was not just a transcendental experience, it must also incorporate true philosophical knowledge. This true knowledge must include the certainty, through the light of human reason, that God exists.

In the Nyāyakusumāñjali Udayana gave the following nine arguments to prove the existence of a creative God.

Kāryāt (lit. 'from effect'): The world is an effect, all effects have efficient cause, hence the world must have an efficient cause. That efficient cause is God.

Āyojanāt (lit., from combination): Atoms are inactive. To form a substance, they must combine. To combine, they must move. Nothing moves without intelligence and source of motion. Since we perceive substance, some intelligent source must have moved the inactive atoms. That intelligent source is God.

Dhṛtyādéḥ (lit., from support): Something sustains this world. Something destroys this world. Unintelligent *Adṛṣṭa* (unseen principles of nature) cannot do this. We must infer that something intelligent is behind it. That is God.

Padāt (lit., from word): Each word has meaning and represents an object. This representational power of words has a cause. That cause is God.

Pratyayatah (lit, from faith): Vedas are infallible. Human beings are fallible. Infallible Vedas cannot have been authored by fallible human beings. Someone authored the infallible Vedas. That author is God.

Shrutéḥ (lit., from scriptures): The infallible Vedas testify to the existence of God. Thus God exists.

Vākyāt (lit., from precepts): Vedas deal with moral laws, the rights and the wrongs. These are divine. Divine injunctions and prohibitions can only come from a divine creator of laws. That divine creator is God.

Samkhyāviśeṣāt (lit., from the specialty of numbers): By rules of perception, only the number 'one' can ever be directly perceived. All other numbers other than one, are inferences and concepts created by consciousness. When man is born, his mind is incapable of inferences and concepts. He develops consciousness as he develops. The consciousness development is self-evident and proven because of man's ability with perfect numerical conception. This ability to conceive numerically perfect concepts must depend on something. That something is divine consciousness. So God must exist.

Adṛṣṭāt (lit., from the unforeseen): Everybody reaps the fruits of his own actions. Merits and demerits accrue from his own actions. An Unseen Power keeps a balance sheet of the merit and demerit. But since this Unseen Power is Unintelligent, it needs intelligent guidance to work. That intelligent guide is God.

If the entire nature of the universe is a continual series of temporary causes and effects, how could the universe exist at all? The temporary must necessarily be insubstantial; therefore there must be a permanent substance on which these impermanencies depend. For the materialist the totality as a whole has a fundamentally different nature to all of its parts. This seems a contradiction. Modern atomism leaves nothing solid like the older atomism. Particles are subject to continual change. The existence of the ultimate particle is probably fleeting.

St Thomas Aquinas

> On the contrary, It is said in the person of God: 'I am Who am.' (Exodus 3:14)
> The existence of God can be proved in five ways. The first and more manifest way is the argument from motion. It is certain, and evident to our senses, that in the world some things are in motion. Now whatever is in motion is put in motion by another, for nothing can be in motion except it is in potentiality to that towards which it is in motion; whereas a thing moves inasmuch as it is in act. For motion is nothing else than the reduction of something from potentiality to actuality. But nothing can be reduced from potentiality to actuality, except by something in a state of actuality. Thus that which is actually hot, as fire, makes wood, which is potentially hot, to be actually hot, and thereby moves and changes it. Now it is not possible that the same thing should be at once in actuality and potentiality in the same respect, but only in different respects. For what is actually hot cannot simultaneously be potentially hot; but it is simultaneously potentially cold. It is therefore impossible that in the same respect and in the same

> way a thing should be both mover and moved, i.e. that it should move itself. Therefore, whatever is in motion must be put in motion by another. If that by which it is put in motion be itself put in motion, then this also must needs be put in motion by another, and that by another again. But this cannot go on to infinity, because then there would be no first mover, and, consequently, no other mover; seeing that subsequent movers move only inasmuch as they are put in motion by the first mover; as the staff moves only because it is put in motion by the hand. Therefore it is necessary to arrive at a first mover, put in motion by no other; and this everyone understands to be God.
>
> Thomas Aquinas, 'The Existence of God', *Summa Theologica*

To be certain that there is a God we have to go beyond the immediate experience of all human beings. But to be certain that there isn't a God we also have to go beyond the immediate experience of all human beings. Now to experience experience beyond experience is an absolute impossibility for the materialist or phenomenologist. Whereas to know that there is something beyond experience is a possibility for the realist. I am a realist because I know that a phenomenon is an appearance of something. I know that something else, must lie beneath a phenomenon, but I may not know what that something is in any distinct or detailed way. In short I can know that I do not always know. The mistake of the pure phenomenologist is that he thinks that he knows everything. He thinks, that what he accurately knows, is all that exists.

The slightly subtler phenomenologist may say there are places like Australia, perhaps, that I have not been to but I know that they exist. But I do not know anything at all about other metaphysical realms of Being. I may simply reply and I do not know of any 'either/or' and 'black and white' distinction that divides Being into two separate halves. What I know in an immediate sense, to what I know of nuclear and sub-nuclear realities, to what I know of mental, spiritual or divine beings, are all part of the spectrum of reality. The only 'black and white' distinction of which I can be sure is that between Being and Nothingness. I assert that between Being and Nothingness there is no third. Thus something must lie behind the phenomena. Phenomena in themselves are not a third between Being and Nothingness.

The next thing to consider is that all finite beings are transient. They exist and then they do not exist. A world of purely finite beings cannot exist on its own any more than a world could exist, made purely of phenomena. But someone may say perhaps all the nuclear and sub-nuclear entities, or appearances if you will, simply depend on an ultimate mass of solid particles, which science will eventually discover. We must reply that at the moment this is a purely metaphysical supposition.

Russell has said that God might exist, but that is as unlikely as a tiger being in the next room. But if we can only know the material world, if we cannot go beyond the here and now, how can we possibly know which transcendental entities are less likely or more likely. If we can say how likely the existence of God is, we have truly travelled into the metaphysical realm.

The early Nyayikas and the Mimamsa thinkers, just as the earlier Samkyas, speculated about metaphysics. The first Samkyas thought that the souls and matter were ultimates. The souls and matter could then explain everything. Other earlier thinkers saw the universe as produced by an unseen power [*adṛṣṭa*]. Others thought that the universe was produced by destiny.

The universe is, as we see, entirely transient. Is it possible that the totality is entirely different from every visible part? Is it possible that while every particle of the universe lives and then dies, that the entire universe is permanent? Well, if we can never see the totality of things, we can never know that permanence. If, on the other hand, the expansion of our minds to see the totality of things is a valid act then we can know that there is an ultimate permanent Being who is uncaused, but who causes.

> *Ayojana* is the second reason. Here it means *motion.*
> The inference is as follows:
>
> The universe consists of material atoms,
> but there must be a prime mover of these material atoms.
> This prime mover is God.
> So God exists.
>
> *Objection*: The atoms themselves may produce motion because of *adṛṣṭa*. *Answer*: *Adṛṣṭa* cannot reside in material atoms; moreover *adṛṣṭa* can never be the complete cause of anything, for if it were no cause would ever be needed. Even for the production of a pot, no potter would be necessary, since *adṛṣṭa* alone would suffice.

Thus there may be an unseen force [*adṛṣṭa*] of a cosmological nature that creates all things; but it must be separate from the atoms, which do not appear to possess that power. And then if that *adṛṣṭa* did exist, perhaps it could, as it were, produce pots without being a potter. But I have no way of knowing that such an *adṛṣṭa* exists.

Thus the existence of a God, a prime mover, initiating subsidiary movers, seems a necessity.

Russell has said that he had experienced deep mystical states, but that he did not presume that they came from a source other than within him. But any one else who has experienced such states may equally well think that they do come from a source beyond his inner self. Thus Russell's statement that he does not presume *x*, does not mean that he does not presume. He presumes that mystical experiences come from within him. He does not *know* that they come from within him.

My experience of God seems to me to be of a God who is beyond. To doubt my belief I would have to have a very strong reason. I actually have no reason.

Thus I accept Udayana's proof. But I regard it as and induction and not a deduction, because the universe cannot contain an infinite God. The induction is probably not one I could rise to if I did not already have a clear idea of God through the teachings of religion. But, given that I do have such an idea, this unusual induction seems valid.

I respect the views of all atheists who either do not have my experience, or who interpret that experience as coming from their own inner selves. They are only being honest which is the best any of us can do.

Udayana says:

> All conditional arguments advanced against the theistic inference are fallacious as 'God' whose being is sought to be repudiated by the arguments is their common qualificand ... So the arguments turn out to be self-contradictory. Thus the charge of fallaciousness urged against the theistic inference is rendered infructuous. As against this the theistic inference is supported by the conditional argument based on causality. The denial of causality would entail the denial of the origination of any effect. This is the favourable feature of the theistic inference.
>
> To explain: If there is no causal operation no effect can come into being. It is well-known that the actions (or processes) of the sentient and insentient are related one with another as cause and effect. So, as in the absence of other kinds of causal conditions, even in the absence of the causal agent the effect cannot come into being. Even the agent is one of the causes of the effect. Some one (the Buddhist for example) may contend against this: Positive and negative associations confirm the causal relationship of those things alone which are visible, not invisible ... If association of a visible cause and its effect led to the knowledge of the invisible effect too then the knowledge that smoke is caused by fire could yield the knowledge of the presence of bodily

heat too if smoke is perceived to be present at a place. Similarly the fluttering of the branch of a tree while leading to the knowledge of the presence of air may lead to an inference of invisible still air. But such is not the case as only the breeze whose movement is felt is regarded as the cause of fluttering. In the case of the world also (in the theistic inference), only an embodied visible cause of it should be supposed to be inferable. Such a contention however is simply wrong.

Our Awareness of God

Many people are aware of a sense of God within themselves. Some people have no such awareness. Of those who possess this awareness, some think that it is the evidence of God's existence, others that it is simply an illusion, or at best a benign thought.

Here each individual makes his own choice. No one can prove him wrong by pointing to external facts, or by citing objective, logical arguments. The inner judgement hovers above earthly reasoning. The inner judgement, be it positive or negative as to God's existence, is transcendental!

Cardinal John Henry Newman [1801-1890], a thinker of modern times, has emphasised this fundamental truth. This truth frees us all from the tyranny of the philosophical expert. Perhaps the twenty-first century will see a universal acceptance of each individual person's inner freedom. Without the development of a strong sense of the inner freedom of each individual, political conviction and political freedom will be null and void.

> Do not make man your master; get good from all; think well of all persons, and you will be a wise man.

The reader may wonder about Hindu concepts of energy. Are these energies entirely different from the energies of nuclear physics? Are they forms of energy we do not know? Or are they the energies that we do know – electricity, gravity and the like? Are there only two realms of Being – matter and spirit? Is there only one realm – matter? And if there is only one realm is that one realm rather a substance neutral as between matter and spirit? Or are there again many kinds of Being; ranging between matter and spirit?

The Vision of A. J. Ayer

Professor Alfred Jules Ayer [1910–1989] was an outstanding proponent of logical positivism and a lifelong convinced atheist. His thesis was that only matter, so to speak, mattered. He rejected all proofs for the existence of God, or for the existence of souls, as invalid. Before he died, however, inner experiences, during a heart attack, made him aware that there could possibly be existence after death. His heart stopped for four minutes and during this period he attained a supra-conscious state. He realised that there was thus a possibility of consciousness after death. This represented an extraordinary change in his philosophy. He added, with dry humour, that on the whole, he rather hoped there wouldn't be. He died the truest empiricist.

During the twentieth century there was an extraordinary concentration on external observation as a means of knowledge.

Reports of inner experience have been part of medical science, where specific pains reported by patients have been counted as evidence of specific bodily disorders. The study of mind, however, has often been reduced to the study of brain. Well-known thinkers of the positivist school have taught that the notion that self-consciousness yielded a whole realm of other knowledge was simply the result of a muddle in the minds of the philosophically underdeveloped. However, the twenty-first century will see a full development of the study of mind and its inner experience. Through the enormous interest that the west is developing in the practice and study of yoga, the chakras, or centres of consciousness, will be externally recognised, not only as ganglia of nerves around our endocrine glands, but as successive centres of consciousness wherein the awareness of different philosophical positions may appear to be located. That is if in normal waking consciousness a subject is convinced that all existence is material, that waking consciousness most probably locates itself in his lower chakras.

CHAPTER 11

YOGA

'Yoga' can mean many things. The English word 'yoke', meaning the wooden piece that lies on the necks of two oxen, may be connected with the Sanskrit *yoga*. The word *yoga* means: employment, use, application and performance. The word may also mean, 'fitting an arrow into the bow'; and thus 'concentrating the mind'. The Sanskrit root is *yuj*, meaning: join, or link. The 'Hatha Yoga Pradipika' of Yogi Swatmarama [*svātmārāma*], who lived during the fifteenth and sixteenth centuries AD, is the earliest explicit text of the Yoga asanas, or positions, as we now know them and practice them. The word *āsana* means: sitting, seat and posture.

Yoga can simply mean philosophy. The philosophy of the Upanishads is of an earlier date than the regular use of the term 'yoga'. I tend to think of my book as a book of philosophy rather than as a book of 'yoga'. Perhaps, I regard it simply as a book about knowledge [*jñāna*].

The Indian may perform his puja on a mat of kusha [*kuṣa*] grass or sit upon hanks of kusha grass to meditate or to perform his asanas. The westerner may use a thin blue rubber mat to carry out his yoga exercises in the village hall; and at first he may merely want to become fitter, or improve his health. The Indian always realizes the importance of philosophy; the westerner will certainly come to that if he becomes a yoga teacher.

Thus there are four kinds of Yoga:

Hatha yoga, or Raj yoga - Yoga as understood in Europe and America. Here there is a primal interest in physical and psychological health. The practice is based on the physical asanas as in the 'Hatha Yoga Pradipika'. Sessions begin and end with peaceful meditation. For Swatmarama, Hatha yoga is the highest state of yoga.

Karma yoga - the yoga of service. All that we experience today is caused by our actions in the past. By acting purely for the sake of the goodness of the action itself, rather than for the good of the result achieved, we obtain release into eternity - Bhagavad Gita.

Bhakti yoga - the pathway of loving God. Here our feelings of love for the individual people we know mingle with the love of God. Mother Teresa of Calcutta [1910-1997] sets us an example of bhakti yoga. Her life is also an example of karma yoga. The Bhagavad Gita also has a strong element of bhakti yoga in that the personal love of Krishna can be the purest motive for action.

Jñānayoga - the path of philosophy

Tantric yoga is sometimes considered as a fifth path. The tantric yogi lives a life of extreme asceticism. He meditates for many hours a day, concentrating on careful breathing and experiencing consciousness in the different locations of the body, or the chakras. Such concentration, however, can also be the aim of those who practice Raj yoga.

Om

'Om' is really *aum*. The first sound is 'a'. The second sound is 'oo'. The third sound is 'mm' through your nose. The silence round the word is, as it were, the fourth sound. Thus the whole word represents the four states of consciousness. The *aum* is the neuter plural form of the Sanskrit adjective, meaning: everything, all things, and thus, the totality. The *aum* is related to the 'om' of the Latin word *omnibus* [for all]. Think of this whenever you get on a bus!

As the Mandukya Upanishad says Om is all. Om is the Atman. The Atman is possessed of four quarters; the four states of consciousness:

> The first quarter is *vaiśvanava*, the waking state.
>
> The second quarter is *taijasa*, the dream state.
>
> The third quarter is *prājña*, deep sleep. Everything becomes undifferentiated, a mass of empty consciousness, the doorway to experience, of both dream and waking states.
>
> The fourth quarter is *turya*, not dream, not conscious, not unconscious, uninferable, unthinkable, and indescribable. It is the pure unchanging non-dual self: Om.

The Yoga Sutras of Patanjali

As has been said, little is known of Patanjali. His 'Yoga Sutras', however, are now well known in the west. His basic conception of Yoga is a method of activities leading to union with the divine. These activities are a system of meditation and breathing, with the practitioner sitting straight upright on the floor, or on a small mat, cross-legged. Yoga was an attitude to life and a way of life, and it did not necessarily depend on the different physical asanas of yoga as we imagine them and practice them today. These activities and this way of life can lead to release [*moksa*] from the worldly attachments of *samsara*, or 'wandering on'. Finally, after death the yogi passes into *samādhi*, when he is absorbed into the *ātman*.

Patanjali accepted the Samkhya system of metaphysics.

> 1. 33. Undisturbed calmness of mind is attained by cultivating friendliness towards the happy, compassion towards the unhappy, delight in the virtuous, and indifference towards the wicked.
>
> 2. 1. Austerity, study, and the dedication of the fruits of one's work to God: these are the preliminary steps towards yoga.
>
> 2. 5. To regard the non-eternal as eternal, the impure as pure, the painful as pleasant and the non-Atman as the Atman - this is ignorance.
>
> 2. 6. To identify consciousness with that which merely reflects consciousness - this is egoism.
>
> 2. 28. As soon as all impurities have been removed by the practice of spiritual disciplines - the 'limbs' of yoga - a man's spiritual vision opens to the light-giving knowledge of the Atman.

2. 29. The eight limbs of yoga are: the various forms of abstention from evil-doing [*yāma*], the various observances [*niyama*], posture [*āsana*], control of the prana [*prāṇāyāma*], withdrawal of the mind from sense objects [*pratyāhāra*], concentration [*dhāraṇā*], meditation [*dhyāna*] and absorption in the Atman.

2. 30. Yama is the abstention from harming others, from falsehood, from theft, from incontinence, and from greed.

2. 31. These forms of abstention are basic rules of conduct. They must be practised without any reservation as to time, place, purpose, or caste rules.

2. 32. The niyamas (observances) are purity, contentment, mortification, study and devotion to God.

2. 49. After mastering posture, one must practise the control of the prana [*prāṇāyāma*], by stopping the motions of inhalation and exhalation.

2. 50. The breath may be stopped externally, or internally, or checked in mid-motion, and regulated according to place, time and a fixed number of moments, so that the stoppage is either protracted or brief.

> 2. 51. The fourth kind of pranayama is the stoppage of the breath, which is caused by concentration upon external or internal objects.

If we compare and contrast two different translations of the Yoga Sutras we might consider whether we are looking at two different pictures of reality. The James Haughton Woods translation of the Harvard Oriental Series [1914] seems the more literal. The second translation by Swami Prabhavananda and Christopher Isherwood [1953] may be taking the Sutra in a direction — towards an Advaita view. Swami Prabhavananda is undoubtedly an Advaitin. The commentary in his book talks of chakras and of nadis, or passages in body or soul. But the chakras and the nadis do not appear in the original Sutra of Patanjali.

> 2. 21. The Being [*ātman*] of the object-of-sight is only for the sake of it (the self).

> 2. 21. The object of experience is only to serve the purpose of the Atman.

Patanjāli appears, from the earlier text quoted above, to have been, not an Advaitin, but a Dvaitin — holding a dual view of reality, like the Samkhyas that he followed. However, the being of the object of experience is nevertheless totally dependent on the Being of the *ātman*; yet distinct.

> 1. 42. When the mind achieves identity with a gross object of concentration, mixed with awareness of name, quality and knowledge, this is called savitarka samadhi.

> 1. 43. When the mind achieves identity with a gross object of concentration, unmixed with awareness of name, quality and knowledge, so that the object alone remains, this is called nirvitarka samadhi.

This distinction between two different kinds of concentration and awareness is similar to the view of Madhvacarya as we shall see in the next chapter.

Chakra

Drawings of the chakras [*cakra*] often present an outline of a human figure and then mark the centres of consciousness, one above the other, from the genital area to a point above the head. The number of these centres is seven. The Muladhara Chakra sits under the genital area. From it emanates the physical body and its essence is solid and stable. The Svadisthana Chakra sits in the sacral centre and its essence is liquid and moving. Each chakra controls its sheath of being [*kośa*], relative to the physical body, one sheath inside the other like Russian dolls, or Russian eggs. If we imagine each of the concentric eggs to be transparent and to possess a glowing point, those points will appear one above the other. Western commentators on tantrism often associate the chakras with the etheric body alone.

But when, for example, Iyengar speaks of the 'etheric body', he probably means the set of five concentric energy bodies [*kośa*], the outer one being the physical body.

Just as Shri Krishna resides in his *loka*, which is his residence in the *cakra*; so the chakra or centre of consciousness resides again at the centre of its own body, or sheath. This sheath [*kośa*] is the emanation of the chakra. The outermost sheath [*kośa*] is the physical body. The physical body is again the object of the god's consciousness and it is produced by his consciousness and thought.

When a tantric text states that the child Brahma sits in the Muladhara chakra with his queen Dakini, it means that the original form of the creator, Brahma, becomes the chakra in the specific instance of the existence of this individual man. Dakini is simply the man's physical body, seen as an emanation of Brahma for this man; and thus the emanation of the man's Muladhara chakra. The physical body is thus the *loka* of Brahma and therefore his queen in this instance.

The material universe is the *loka* of Brahma on the macrocosmic level; just so, in the microcosmic realm, Brahma sits in his *loka* of the Muladhara chakra, from which our physical body emanates

The whorl of energy, which each chakra is, may be thought of as a movement [*spanda*], may be seen as a pattern of light [*yantra*], or may be heard as a meaningful sound [*mantra*]. The technique of concentrating on the *spanda* is called *tantra*. The meaning of tantra is basically 'technique' and then: theory, loom, scientific work, row, happiness, series and doctrine. 'Tantra' is one of those amazing Sanskrit words.

The seed mantra [*bīja*] of the Muladhara chakra is *lam*. This means that *lam*, the audible or manifested sound [*śabda vaikarī*], is the closest sound we can hear, or make, to the subtle sound, which that chakra in fact is. The pattern, or *yantra* of the four petals of the chakra, is as it were the division of *lam* into four further subsets of vibrations: *va*, *ṣa* [palatal], *śa* [cerebral] and *sa*. This fourfold division of *lam*, its emanation from one to many, is classically of the pattern of Hindu thought. It is in this sense that Iyengar speaks, at moments, of a single 'etheric body'; but that etheric body surely emanates into the five koshas.

The power in Brahman, which makes the subtle shabda and the chakras into possibilities, is called the *bindu*, meaning: point, dot, drop, mark, spot; a mark made by the teeth of a lover on the lips of his mistress; and the sudden development of a secondary incident in the plot of a drama (which, like a drop of oil in water, expands and furnishes an important element in the plot). Some Hindus wear their hair twisted into a topknot behind the crown of their heads. They believe that at death God can grab it and pull them into heaven. This is a sort of metaphor for the *bindu.*

When we imagine Brahman as a sphere, and the seed of the universe as a spiral [*mahakuṇdhalinī*], coming off the surface of that sphere; then the *bindu* is the point, as it were, on the sphere, from which the spiral originates. Sphere, point and spiral are, of course, partly metaphorical.

Koshas

hiraṇmayikośa	- sheath of golden consciousness, close to atman.
ānandamayikośa	- self [*chitta*] sheath of bliss

vidyāmayikośa	- ego and intellect
vidyāmaya	- [absorbed in knowledge]
manomayikośa	- mind [*manas*]
pranamayikośa	- vital air [*prana*]

The sixth kosha, or outer sheath, is our visible, human body.

Each chakra is, or has, a god [*deva*] who presides over, and a goddess [*devi*] who is, the loka [*loka*]. The loka is the subtle sheath [*kośa*] of the chakra and the realm of activities pertinent to that level of consciousness. Just in the same way the Hindu wife is the embodiment of the home, which is the loka of her spouse. The gods are really aspects of God, or emanations of God, as he presides over different realms and heavens of the universe, and of the human body. Shiva is lord of the physical world, which is, as a goddess, Dakini, or nature.

Sir John George Woodroffe [1865–1936], also known by his pseudonym Arthur Avalon, was a British orientalist whose work helped to unleash in the West a deep and wide interest in Hindu philosophy and yogic practices. He translated the Satchakra-nirupana of Swatmarama, which was written the sixteenth century AD. This book is the first known description of asanas [*āsana*], or poses, of physical yoga practice.

The following table of the chakras is based on the Sat-chakra-nirupana – Description of the six Chakras. Some modern chakra theory closely relates nadis and nerves. Ganglia, or groups of nerves, surround the endocrine glands. These groups of nerves are normally part of the unconscious nervous system, but with the practice of yoga we can become aware of them. Some people can feel their chakras; some people can't.

Muladharachakra

mūlādhāra – root place

location in the physical body – adrenal gland

Colour – yellow

Shape – square

Number – 4

Element – Earth [*privṛthi*]

Position – base of spine

Sense – smell

Mental activity – cohesion

Action [*karmendriya*] – feet

Guna – tamas Bija [*bīja*] – *lam*

Deva – Brahma Devi – Dakini

Svadisthanachakra

svadhiśthāna – self abode

location – testes and ovaries

Colour – white

Shape – crescent

Number – 6

Element – Water [*ap*]

Position – sacral centre

Sense – taste

Mental activity – contraction

Action – hand

Guna – tamas Bija – *vam*

Deva – Vishnu Devi – Rakini

Manipurachakra

maṇipūra – city of jewels

pancreas and spleen

Colour – red

Shape – triangle

Number – 10

Element – Fire [*tejas*]

Position – solar plexus

Sense – sight

Mental activity – expansion (heat)

Action – Anus

Guna – rajas Bija – *ram*

Deva – Rudra Devi – Lakini

Anahatachakra

anāhata – non-vibrating

thymus gland

Colour – smoke

Shape – six-pointed star

Number – 12

Element – Air [*vayu*]

Position – heart centre

Sense – touch

Mental activity – awareness of movement

Action – Penis

Guna – rajas Bija – *yam*

Deva – Isa Devi – Kakini

Vishuddhachakra

viṣuddha – purification

thyroid gland

Colour – sea blue

Shape – circle

Number –16

Element – ether [*akaśa*]

Position – throat

Sense – hearing

Mental activity – sense of space

Action – Mouth

Guna – satva [*sattva*] Bija – *dam*

Deva – Sadasiva Devi – Sakini

Ajnachakra

ajña – unknowing, obedient

pituitary gland

Colour –snow white

Number – 2

Element –mind [*manas*]

Position – brow

Mental activity – thought

Guna – satva Bija – *aum*

Deva – Sambhu Devi – Hakini

Sahasrarachakra

sahasrāra – thousand petal lotus

peneal gland

Tantrism

The tantric yogi is frequently a devotee of Shiva, the lord of *tapas*, or asceticism. Union with Shiva inspires his life long pursuit of breathing exercises, physical asanas, and the denial of food and sleep. He also studies constantly. In the Puranas, Parvati (Shakti) drew Shiva from asceticism to marriage and eroticism. Shiva thus has an aspect of Brahman, who purely exists in Himself, and also an aspect of Lord and Creator, who brings winter and then spring – death and then rebirth.

The chakras are based on the polarity of Shiva-shakti. The Deva Isa of the Anahata chakra and his queen Kakini (Shakti) are the lord and lady of creation and of the element air, the subtlest of the four gross tattvas. The tattva, or element, of *vayu* subsumes the other three elements as the Lord of the worshipper subsumes the other gods. When the consciousness of the yogi regularly rises above this chakra, he then ceases to contemplate god as the Creator and his spirituality is proceeding beyond devotion.

The reader can think about the design of the yantras. The Muladhara chakra is the chakra of earth and therefore its yantra is rectangular; representing the four gross elements of which the earth is made, the four directions and so on. There are endless correspondences.

Tantric cosmology

Like many Indian believers, tantrics viewed creation as a unity, or non-duality, in which everything is Brahman, the universal spirit. All things derive from this single reality, which, according to tantrics, can be expressed only through diametrical polarities or opposites. The world, or the macrocosm, is generated through these polarities, which are also expressed within each of us — in the microcosm. The Sanskrit word *ṣakti* means: ability, energy, power and strength. The word *ṣiva* means: gracious, benign and favourable. Only later, as devotional Hinduism developped, did *ṣiva* become the name of God, the destroyer. But even so, Shiva is honoured and loved as a beneficient force. All earthly things have to be brought an end.

The followers of Tantra are often branded as *nāstika* by the upholders of the Vedic tradition. From the Sanskrit *asti* meaning, 'it is', or 'it exists', *āstika* means: one who believes in the existence; and thus: orthodox and pious. Thus *nāstika* means those who do not accept Vedic authority — the Buddhists and Jains for example; it does not imply that they are atheists: some thinkers, Samkhya or Mimamsa, who do not accept God but who accept the Vedas, are considered *āstika*.

Ha	Tha	Comment
Subject	Object	philosophical / abstract
Good	Evil	
consciousness	unconsciousness	psychological / physical
realisation	compassion	
wisdom	power/energy	
active	passive	
day	night	symbolism of sun and moon ida and pingala
death	life	
man / male	woman / female	the tantric paradigm for polarity
Shiva	Shakti	divine expression of polarity

All these polarities are aspects of oneness — they all exist as opposite sides of the same coin. Death has no meaning without life; male cannot be, except with regard to female; good implies its opposite evil, and so forth.

Life's goal is to achieve liberation from the cycle of life, death and rebirth by realising this all-pervading oneness within us. While the philosopher aims for a perfect intellectual understanding of this principle, the tantric, or yogi, wants to realise this truth in a completely different way. He wants to transform all polarities within himself so they merge; and oneness is experienced in every fibre of his being. Once the yogi is free from all dualities, he is free from life and death — and liberation from the cycle of rebirth is achieved.

The tantric goal

The goal of tantrism is to exercise control over the flow of energy, or prana. This can be used to awaken and raise *kuṇdhalinī*.

When *kuṇdhalinī* enters the crown, or *sahasāra* chakra, Shakti merges with Shiva. All polarities merge and compete union [*yoga*] is achieved. Union of life and death is transcendence over the polarities. This is release [*moksa*], from the worldly attachments of *samsara*, into *samādhi*. This release is beyond description and beyond the cycle of death and rebirth.

Purposeful control of prana releases blocks within us that impede the natural flow of energy through our physical bodies and the natural flow of prana through our subtle bodies.

We may then move energy or prana at will to particular regions of our bodies, to particular chakras

Awakening Kundalini

The Muladhara chakra, the lowest chakra in our bodies, is the place where our natural power resides — the energy within us that we derive from 'mother nature'. This power is always regarded as a female principle and yet it is our embodiment of the divine energy [*śakti*], which is masculine. This energy is visualised as a potential lying coiled, like a spring, and is often represented in tantric texts as a coiled snake. In a worldly person, whose life is totally focussed on material desires, this potential lies dormant, unmoving.

In animals and ordinary people prana flows through the left and right channels, or nadis [*nādhi*], the *idhā* [praise, commendation] and the *piṇgalā* [golden brown]. This energy does not always flow smoothly. Through practise of physical yoga, and meditation, prana flows more readily and finally reaches into the base of the *suśumṇa* [gracious] nadi, the central channel. Here, in the Muladhara chakra, it awakens *kuṇdhalinī*, which can now rise up through the central channel [*suśumṇa*]. The more practised and focussed the yogi becomes, the higher *kuṇdhalinī* rises, piercing each chakra as it does so. Finally, in perfect meditation, Kundalini reaches *sahasrāra*, the crown, the seat of divine wisdom, or Shiva. So Shakti, the female principle, and Shiva, the male, merge in oneness.

Moksha

The merging of Shiva and Shakti releases perfect wisdom into the divine energy within us. Through this all opposites are joined in both our understanding and in our experience, which themselves become one in meditation. As all oppositions fall away in our 'oneness', so the polarity of life and death disappears and the cycle of rebirth is transcended — the individual is released from worldly attachment into *samādhi*.

Gurus

Bellur Krishnamachar Sundararaja Iyengar [1918–2014], better known as B. K. S. Iyengar, was the founder of the style of yoga known as 'Iyengar Yoga'. He was born in the village of Bellur, in Karnataka. Then his family moved to the regional capital, Bangalore. Throughout his childhood and early years he suffered from very poor health, but eventually he was strengthened by the power of yoga. He became world famous as a yoga teacher. In many parts of India he is not well known, yet somebody in Orkney or Lewis, if you will, or any part of Britain will be found to teach his method. His method involves three stages of development. Each consists of a progressive and exact series of poses, using, in the earlier stages at least, a set of props and supports. His yoga is sometimes called 'Hatha Yoga'.

The meaning of *haṭha* is: force, violence, absolute and ultimate necessity. A modern British and American view is that 'Ha' and 'Tha' mean 'sun' and 'moon'. Yoga is the union of what appear to be opposites, Ha and Tha; thus 'Hatha Yoga'.

Satyananda Saraswati [1923–2009], was a sannyasin, yoga teacher and guru. He was born at Almora in the state of Uttaranchai in the north of India. At the age of six years he began to have deep spiritual experiences, falling into a kind of mystical sleep. In 1943 at the age of twenty, he met his guru Sivananda Saraswati and went to live at Sivananda's ashram. In 1964, he founded the Bihar School of Yoga at Munger. He developed a gentle form of yoga practice where states of consciousness were emphasised, aiming at Yoga Nidra [*yoganidrā*], the state of dynamic sleep.

Sivananda Saraswati [1887-1963] was born at Pattamadai in Tamil Nadu. He came from a wealthy brahmin family and qualified as a doctor. He worked for some years in a hospital in Malaya. All his life he continued to help the poor and sick, developing ayurvedic medicine as well as using scientific medicine. He spent many years as a wandering monk [*parivrājaka*], healing and teaching.

Sri Aurobindo [18720-1950] was born Aurobindo Ghose in Calcutta. His father was an assistant surgeon in Bengal and connected with the Brahmo Samaj religious reform movement. He was sent to school at the Loreto convent in Darjeeling, where Mother Teresa served her novitiate many years later. He was brought up to speak English but spoke Bengali to the servants. Later he was sent to London where he attended St Pauls School. Aurobindo Ghose then studied for the Indian Civil Service at Kings College Cambridge. Returning to India he carried out administrative duties for the Rajah of Baroda in the state of Gujarat. He wrote articles opposing British rule and was imprisoned for a short time, in 1909, until his trial at which he was acquitted. During his imprisonment he experienced mysticism. After his release he moved to Pondicherry where he began to pursue spiritual work. He developed the whole philosophy and practice of 'integral yoga', where everything we do, and are, leads to God. In his philosophy he notably rejected the teachings of Shamkara and the unreality of Advaitism. The doctrines of Advaitism, Sri Aurobindo taught, were fundamentally negative and interfered with the positive transformation of the world into the divine. The provision of cleanliness and comfort for human beings was an important part of this transformation.

> The Spirit shall look out through Matter's gaze.
> And Matter shall reveal the Spirit's face.

According to the view of Shri Aurobindo, at moments, we may see the universe as purely matter; and then again, at other moments, the duality [*dvaita*] of matter and spirit reveals itself. At the highest levels of our consciousness, reason and intuition combine.

> We will put aside the trenchant distinctions of a partial logic which declares that because the One is the reality, the Many are an illusion, and because the Absolute is *sat*, the one existence, the relative is *asat* and non-existent. If in the many we pursue insistently the one, it is to return with the benediction and the revelation of the one confirming itself in the many.

CHAPTER 12

MADHVA

The Dvaita Philosophy of the Atman

Shri Madhvācārya was born in 1238 AD, at Pājaka Kshetra — a small village near Udupi, now in the Karnataka State (southwest India). He died in 1317 AD. His parents called him Vasudeva, meaning 'beneficient and divine' — the name of a character in the Mahabharata.

At an early age he is said to have run away to the ashram at Udupi, where he was named Purnaprajna. Here he shone at once, both at learning and debate. After his brilliant argumentative skills had defeated foremost scholars who had come to debate at the ashram, he was given the name Anandatirtha, which was a title implying that he would inherit the headship of the order. When he began writing he took the name, Madhva. This name implied that he was an avatar of Vayu, the god of the wind and of inspiration. He often identified himself as the third incarnation of *mukhya prana*, the Primal Breath, revealed in the Rig Veda, one form of which is Vayu. The first incarnation of *mukhya prana* was Hanuman, the monkey-headed god.

In 1278 Madhvācārya founded the Krishna Mat at Udupi. The Krishna Mat is still the centre of Madhva's following. Later in life he is said to have made a tour of India, reaching the Himalayas.

Madhva is said to have written thirty-seven works. These include commentaries on the Upanishads, on the Bhagavad-Gita and on the Brahma-sutras, also on the Mahabharata and the Bhagavata-purana.

Madhva was a social reformer. He banned animal sacrifices from his temples and he did not allow the use of liquor during ceremonies.

Madhva's followers called his philosophy, 'the way of thusness' [*tattvavāda*].

Ontology

Madhva taught that reality is dual [*dvaita*]. There is the Being of God [*parātman*] — the fullness of infinite qualities. And there is the being of souls and matter, which depend on the Being of God. The being of souls and matter is different from the Being of God.

> The philosophy of Madhva is regarded as the philosophy of difference [*bedha*]. Reality presents us with five basic differences [*pañca bedha*].
>
> 1. The difference between God [*īśvara*] and souls [*jīva*].
> 5. The difference between souls and souls.
> 6. The difference between souls and insentient matter [*prakṛti*].
> 7. The difference between different items of insentient matter.

8. The difference between God and insentient matter.

Shamkara [*śaṁkarācārya*] probably lived during the eighth century AD. He was born in Kerala and he travelled all over India and died in Kashmir. He had denounced caste and meaningless ritual. He had taught both the love and the understanding of God. He had rejected the Buddhist doctrine of emptiness. Shamkara's *advaita* view saw reality as simply one — 'non-dual'. But his teaching had a sense also that what we humans think of as reality, in our ordinary lives on earth, is threefold.

Firstly there is the real Being of God [*pāramārthika*].

Then, Shamkara said, there are two kinds of unreal being. The first kind — things that appear in this world — are only 'apparent being' [*vyāvahārika*]. They seem to have regularity of pattern and continuity of existence; but their duration is temporary. The second kind of unreal being is formed by the pure fantasies and illusions of our private worlds of thought — we may hold these illusions as individuals, or as groups of people. These last are *prātibhāsika*, or 'illusory'. Neither of these two kinds of temporary being, however, have real existence. Real Being must be eternal. It is ultimately One. Reality is 'non-dual' [*advaita*].

But Madhva's view is that there is no mean between existence and non-existence. There is only existence. The Hindu scriptures, he says, do not maintain that world appearance is different from both existence and non-existence [*sad-asad-vilakṣaṇa*]. Non-existence is not another kind of existence. Between existence and non-existence there is not a third.

Not only does God exist; but also He can create entities beyond Himself. He eternally creates *ākāśa* — the primal cosmic energy. The *ākāśa* can never cease. The *ākāśa* is real Being. It does not lie between Being and Nothingness [*sad-asad-vilakṣaṇa*]; and it is eternal. The *ākāśa* is entirely dependent on the Being of God; though both God and *ākāśa* are eternal. Madhva accepted God as total creator; the *ākāśa* is equally eternal, yet dependent.

Only the objects of true knowledge exist. When we are misled, it is not that we know another object different from the object of true knowledge, but that we know the same object in a different, erroneous way.

When we think of the horns on the head of a man, our knowledge is not of an existing entity, but of a non-existent entity. Thus we can know a non-existent entity as not existing. It does not, because of our consideration, somehow come to be.

When we think of a jug that the potter is about to produce, we can know something that is at present non-existent. Thus it is erroneous to say that the conch-shell silver cannot be non-existent because it is known; we can obviously know that which is non-existent. We can either know it as being non-existent, or we can think that it is existent, when that is not the case.

There is a sense in which the non-existent can be thought; but it cannot be directly perceived as an existent. One does not find horns on the head of a man as one does on the head of a cow.

The conch-shell silver is directly perceived as an existent. It is not perceived as indefinable [*anirvacanīya*], as the Shamkarites would have it, but as real. The point about making mistakes is that, at the moment of error, we think that what we perceive is real. The conch shell silver appears as real, and later is seen to be unreal. While we are mistaken, there is an appearance of a 'this' as identical to the silver [*idam-rajatayoḥ*].

But, for the Shamkarites, there is a double falsity, where the illusory appearance is both false in itself and again in its association with the silver. This automatic falsity of all appearances thus leads to an infinite regress. The holders of the *maya* doctrine admit this. Yet they do not see that the illusion is a vicious infinite [*anavasthā*]. If the illusion did not appear as if it was of the nature of ordinary phenomenal experience, if it appeared as illusory [*prātibhāsika*], no one would bother with it. To be illusory it has to appear to be of the nature of phenomenal experience. Otherwise it could not be illusory, it would be merely a daydream. It has to be wrongly defined as a conch shell in order to then be defined as illusory. Again, if the appearance (of being silver) is itself indefinable, as is the silver itself, then truly a vicious infinite regress appears. We thus simply have to accept that the unreal and non-existent may appear as the real and that the world appearance cannot be defined as being indefinable [*anirvacanīya*] .

But reason has its limitations. We live in an empirical world, where we constantly encounter individuals. We only meet the universals, about which we reason, through individual instances. These individual instances always possess special characteristics in addition to the characteristics that render them members of a class or genus. Pure abstract reasoning, about the nature of a hare's horns, for example, cannot establish the actual existence of anything. God, as Vishnu, is a real living individual, who speaks to us through the Vedas. He is not just an abstraction, which is reasoned to but not apprehended.

> One should not imagine on the basis of inference/reason that there are other causes than *Viṣṇu*, for the creation, sustenance, etc. of the world. A person who has not studied the *Vedas* or who has no clear understanding of the *Vedas*, cannot know the Perfect Being, who is all knowing and also the creator of all. This creator of the world is knowable only by the *Upanishads* (*upaniṣadaḥ purusa*). Hence, the creatorship is known only through *vedas* (*veda vedya*).

> Again, inference or reason is not necessarily always valid. In this regard *Kūrma Purāṇa* states — *anumāna* or reason unsupported or unaided by *Shrutis* cannot conclusively establish anything regarding specific or particular objects ... Perception (experience) and inference (Reason) aided and supported by the *Shrutis* and the *smirtis* are valid sources of knowledge in respect of imperceptible objects ... One should therefore avoid barren reasoning (unaided by Śruti and Smṛti). It is possible to reason about anything including the things like *Hare-horns*, etc.

The knowledge we receive from the Vedas is the knowledge of God, as He is, in Himself. He is pure God, quite independent of objects.

As such He cannot be directly reasoned to from our knowledge of objects.

Thus Madhva offers no proofs of God's existence.

Narrative and poetic forms are equally important for the promulgation of Indian philosophies. The drama of the Chandogya Upanishad (VI. xii. 1-3), where the boy, guided by his guru, explores the significance of the Nyagrodha seed, reveals to our conscious selves the truth hidden deeper within consciousness. The narrative develops an attitude; awakens within us truer sympathies, as in the story of the hunter and the bird.

In this tale a hunter pursues a bird all day until the bird lands at the feet of a king and begs his protection. The hunter appeals to the king to let him kill the bird so that he can feed his family. The king sees both points of view. Each person is right from his own perspective. So the king cuts off a piece of his own flesh, equal in weight to the bird, and gives it to the hunter. The bird flies away. Thus the narrative can intrigue the reader and entice him toward the metaphysical.

In Indian Philosophy illumination is as important as argument. In daylight the pilot steers the ship by the vision of the land in the distance. But at night he steers his vessel in the dark, by his compass or by the stars.

The story of Agni, the fire god, and of his concealments and his manifestations, thus contains the seeds of the unveiling of the deceit – Agni is his own manifestation. But any living thing is Agni.

The Upanishad is a 'trojan text'; it appears to lead us in one direction, but actually it takes us another way entirely.

Substance and the Categories

Substance [*dravya*] is a material cause — it is a thing, or what a thing is made of. Substance is the basis of the changes [*pariṇāma*] in the development of things. God is a substance, but He does not change. Souls are permanent, they exist eternally; however, they may be manifested [*abhivyakti*], or unmanifested. Souls, however, can grow in perfection. Material substances are not permanent. The other categories of Being depend on substance. They are thus subordinate modes of Being.

The categories are as follows:

dravya — substance

1. *guna* — quality
9. *karman* — action
10. *sāmānya* — class-character
11. *visesa* — particularity
12. *visista amśī* — qualified whole
13. *śakti* — power
14. *sādṛśya* — similarity
15. *abhāva* — negation

dravya

The senses of *dravya* are: object, matter, property, implement, substance and thing. The word 'substance' is included in Sanskrit-

English dictionaries as a possible translation of *dravya*. Now the Latin word 'substance' has a sense of that which underlies qualities or appearances, but the word *dravya* has no such resonance. Madhva defines *dravya* as *upādāna kāraṇa*. The sense of *upa* is often that of: secondary or by the side of; and *adāna* means: receiving; and *kāraṇa* means: action. Thus *dravya* has a dynamic sense of 'coming to be' and yet a sense of secondariness, or subordination. The Being of God himself is not *kāraṇa*. The words 'thing' and 'thinghood' would also be good renderings of *kāraṇa*; provided it is understood that 'thingness' is not the deepest kind of reality. The idea of *dravya* is that of thinghood. There is no suggestion of any duality of levels; *dravya* are just what they appear to be. For Madhva, we see what is.

guna

The idea of *guna* is purely metaphysical. The gunas never appear in themselves. They are the underlying roots of quality. The things that we see have different qualities, because they are formed of different combinations of the three gunas — *sattva*, *rajas* and *tamas*. The gunas are the primary metaphysical qualities, which exist prior to the existence of any physical or spiritual body. Thus they are not 'qualities' in the simple sense of being aspects of substances, but substances are what they are because of their gunas. At first the idea of *guna* is difficult.

Even in the time of the dissolution of the universe [*vilaya*], pure *sattva* exists as a distinct part of the totality of *brahman* with His inner differences, just as the totality of all of the jivas also permanently exists within Him. For Madhva again the eternal and empty *ākāśa* remains the same both at the dissolution of the universe [*vilaya*] and when it has re-evolved. But as the evolution of the universe begins, the pure sattva guna [*śuddhasattva*] devolves the rajas and tamas gunas and the universe we know takes real and positive form.

The gunas hover between thing and quality, and are the ultimate constituents of all created things, other than souls. The *sattva* guna can exist on its own in Madhva's system; *rajas* and *tamas* never exist separately from admixture with one another and with *sattva*. Living bodies, ether bodies, rocks and trees are all composed of the gunas; the gunas are the pre-substantial components of substances. Thus they exist as a category separate from substance [*dravya*]. God and souls have no gunas.

karma

The choices and actions of souls are *karman*. There are no human actions that are morally indifferent.

There are three kinds of *karman*. There are actions enjoined by the scriptures [*karman vihita*]; those prohibited [*karman niṣiddha*]; and those not considered by the scriptures [*karman udāsīna*]. We notice here that the ideas 'right' and 'wrong', as well as being moral concepts, are clear metaphysical concepts, relating to things that engender release [*moksa*]. Actions not considered by the scriptures [*karman udāsīna*] nevertheless have a moral force if they take us closer to, or further from, spiritual release. This is typical, not only of Madhva, but perhaps of all Indian thinkers.

Since the *Śruti* has mentioned *Brahman* as the independent agent of action, He alone causes *Karma* to work, according to *Bādarāyana*.

The Lord and *Karma* are both the causes of the fruits of *Karma*, even then, *Karma* does not make the Lord to act, but it is the Lord who causes *Karma* to function. 'Through this (*Udāna*) He leads *Jīva* to heaven by his merit and to hell by his (the jiva's) Sin. By the two viz *Puṇya* and *Pāpa*, He leads him to the world of men.' (Pra. 3.5). In this way *Śruti* declares *Brahman* to be the agent. Moreover, *Smṛti* also states that '*Dravya, Karma* and *Kāla* are all dependant on God and regulated and controlled by God'.

Thus God is not only the independent Agent, but also the bestower of the fruits of action.

sāmānya and visesa

The doctrine of *visesa* is important in the philosophy of Madhva. The meaning of *visesa* is: difference, kind and distinction. The meaning of *sāmānya* is: common, general and ordinary. The *visesa* is any particular quality a thing might possess. Again the *visesa* is distinguished from the class-character [*sāmānya*]. We might wonder why the *visesa* and the *sāmānya* need be distinguished. The *sāmānya* is closely related to the individual nature of the thing considered, making it recognisable and different from things of other types. The *visesa*, on the other hand, is any characteristic that anything might possess; including all the myriad characteristics things might possess from differing points of view. We do not need here to consider the difference between genus and species. In the logic of Aristotle there is a hierarchy of classes such that the lower class, or species, is subordinate to the higher class, or genus. Thus the terms 'species' and 'genus' are relative. The term *sāmānya* simply means 'class'. As in the logic of Principia Mathematica, in Indian logic there is a simple hierarchy of classes; and there is no need to distinguish subordinate and superior categories.

In the Being of Brahman there must be quality. In despite of the unity of Brahman there must be, within His Being, an excellence, eminence, pre-eminence or superiority which we can call *atiśaya*. Because of this *atiśaya* creation can exhibit variety and differences.

> ... it has to be admitted that in the unity of Brahman there is some special virtue [*atiśaya*] which represents difference and serves its purpose; there is no other way of solving the difficulty ... this special virtue, which serves to hold and reconcile plurality without sacrificing its unity, is called by the Madhvas *viśeṣa*; this *viśeṣa* exists not only in Brahman, but in all other things. Thus, for example, a cloth is not different from its whiteness, since both of them form one indissoluble whole.

The relationship of a piece of cloth to its own whiteness is, to me, actually just as mysterious as the relationship of *atiśaya*, in Brahman, to the Being of Brahman. The meaning of *atiśaya* is simply 'pre-eminent quality', or 'excellence'. Materialists often say that talk of God is meaningless because the idea of God contains contradictions, including that of supporting pairs of opposing attributes. Indeed, He is one and many. Ultimately His being both one and many is not understandable. Thus the idea of God leads to the mysterious; but for all that it is not to be denied.

But the separation of the idea of the cloth from the idea of its whiteness, in the case of a white piece of cloth, is also perplexing. There is a oneness in quality and substance. Yet cloth and whiteness are different. We might say that the idea of the cloth and the idea of its whiteness lie in different and distinguishable categories. The notion of categories is 'mind-relative'. Things in themselves do not submit wholly to categorisation. There is a oneness about the cloth and its whiteness, as the cloth exists, unconsidered and in itself. (So materialists, who say that the idea of God is meaningless, might equally say that the idea of a piece of white cloth is meaningless.)

The *visesa*, or quality, is a different idea from that of the class character, or *sāmānya*. There are innumerable qualities in each object as it is seen from different points of view. But one particular quality in an object makes it the member of a class. This is its class character or *sāmānya*.

visista amśī

Again *visista amśī* — the qualified whole — is a special category in Madhva's view. The relationship of inherence [*samavāya*], important in the thought of the Nyāya School, is not accepted by Madhva. For the Nyāya, as for the Samkhya, the cause appears in the effect. For Madhva this is enigmatic. Surely the relationship between cause and effect cannot be simply one of contact [*saṁyoga*], because without a cause there is no effect and without an effect there is no cause. According to the Nyāya the relationship is one of inherence — *samavāya*. Madhva immediately senses an infinite regress here. If there is an inherence between cause and effect, is there another inherence between the cause and the first inherence and again yet another inherence between that first inherence and the effect? — And so on *ad infinitum*.

Again, if there is a relationship between quality and substance, is there then an infinite regress of further relationships between (1) the quality and the relationship and (2) the relationship and substance?

For Madhva the gap is bridged by the special category of the 'qualified whole' [*visista amśī*]. The 'qualified whole' is distinct from the quality [*guna*] and substance [*dravya*].

The problem here is 'reification' — making a thing out of an abstraction. If we keep talking about 'qualities' they begin to sound like things (substances). If we keep talking about 'substances' substantiality itself seems like a quality a thing can possess. The inherence between substance and quality is not a third item in addition to the substance and its quality. Things are related to one another by their qualities; but the relationship is no more than those qualities. Only substances exist. They are qualified, but these qualifications are not further existences. Thus the qualified whole [*visista amśī*] seems an unnecessary category at first sight; but enables Madhva to clearly explain the situation. However, I think Madhva is incorrect in thinking that the Nyāyika is so mistaken.

śakti

There are four kinds of power:

acintya-śakti — mysterious power as in God

kāraṇa-śakti — causal power (naturally existing in things)

ādheya- śakti — a power brought about by a new operation

pada- śakti — the signifying power of words.

sādṛśya

The similarity [*sādṛśya*] between two objects makes inference possible. Only in the eternal substances, such as the souls [*jīva*] can there be said to be permanent qualities, or universals [*jāti*]. The relationships between such universals are examples of perfect concomitance [*vyāpti*]. But in the world of material objects there are no permanent universals, which transcend individuals. When objects are destroyed there are no permanent entities that somehow, or other, transcend these individual existences. Material objects are not related to a transcendental realm that is utterly permanent, or indeed certain. But inferences can be made on a basis of similarity [*sādṛśya*]. Just so, again, we name things on a basis of a close similarity. Thus there are no immutable universals hovering over the realm of material things, as Plato thought.

Madhva again distinguished between a primary universal like cow [*gotva*] and a secondary and derived universal like 'cognisability' [*prameyatva*], which can only be known when we reflect on our cognisance of basic universals. This secondary universal he called a 'limiting condition' [*upādhi*]. Madhva did not consider that these secondary universals, and the talk about secondary universals, required a tertiary level of universals, and so on, until we find ourselves in the morass of another infinite regress. He taught that the primary universal [*jāti*] and the secondary universal [*upādhi*] were of qualitatively different kinds; so there was no danger of an infinite regress, though there can be numerically as many levels of secondary universal as we require. Madhva is always deft in the avoidance of the infinite regress.

What is the nature of the similarity between individuals whose catergorisation places them under one, universal term? Well, according to Madhva, in a group of terms that are similar, the similarity obtaining between one pair of objects may be different to the similarity holding between another pair.

Groups of things or sets of parts can be seen under another category altogether. The relation of inherence [*samavāya*] is important in the Nyāya-Vaiśeṣika school, who see the effect as inhering in the cause. Although the appearance of cause in the effect and of qualities in the substance might indeed be the special relationship of *samavāya*, because it cannot be a simple relationship like contact [*saṁyoga*], there is a further problem. The inherence [*saṁyoga*] itself may need other relationships to relate it to the inhering quality and substance within which that quality inheres. Thus Madhva deftly plays the infinite regress card again. To solve the problem he simply devises a new category — the qualified whole, *visista amśī*. This whole is neither the relationship between substance and quality, nor that between cause and effect, nor again that between any parts of a thing. It is, in short, not a relationship. It is a recognisable, individual entity.

Madhva does not admit any difference between things and their qualities [*gunaguṇyabheda*].

abhāva

Finally there is the category of negation [*abhāva*].

> There are four kinds of negation:
>
> *prāgabhāva* — negation before production
>
> *dhvaṁsābhāva* — negation after destruction
>
> *anyonābhāva* — otherness (the negation of the pot in the jug and of the jug in the pot)
>
> *atyantābhāva* — the non-existence of impossible entities.

Here it is important to say that negation is simply nothing. 'Nothing' is not a weird kind of something. Thus objectively there are not different kinds of nothing. To say that there are 'four kinds of negation' is a manner of speaking.

Madhva clearly argues the reality of space and time. These are substances [*dravya*]. His arguments are well expressed by Radhakrishnan. We cannot perceive, in a direct physical sense, the totality of space and time, and yet we do seem to know that totality.

> Every explanation of avidyā implies the presuppositions of space and time, and so the latter cannot be explained away as the products of avidyā. Space and time are regarded as real wholes having parts. If they have no parts, we cannot

> have distinctions of here and there, now and then. We are presented with parts of space, for it is incorrect to hold that everything presented to us occupies all space, unlimited and invisible. We are conscious only of limited bodies occupying portions of space and resisting one another. We perceive parts of space and time, and so they must be regarded as existing. According to Madhva, they are objects of perception to the witnessing self (sākṣin).

Time [*kāla*] and universal space [*avyākṛta ākāśa*] are made from the superior *prakṛti* at its most fundamental level. Time and space are clearly substances [*dravya*], which exist in themselves [*svagata*] and are vehicles [*ādhāra*] of everything else. Time and space are vehicles of the production of things. Universal space must be connected to the material objects that exist within it and therefore must also contain its own instances of *visesa* (individual quality).

The categories are the ways we can think about the objects of our thought. The list of categories is the list of the different kinds of objects we can think about. To what extent the differences between the categories depend on our thinking and to what extent these different kinds of things exist outside our minds and in the real world, it is difficult to say. The distinctions on which the categories depend are cases of distinctions of the mind with foundations in reality [*distinctio mentis cum fundamentum in re*], rather than cases of pure distinctions of the mind [*distinctio mentis*] or real distinctions [*distinctio realis*], as St Thomas Aquinas might have put it.

God

God [*paramātman*] has two forms on account of His emerging from, and merging in, Himself. His perfect unevolved form is *pralaya*. His perfect evolved form is *avatāra*.

> The original form of the Supreme is Perfect. His avatāra form also is perfect. This perfect form (at the time of creation) emerges from the perfect original form. At the time of dissolution, this perfect *avatāra* form, merges in its perfect original form, and is perfect. (Br. up. 5.1.1). This Atman (at the time of creation) emerges himself from His original form, as *avatāra* form; (at the time of dissolution) he merges Himself in Himself. That lord, who is *Nirguna* (has no *prākṛta* attributes, free from imperfections and faultless, (creator at the time of creation) takes on different *avatāra* forms and again at the time of dissolution, becomes one with His original form and attains *yoga nidrā* ... There is no merger of the faultless Lord in the *gauṇātmā* (i.e. *jīva*). None of the *shākhās* of the *vedas* say anything different from this.

God is the only independent [*svatantra*] reality. The rest of reality [*padārtha*] is dependent [*paratantra*]. God has two forms: His perfect, original, *pralaya* form and His evolved, *avatāra* form. This *avatāra* form includes all the dependent beings. Though these beings are indeed dependant on the Being of God, they are nonetheless distinct and different from Him. These beings [*bhāva*] are of two kinds: conscious beings [*cetanā*], or souls, and unconscious entities [*acetanā*] like matter and time.

The term *yoga nidrā*, as applied to human beings, is a state of half sleep and half meditation in which knowledge is very full.

The form of God seen, or experienced, in meditation is not the ultimate *brahman* as He is in Himself.

> *Brahman* transcends even the form seen in meditation.
>
> Whatever is seen in the mind by the seeker, during meditation, is the form of the Lord. Then how is He unmanifest? To this *Sūtrakāra* points out *Brahman* is different from the form seen during the meditation.
>
> Even as the Lord's attributes of Bliss and knowledge are different from those of the *Jīva*, in the same way, the *Brahma* is different from the form perceived during the time of meditation. 'That which is not thought of by the mind, but by which the mind is said to be known, know that to be *Brahman*. The *Jīva* is not *Brahman*. *Brahman* is close by you as your controller.' (Kena. 1.6). In this way, what is seen by the mind is not *Brahman* is stated. 'Whatever is reflected in the mind (the mental construct) at the time of meditation is called *Brahman* by courtesy and that is what is perceived by the mind during meditation. Since the *Brahman* abides in the reflection which bestows the fruit of *Aparokṣajñāna* on the meditator, as in the case of the ardent worshipper of an image. *Brahman* is perceived by *Aparokṣajñāna* that one has by meditation and by God's grace.' Thus is stated in the *Brahmatarka*.

The meaning of *aparokṣajñāna* is simply: knowledge that is not invisible and, thus, perceptible. When we see a picture of a friend we recognise that picture as being 'of him'. In the same way the image of Brahman that we experience in meditation is 'of Brahman'; though not actually Brahman as He appears to Himself.

The Beatific Vision of the Christian theologian is the vision enjoyed by the souls in heaven. This vision rarely happens during earthly life. The experience of God during mystical prayer, or during an ecstatic moment, which probably happens to nearly all souls once or twice in a lifetime, is not the Beatific Vision; but it is an approximation to that state.

Souls

The souls [*jīva*] are infinite in number and are tainted. They are subject to cycles of transformation. When the *avatāra* form of God emerges, they appear. They are reflections of the Being of God. But they are not pure or perfect. This imperfection is not their fault in the full moral sense understood by some thinkers because, for Madhva, they are not free. Their being is separate from the pure Being of God; but they are reflections [*pratibimba*] of that Being. God is the source [*bimba*].

> *Jīva* is sentient. But being dependent like stones and other things, they cannot be regarded as an independent agent. 'O *Janamejaya*, even as a person, makes a wooden puppet to dance, to move its hands, feet and fingers by pulling the strings, in the same way

> the Lord propels every being to do their respective role' (Mbh). So it is said in *Mahābhārata*. (In conclusion, the Lord directs and controls all).

There are three kinds of souls. The highest kinds are souls fit for emancipation [*mukti-yoga*]. The gods such as Brahmā and Vayu; or the sages like Nārada and great kings; or the original ancestors [*pitṛi*] and advanced men are of this highest kind of soul. They can see God as being bliss, knowledge and *ātman*. The second class is of souls that experience transmigration. They enjoy the pleasures of heaven and suffer the pains of earth and hell. The third class of souls are ghosts and demons and they never experience emancipation.

The souls of whatever kind possess eternity.

> Hence, if the *Devatas*, propounded by the eternal *vedas*, are accepted to be non-eternal, there will be a contradiction. For there is no valid authority to prove, that when one *Devatā* disappears another one rises in its place. This is not correct.
>
> Because, even as the creator, sustainer and protector of the universe, created the sun, the moon etc. in the past *kalpa*, in the same way, in this *kalpa* also he created (Rv. 1.19.3). Even as in spring, there is natural law regarding the flowers and flowering plants, in the same way in every *kalpa* there is a rule regarding the creation of the *Devatas* in each *kalpa*. Hence just as the universe is known or seen in this *kalpa*, in the same way and in the same form it will be seen in the next

> *kalpa* and at no time different from it etc. On the basis of such Scriptural authority it is established that there is a rule regarding the origin of the *Devatas* (*Devatas* are eternal due to continuity).
>
> To the realised souls who know the past and the future, the eternity of the *Devas* due to continuity (in each *kalpa*) is a matter of direct perception. The others can infer that since there are *Devatas* in the present *kalpa*, there will be *Devatas* in the future also. Hence the *Devatas* are eternal due to continuity from *kalpa* after *kalpa*.

Because the souls are substances different from God, they are intrinsically different from one another. They are not differentiated merely by their bodies and minds, as the Shamkarites would have. Each soul possesses distinct qualities and has distinct experiences. Thus also the blindness [*avidyā*] of each soul is also distinct.

This blindness [*avidyā*] is a negative substance. It is a form of *prakṛti* and it has two kinds: 1) *jīvācchādika* — that which obscures the spiritual powers of the *jīva* from itself; and 2) *paramācchādika* — that which hides God from the gaze of the *jīva*.

> *Jīva* is atomic. Even then it can pervade the whole body. Even as a drop of superior sandal paste, which is applied at one place on the body, its fragrance is all over the body, in the same way, the *Jīva* pervades over the whole body, though atomic. This atomic *Jīva* pervades all over the body by its many aspects; like a drop of

> a superior sandal paste which pervades all over the limbs. Thus it is said in the *Brahmānda Purāṇa*.
>
> *Jivas* having aspects, does not conflict with its indivisibility, as these are colourfully identical (*Saviśeṣabhinna)*.
>
> If it is said that on account of the special position of the drop of sandal paste, the fragrance spreads all over the body. This is not the case with *Jīva*. We say. The *Jīva* also has a special position in the heart alone, is admitted in the scriptures.

The *jīva* is atomic, that, is it is minute, or the size of an atom. As the jiva is spiritual it is not atomic in nature as bodies are. The meaning of *saviśeṣabhinna* is 'distinct with differences'. Continually we confront the mystery of the one and the many in the philosophy of Madhva. But the strength of Madhva is to face this mystery rather than somehow avoid it. Each soul is different from other souls and each soul is one in its own self; even while absorbed in Brahman. Souls differ from one another, being separate individuals with distinct qualitative differences.

> ' ...The supreme Being is different from the entire group of *Jivas*. He is not inferable, He is unthinkable. The Lord is perfect, the *Jivas* are imperfect. Because God is ever free the *Jīva* seeks from Him freedom from Bondage through His Grace'. As thus the *Kauṣika Śruti* explains ...

On the other hand:

> Even as the world is said to be non-different from *Brahman*, *Jīva* too whose properties of knowledge and Bliss resemble those of *Brahman*, is said to be non-different from *Brahman*.

> Bliss, knowledge etc., which are the essence of being of the *Jivas*, resemble those of *Brahman*. Hence it is said to be non-different from *Brahman*. These qualities are all found in *Brahman*, and hence it is said, 'All this is *Brahman*', so too should it be understood in respect of *Jīva*. In this respect it is stated in the *Bhaviṣyat Parva* — *Jīva* is different from others and *Brahman* is different from *Jīva* too. Even then, since all of them resemble in their nature as knowledge, in the vedas, they are said to be non-different.

The relation between Brahman and the soul can be said to be that of *amśa* and *amśi* — roughly, part and whole — though if a more complicated explanation is preferred — ectype and archetype. There is a clear distinction, on the one hand, between an apparition of God, which is also His *amśa*, but which is in no way distinct from Him and, on the other hand, the jiva, which is the *amśa* of his *amśi*, but which has authentic and separate existence.

> The *Avatāra* form of the Lord though an *Amśa* is not an *Amśa* in the sense in which the *Jīva* is an *Amśa*. Though the light of the glow-worm and the fire of the final deluge are both the *Amśa* of fire, they are not of the

> same kind (i.e. their essential nature is not the same) or even though ocean and urine, mount Meru and the excreta are the *Amśa* of the elements water and earth etc, they are not identical with their *Amsis* viz water and earth.

Again, of the apparitions of the Lord, the text continues:

> These incarnations, *Varāha* and others of the Lord are the Lord's *Svarūpāmśa*, and they are in fact the Lord only. These protect the people tormented by the demons in every yuga. But that which is different from this Supreme Being, which is not an effect or modification of anything, which has the beginningless Sattva guna, the conscious being is *Jīva*. This *jīva* takes birth again and again, since he has had no *Śravaṣa* and *Sākṣātkara* of the Lord (Bhagavata 1.3). '*Svāmśa* and *vibhinnāmśa* are two kinds of *Amsas*. Whatever is the nature, power and condition of supremacy etc of the *Amśi* (the original form) the same holds true of the *Svarūpāmśa*. There is not an iota of difference between the *Svarūpāmśa* and the *Amśin*. But the *Bhinnāmśa* is of limited power and has resemblance with *Amśin* to a very slight degree' (so it is said in *Varāha Purāṇa*).

As with the Samkhya system there are twenty-five categories of Being which devolve in a similar series. However, there is a more complex development of detail furnished by Madhva than is provided by the early Samkhya. Manas is both a category and a sense organ. As a sense organ again it is eternal and non-eternal.

As eternal it is the very own essence [*svarūpa bhūtam*] of God, of gods and of souls.

> As non-eternal, manas again belongs to God, to gods and to souls. The non-eternal manas can then be divided into five kinds:
>
> *manas* — providing imagination and doubt
> *buddhi* — the function of decision
> *ahamkara* — thinks unreal things are real
> *citta* — causes memory
> *cetana* — intelligence
>
> These are the functions [*vṛtti*] of manas.

For Madhva our perception of self is quite beyond the activity of mind, or manas, even in its *cetana* functioning. He has a special sense — *sākṣi-jñāna* — that always leads to unerring truth about the self as ego [*aham*], as self-conscious self. This sense of self also includes the truths of pure sense perception. This perception is also perfectly reliable, when the senses are not interfered with. Weakness in the sense organs, or distortions in the media of light and so forth, can cause the senses to fail. When *ahamkara* is not distorting our judgement, what we actually see, has both subjective truth and objective truth.

Also through the *sākṣi-jñāna* we recognise time and space.

The universe could not have created itself; nor could pure negation have created the world. Such views confuse the most fundamental distinction between Being and Nothingness; and make nothing, somehow, become something. They are bad philosophy.

> Primordial antecedent negation is not the creator or the cause of the world.
>
> If it is said that Primordial Antecedent negation (*Viśva prāgabhāva*) is the cause of this universe, we say it is not correct. Because it is only an object of mere negation ... In these *Shrutis* the *Asat* is stated to be the cause of this universe. As a result, they are opposed to the *Shrutis* which state that *Viṣṇu* is the cause of this universe.

Some Hindu thinkers have taught that matter existed independently of God. They have taught that the act of creation is a reorganisation of matter. This error is wholly rejected by Madhva.

> *Brahman* is the one independent world cause.
>
> This universe has no independent cause, other than the Lord. Because, the *Shrutis* have rejected an independent material cause and there are reasons for the same.
>
> In this world, it is seen, that things are produced (or created like pot and cloth etc) by the use of many independent means. But not so with *Brahman*. The

creation of this universe takes place, by His own natural capacity only.

When God creates the universe He uses accessories that are dependent on Himself.

The accessories dependent on the Lord are (admitted) accepted in the *Shrutis*.

A possible doubt may be raised viz when we have such *Shrutis* statements like 'Born of water' 'by the Earth'. (Tai. Ar. 3.13) how do you say there are no *Pramanas* for the other means?

To clear this doubt, the *Sutrakāra* points out, the *Shrutis* have accepted the dependent accessories. Hence, there is no problem of contradicting the position ... 'Whatever then existed (at the time of dissolution) was *Kāla* (Time), *jīva* (Self) and the Lord and they were covered by Him and were under His control (dependent on Him). Hence, the Lord only existed at that time. This universe was born of the Supreme Being, because, it was not in existence before.' Thus says *Kāṣāyaṇa Śruti*.

Creation is not, on account of having a purpose. If it is said that God created the universe for the fulfilment of certain purposes which he did not have before creation, then he must be imperfect ... In everyday life ecstatic persons out of sheer overflow of joy dance and sing spontaneously and sportively, and there is no purpose

> for their activity, the same is the case with the Lord - His activities of creation etc. The Lord therefore does not create the universe with any motive.

I think it is clear that, for Madhva, God is the creator of every thing. Creation is really a series of emanations from the divine Being. Then there is a reabsorbtion of realities, one into another, and then finally back into God. The created universe is not separate in its being from the Being of God. For Madhva, God creates the universe out of Himself: for Christianity, God creates the universe 'out of nothing' [*creatio ex nihilo*].

The difficulty of Madhva's view of God is clear. Surely a just God could not deliberately create evil souls, who then automatically go to eternal suffering? Is karma, then, beyond the control of God? The simple answer seems, according to Madhva, to be, 'Yes'.

> If it is said '*Karma* cannot be accepted, because it is due to God Himself and depends on Him', we say this is not correct, because *Karma* is beginningless ...
>
> Because, the *Karmas*, which the *Jivas* are made to perform by God, are due to the *Jīva's* previous *Karmas*. Thus the chain of *Karmas* goes back indefinitely and enables God to consider them at the time of making *Jīva* to perform its *Karma*. Thus *Karmas* have no beginning or are *Anādi*. Hence, the fault of partiality and cruelty cannot be attributed to God.

From a western point of view, those who do not believe in freedom either attribute partiality and cruelty to God, or they regard Him as lacking in power. Christianity accepts the free creation of beings who possess free will; and who, if they do wrong, deserve punishment. Freedom is of course mysterious too, just as is karma.

The meaning of *anādi* is 'without beginning'. If things react and interact at all, they have to do so according to the law of karma, which is eternal and without beginning.

Maybe further research into the philosophy of Madhva will reveal answers to some problems that are, at first sight, insoluble. Yet his work is a meeting of ancient and modern philosophy — a vision that recognises a creator God and yet is bound by an earlier and pre-theistic vision of a total causality. Perhaps the thought of Karl Marx was a return to that vision of karma, or material causality, as controlling everything; and a view of free will as an illusion. If we view free will as an illusion contradictions are involved. Perhaps I can only truly imagine that other souls are unfree, while I myself must have free will. If I myself do not possess freedom of will, how can I know that some causal force is not controlling my mind and forcing me to think I am free, or, indeed, unfree. True knowledge requires that we have the freedom to truly respond to what we see. Freedom of action is an adjunct of the freedom to know.

> The *Shrutis* which state that *ākāśa* is beginningless should be understood only in a figurative sense. Otherwise there would not be statements saying *ākāśa* has origin.
>
> This *Ākāśa* is *Anādi*, it is subtle and supersensible, such *Shrutis* are to be understood in a figurative sense,

> otherwise there would be no statements regarding the genesis of *Ākāśa*, in such a large number ...
>
> '*Puruṣa (Jīva), Prakṛti, Paramātma* and *Kāla* or time are all eternal. *Prāṇa* (Breath), *Śraddhā* (his spouse the five elemental substances and their effects (body etc) are all non-eternal. Those which have origin are non-eternal and those which have no origin are eternal. *Puruṣa, Prakṛti, Paramātma* and *Kāla*, (have never originated) or have no origin and hence, they are not destroyed. *Mukhya Prāṇa, Śraddhā, Ākāśa* come into being partially, hence they have origin and also have no origin' so says *Bhāllaveya Śruti*.

At the end of the sacrificial meal of Hindus the Brahmin leaves part of his portion to be eaten by his students. This leaving [*seṣa*] represents that part of creation that, according to the Vedas, is never absorbed into Brahman when the universe is absorbed into him at its dissolution [*vilaya*]. Thus Madhva has this difficulty. His thought brings him to the idea of the infinite God of philosophy, who is the creator of the entire universe. But the Vedas insist that the dissolution of the universe is not total. Madhva thus develops notions of the souls [*jīva*] and even that part of prakṛti that he taught was purely sattvic, as having a sort of permanent existence, during the dissolution [*vilaya*], within God. Thus we have Brahman as total creator and total destroyer of the universe, and yet souls who have eternal existence in some form or another. Again the special pure form of Sattva, which at the first moment of creation emerges to form subtle beings, has not, at the dissolution, been entirely absorbed into the divine Being.

The creation of the souls and of the universe in Indian philosophy is not 'creation' in the western sense. It is the 'emanation' of beings from God and then one from another in a sort of 'gnostic' sense. St Thomas Aquinas taught that, philosophically speaking, God could have created matter from eternity without beginning, but we know, from biblical revelation, that He created the universe in time. Aquinas of course made the clearest distinction between reason and faith. The Hindu thinkers regard truths arrived at through reason and truths revealed to us by the Vedas as, equally, knowledge — *jñāna*.

Pramana

An important successor to Madhva was Jayatīrtha who lived towards the end of the fourteenth century. Legend has it that in a previous incarnation Jayatīrtha had been the bull that always accompanied Madhva on his journeys. The most important work of Jayatīrtha is the Nyāyasudhā, a commentary on the philosophy of Madhva. Jayatīrtha is said to have brought his master's philosophy to the common man.

Madhva made important strides in the development of Indian logic. Hitherto the act of perception had been treated as an abstraction. Madhva treated each act as a concrete, individual event. An act of perception had its universal, true and abstract aspect, but also its individual and subjective aspect.

Both Madhva and Jayatīrtha defined *pramana* as agreement with the objects of knowledge [*yathārtha*]. The knowledge of an object is usually not a matter of one, single, individual act of perception, but usually includes a series of such acts and the memory [*smṛti*] of those acts.

Jayatīrtha insisted on the importance of the memory of a perception as a valid act of perception. There is no necessary connection between a perception's being valid and its taking place in present time, or its having been previously unacquired – 'unobtained realness' [*anandigatārtha*]. Other systems of Indian philosophy regarded memory as less important, or as unreliable. However, the reliability, or the unreliability of memory, does not set it in a different logical category from immediate perception. Both can be erroneous. To err is human. To consider the problem of knowledge properly, we have to consider it in abstraction from present time. This is what so many philosophies, ancient and modern, have failed to do. But we also have not to make that abstract into a false concrete. It is the table that is particularly concrete and not my view of it. The table exists as a continuum, but any one person's knowledge of it is usually the result of a number of instances of seeing it.

Jayatīrtha argues that there is no necessary connection between validity [*pramana*] and any requirement that the object has not been acquired before [*anadhgatārtha*]. If the pastness of a perception of an object made that perception *per se* invalid, then also inferences about objects that existed in the past, or about objects that will exist in the future would also be invalid. When we remember an object we are well aware that it may have changed its state. When we visit a town that we have not seen since childhood we expect there to be changes. Memory grasps an object as it was and is indifferent as to changes of state — 'it was so at that time' [*tadāsan tadṛśa iti*].

The enigma of memory is that all men regard it as a source of valid knowledge, in spite of the failure of individual men's memories in many instances. Memories, however, are no more enigmatic than the perceptions on which they are based.

Jayatīrtha regarded the universality of human experience as the ultimate testimony of all of the means of knowledge [*pramana*]. He criticised the overly empirical approach of some theories of knowledge, which say that only knowledge of something new can be a *pramana*. There are eternal truths. Again there is no necessary connection between validity [*pramana*] and an object's being previously unacquired [*anadhgatārtha*].

The definition of knowledge, or rather the definition of *pramana*, in the Madhva School, is 'agreement with the objects of knowledge [*yathārtha*]'. The general meaning of *pramana* is: measure, school, authority and comparison; but it has a specialised meaning in philosophy: the means of knowing. The simple, everyday meaning of *yathārtha* is: right, or real.

Madhva distinguishes two kinds of *pramana*: *pramana* as true knowledge and *pramana* as the instrument of knowledge. The first is called *kevala pramana*, the second *anu pramana*. The meaning of *kevala* is 'pure': the meaning of *anu* is 'lesser', or 'minor'. Our consciousness [*caitanya*] and our states of knowledge [*vṛtti*] are *kevala pramana*. Of these things we are certain. The basic meaning of *vṛtti* is: rolling and running down (of tears). It then means: course of action and moral conduct; and then again: mode of being, nature and kind. Finally when applied to our minds it refers to our 'states of knowledge'. We know our own states of knowledge for certain.

When I think that I see a tree I know that I think I see a tree. In this sense the internal act of perception is infallible. Our knowledge of the great truths of scripture is also, for Madhva, *kevala pramana.*

When *pramana* is the instrument of knowledge and not the knowledge itself then it is *anu pramana*, or 'little knowledge'. Again it is threefold as perception, inference and scriptures. That any two sides of a triangle are together greater than the third would be *kevala pramana*, but true empirical perception must be *anu pramana.* Reasoning from empirical perception, as when we gradually build the idea of a natural kind from many perceptions and then, from the immediate perception of an individual instance, infer empirical results, is also *anu pramana.*

One might say that in scriptural statements the necessary truths about God's nature would be *kevala pramana* and lesser truths about his appearances might be *anu pramana.*

When we arrive at the truth by guessing, we do not go via a *pramana*, thus guessing is a form of doubt.

Modern systems of logic exclude any knowledge of the knower and concentrate entirely on the object. Thus these systems cannot comprehend understanding, or indeed the full sense of *pramana.*

Recognition is not always instant. Knowing that ducks can swim is a process achieved by a complex combining of impressions over period of time. Thus one of the greatest achievements of Madhva was his recognition of memory [*smṛti*] as a means of cognition.

Śālikaṇātha was a Mimamsa philosopher who lived *circa* 700 AD. He argued that memory should not be regarded as a *pramana*, but only as a reflection. Recognition [*pratyabhijñā*] cannot be part of memory; because recognition implies direct sense contact, or indeed a series of direct sense contacts. He thought that knowledge required direct sense contact; and, in fact, that knowledge was the same as recognition. Jayatīrtha, however, urged that because memory can agree with the object of knowledge, memory is thus a *pramana*. Change of state does not invalidate memory because memory thinks of a thing *tadāsan tadṛśa iti* — as it was at that time. Therefore change of state does not mean that memory is not a *pramana*.

Regarding the origins of scripture and the infallibility of scriptural statements, Madhva's views are similar to the views of the Mimamsakas. For Madhva human testimony, which is due to personal authority [*pauruśeya*], may be fallible. But the Vedas, which are not the composition of any person [*apauruśeya*], are infallible.

Madhva recognised only three means of knowing: perception, inference and scriptural testimony. He regarded comparison [*upamāna*] as a form of inference.

Nature

When Brahman withdraws creation into Himself [*vilaya*] He does not entirely absorb the subtle *prakṛti*. The existence of this subtle *prakṛti* continues in an unmanifested state. In this state the subtle *prakṛti* is pure *sattva*.

In this state again all the souls have continued existence thus, in some way, preserving their identity until they re-exist as fully distinct individuals during the next period of creation [*avatāra*]. Their path to final release [*moksa*] continues across the endless phases of creation. Their number is infinite.

As space *ākāśa* is empty and eternal. It is empty and unmanifested space [*avyākṛta ākāśo dig-rūpah*].

In the evolving state of the universe [*avatāra*], time [*kāla*] is the direct product of this subtle *prakṛti*, which is here taken as substance [*dravya*]. This substance is accepted as *māyā*, the consort of God. It is impure [*doṣa-yukta*] and from it evolve the subtle bodies [*linga-śarīra*] and the three gunas. Sattva exists by itself in its pure form in the Madhva system; rajas and tamas are always mixed with one another and with sattva. Various mixtures of the three gunas are said to create the different evolutes. In the *ahamkara,* there are ten parts of sattva for one of rajas and a tenth part of tamas. The element *ākāśa* [or *būtākāśa*] is the product of the *tāmasa ahamkara* and is limited. It is what material things are made of.

The philosophy of Madhva is the philosophy of difference. God possesses distinct inner differences, which in no way contradict His purity and oneness. In the unmanifested state of God's being the souls and primary *prakṛti* maintain some sort of existence within the being of god. Unmanifested *prakṛti* appears to be homogenous, but it subtly contains different elements, or at least has the power to manifest different elements when aided by God and the emerging souls.

God moulds forms out of prakṛti, which is the material cause and in which he exists himself in various forms. Before we get from the unmanifested prakṛti to he well developed forms of creation, we have twenty-four transitional products of creation, which are mahat, ahamkara, buddhi, manas, ten senses, five sense-objects and the five great elements. These exist in the primordial prakṛti in subtle forms before their evolution.

The three aspects of prakṛti are presided over by the three forms of Lakṣmī — Śrī, Bhū and Durgā.

Ethics

In the ethical emphasis of Madhva *bakti* is of supreme importance. Yet knowledge is the basis of true love of God and knowledge enhances that true love. Again a moral life is essential for salvation [*moksa*]. A moral life helps us to understand the truth. Then truth enables us to live a moral life for its own sake.

Each soul needs to study under a spiritual teacher. This teacher will direct the particular course that the individual soul requires. Here we have the importantly individualistic vision of Madhva. Each jiva is different from every other jiva and each jiva will contemplate its own unique vision of God on its final release; and therefore each jiva must follow its very own, personal, good way [*dharma*].

Only men of the upper three castes have the right to study the Vedas, but Madhva allows the Sudra and women to study the Puranas and the *smṛti*, if they are able. With this study goes the practice of meditation. Through meditation and by the grace of God the soul can arrive at direct and intuitive realisation of God [*aparokṣajñāna*]. Rites and sacrifices are always important, however.

> Bhāgavata Tantra mentions the eligibility of the eligibles. There are three types of *Adhikaris* or eligibles. They are inferior, Middle order and the Best. The Superior *Adhikāri* among human beings comes under the category of *Adhikaris. Risis* and *Gandharvas* are middle order *Adhikaris* and Gods are Superior or the Best *Adhikaris*. This is the natural classification of the *Adhikaris*. There is a second classification based on merit. A human being who has devotion for the Lord (*Viṣṇu*) and has studied the *Shastras* is an inferior *adhikāri*. The one who (in addition to these) is also practising *Śama* (calmness), *Dama* (control of the senses), *uparata* (indifference to the objects of the senses), *titikśā* (who tolerates or bares the opposites like heat and cold, happiness and sorrow), *samāhita* (who has the right knowledge of things) such an *adhikāri* is a middle order *adhikāri*. On the other hand, a person who has realised that the whole world from God *Brahmā* to the blade of grass is non-eternal and meaningless, impermanent and as a result has become dispassionate and non-attached, and has sought the abode of *Viṣṇu* as the only resort, who has offered all the fruits of all his *karmas* to the Lord is to be considered as the superior or the best *adhikāri* (among human beings).

(It is important here to distinguish between God [*brahmā*], who is the creator and who evolves from Brahman, and *brahman* Himself.)

Knowledge alone however cannot produce total release. Freedom cannot be effected without the grace of God. A soul who has the intellectual vision of the truth but has not received God's grace continues to live in the flesh. He is a *jīvanmukti*. Release occurs when unessential forms [*anyathārūpam*] are shed and the pure spiritual existence [*svarūpeṇa vyavasthitih*] of the soul is restored for the last time. The blessed receive a body of pure matter [*śuddhasattva*]; but this body is not subject to karma, nor does the soul experience any attachment to that superior body. The freed retain their consciousness of individuality both in the creation and in the reabsorbtion. The unreleased may experience absorption into Brahman in meditation, or loss of consciousness in deep sleep. Yet they are aware of their own self-consciousness as separate from the consciousness of God.

Worship of God is necessary in order to obtain divine grace; and to this end the rituals of religion are of paramount importance.

In Himself God is unapproachable. We attain advance towards God by the mediation of Vayu, the wind god.

> The Lord should be meditated upon as most perfect. Because such *upāsanā* is the best. It is said in *Brahmatarka* — 'All wise men should certainly meditate on God always, as most perfect, because the word *Brahman* is connotive of greatness and perfection. The Supreme Lord is greater than *Ramā* and other gods.

This knowledge of God, as most perfect and great, creates love for Him in everyone always, everywhere. Whenever *Brahman* is contemplated as the Supreme Lord of all, he should also be contemplated as being most perfect...'

It is said in the *Nārāyana Tantra* — 'If it is not possible for a person to meditate on the attributes of the Lord, due to mental agony, disease, and the mind's interest in other things, he should always remember the Lord as ever perfect. He should never give up such remembrances, as all the attributes of the Lord are included in His being 'Ever perfect'...

One should meditate sitting in a comfortable position, as meditation is possible in the sitting posture only.

Even if one is always meditating, one should do it while sitting, there is less distraction for the mind and hence the meditation becomes possible...

'If the body is steady, then the mind will also be steady. If the body is unsteady, the mind also becomes unsteady,' says *Brahmāṇda Purāṇa.*

The *Smirtis* also say the same.

Smirtis state — 'Seated in a sitting posture, holding the body, neck and head in straight line, the *Sādhaka* should make his mind steady, and concentrating on

> the tip of his nose and without looking in any other direction, one should meditate' etc.
>
> Where and when the concentration of mind is possible there and then meditation may be carried on. Fixed time and place make no difference.
>
> Wherever and whenever the concentration of the mind takes place, one should sit. Where the mind is in pleasant mood, at that place and time, and in that situation (or posture) one should enjoy. Nobody has said that time and place make any difference in meditation. Time and space are to be considered only to make the mind to be in a pleasant mood and not for meditation.' So it is stated in the *Varāha Purāṇa*.

Madhva's direction to the anguished soul, who cannot rest in the simple contemplation of God's excellencies, that he should simply remember that the Being of God is 'ever perfect', reveals the fundamental richness of the *varāha* vision. Unlike the *nirguṇa brahman* of the Advaitins, or the notion of Being held by Russell and other western thinkers, the idea of God's perfection, in Madhva's thought, is the doorway to infinite richness.

prana

The meanings of *prana* are: breath, breath of life, respiration, spirit, and vitality. The *mukhya prana* — or root principle of *prana* — is the undifferentiated, pure *prana*, which emanates from the Being of God. Perhaps there is no difference really between *mukhya prana* and the pure *sattva* that always abides in God, or *śuddhasattva*. The *śuddhasattva*, however, is seen as a pure quality, whereas the *mukhya prana* is an active power. What emanates from God is actually both quality and power.

> Again the *mukhya prāṇa* produces five further pranas:
>
> 1. *prana* — vitality
> 2. *apāna* — outward breath, wind
> 3. *vyāna* — expansion and contraction of the voluntary muscular system
> 4. *udāna* — creative breath, speech
> 5. *sāmana* — digestion and maturation.

In the process of creation *mukhya prana* can take forms, which are more subtle or more gross.

> *Prāṇa* inside the body is atomic and subtle, but *Prāṇa* outside is all pervading.

Nowadays we might call *prana*, 'energy'.

For Advaitins, really, all is prana, and indeed prana is God. But Madhva is the *dvaita* philosopher of real distinctions. Certainly the prana outside the body produces the body itself; and the prana inside the body is that body's life and its living functions. But prana is not God. Prana is part of creation.

> If it is said that there is none superior to *Prāṇa*,
> then the difference of *Prāṇa* from the Lord will

> not be proper, we say, this is not so. Because as mentioned in the *Śruti*, it is reasonable.
>
> If *Prāṇa* is taken to be superior to all, then his difference from the Lord will not be reasonable. This is not so. Because, as mentioned in the *Śruti*, it is reasonable; the *Śruti*, after mentioning the superiority of *Prāṇa* to all *upāsanā adhikarins*, states that the Lord is superior to *Prāṇa*.

The meaning of '*upāsanā* adhikarins' is: approaching claimants.

Brahman

The primal cosmic energy [*prana*] is both a thing and a quality. Active people are said to be 'energetic' or to 'have energy'. Microscopic entities like electrons may similarly be seen to possess energy but also they may be seen to actually *be* energy itself. Prana and electrical energy are realities reasoned to rather than seen and thus can be thought of both as things and as qualities. Exactly thus the bliss of Brahman is a quality that Brahman possesses, and yet is Brahman himself. He is bliss. Though to grasp his qualities as pluralities our minds separately list his strength, his goodness and his happiness. In reality these qualities are not separate or different from one another.

Pure Being is at once a noun, an adjective and a verb. And Brahman is Being.

> On account of the two fold teaching by the *Shrutis*, that *Brahman* is both of the nature of the essence of Bliss and

> also has the Bliss as its property, like the serpent and its coil. 'The knower of Bliss of *Brahman*' (Tai. 2.4). 'He is of the essence of the Supreme Bliss' (Br. 6.3.33) in this way, on account of the two teachings, their relation — i.e., relation between the Bliss and Bliss-ful etc should be constructed as the relation that holds between the snake and its coil, — the snake has the attribute of being in a coil and is also of the essence of the attribute of a coil, i.e., it is both the coil and coiled.

Madhva propounds that life in the world can be divided into two groups, *kśara* and *akśara*. The life of destructible bodies is *kśara*: the life of indestructible bodies is *akśara*. Laxmi is *akśara*, while others from Brahma and lower are ksharas, or jīvas. Vishnu is exempt from this classification, as his body is transcendental.

The western tradition of creation is that God created the universe out of nothing. The Indian theistic tradition is that the universe and souls have evolved from the Being of God. The Nyayikas have generally taught that the existence of atoms has been for infinity and must remain for infinity. They have taught that God has created the atoms, but not at any point in time. Time, they believe, is eternal.

Saint Thomas Aquinas taught that the physical universe has had a beginning, and that it will have an end. But he based that teaching upon Holy Scripture and not upon reason.

> By the word of the lord the heavens were established:
> and all the power of them by the spirit of his mouth:
> Gathering together the waters of the sea, as in a vessel:

laying up the depths in storehouses.
Let all the earth fear the lord: and let all the inhabitants of the world be in awe of him
For he spoke and they were made: he commanded and they were created.

It is interesting that many modern physicists teach that time and space have no existence apart from matter. There was (or is) no 'before the universe' and there can be no 'after the universe'. Time is merely when events happen; and space is where they happen. In modern parlance time and space are adverbs and not nouns. Nowadays we might reason to a finite universe — perhaps!

Logic

Does logic have a metaphysical, or indeed, even a physical status?

Is the first move of the universe a moment of logic?

That is a different question from the question, does mind exist as superior to and more primary than matter.

Perhaps logic is an empirical fact; a something whose existence is primary. Perhaps it is not archetypically theoretical, but simply something real. Thus the vision of Shri Madhvācārya will be developped in Chapter Twelve of this book.

Consciousness

It is almost as easy to reflect on our own self-consciousness as it is simply to be conscious. We merely have to wish to so reflect and we find that we are thus reflecting. Reflecting on our own self-consciousness is not an act of conceptual thinking but a suspension of such thinking. Our self-awareness, which is at the same time an awareness of the totality of objects that we know, underlies and embraces any individual feelings or particular objects that we might experience and consider.

Now Chinese thought distinguishes between two kinds of knowing: *guan* [level tone] means the knowing of the wide vision and general consideration. The character *guan* is composed of the pictogram of a stalk flying and the pictogram of 'seeing'. The meaning of *zhi* [level tone] is 'knowing' in the precise sense of the word. The character *zhi* is composed of the pictogram of 'arrow' and the pictogram of 'speak'. The sense of *guan* is receptive: where the knower simply accepts the broad balance of reality as it presents itself. The stalk has a brilliant eye and an eminent perspective as he flies, but he doesn't have a large brain. Like many animals he sees things as they are in themselves.

The sense of *zhi* is accurate and effective. Here the knower acts positively to understand. The arrow in the pictogram illustrates that this kind of knowing hits the narrow mark. The mouth radical indicates that this *zhi* kind of knowing is closely allied to social needs, communication and speech: i.e., to conceptualisation. Ideas that are *zhi* can be amazingly powerful and true, but the individual focus, dividing reality according to the needs of the hunter and his clan, is a very one-sided way of viewing the generality. Consciousness is all of these kinds of knowing and indeed can be hit with the arrow of *zhi*. We can think about consciousness itself. But the idea of consciousness in itself does not know of any precise details about itself. I am aware of the world in a general way of *guan*, but *zhi* picks out any that details I observe. Thus I can recognise and conceptualise.

I remember once talking to a class of fifteen-year olds and explaining about my philosophy and my book. I suddenly said, by way of explanation, and also in a burst of self-understanding, 'I want to know why I'm me.' A boy in the second row replied, 'That you are never going to know!' And I now ask myself: Is there a set of epithets, which are essential to being human? How do I find out what they are? Is there a more detailed set of epithets, which characterise myself? How can I know? I cannot conceptually grasp the 'me-ness' of me. But I can, of course, experience being me. Experience is a deeper sort of knowing than categorization; broader and more sure. For a conscious being, experiencing is existence. With a conscious being, 'being' and 'knowing' are the same thing. Yet I also know that I can lose consciousness and still exist. This union of consciousness and unconsciousness means I am something like a substance, whether I like the word or not. But if I insist that I am a substance, I am either conceptualising myself, as it were, externally; or simply I am saying that I exist, which statement adds nothing to my real experience.

People may describe me in various ways; but they cannot define my individual, personal essence. They cannot distinguish here between essential and accidental qualities. A scholastic philosopher can describe me as a 'rational animal', indeed, but this description applies to every human being, not just to me.

In a conventional sense of 'personality' the phrase 'my personality' just means myself, in so far as I have certain predictable tendencies in a socially interactive situation. 'Personality' comes from the Latin *per sonare* - to speak or sound through, referring to the mask that Roman actors wore. The mask expressed the predominant mood of the character. From ancient times until the time of Shakespeare and even later, characters in plays had a predominantly 'characterising' vice or virtue. Today perhaps we see one another as possessing a wider range of possible reactions. In the past, and sometimes even today, what women and various social classes were allowed to do was seen as the actual range of their individual potential. But the description of my personality remains an art and not a science. I will never fit a formula. I will always surprise people.

I might say the thinking of the great minds of the past influences my thinking. I carry mask upon mask before (or perhaps behind) my face — the impressions faint or clear of personalities weak and strong: parents, heroes, teachers and thinkers, creating my values and constructing my primary thought patterns. What is it to be a Western European? Is it not to wear the masks of Socrates, of Jesus and of Augustine? If nowadays we wear the additional personae of Newton, Darwin or Marx; or of Goethe, Fichte and Freud; we cannot slough off the deeper layers of our historically evolved personalities. To be modern is to experience conflict. If we one-sidedly accept certain parts of ourselves we must reject others. If we bring one mask to the fore we conceal others. Conflict is an argument between two masks within each self. The fanatic externalises this argument, looking for the other side of himself in an individual, external opponent. I have always been impressed by the relative ease with which many Asians relate to their historic selves.

But is there a real inner face behind these other masks? Here philosophy, along with metaphor, fails.

BIBLIOGRAPHY

Aquinas, Thomas. *The Summa Theologica of St. Thomas Aquinas*. Trans. Fathers of the English Dominican Province. London: Burns, Oates, and Washbourne, 1920. Online Edition, 2008.

Aurobindo, Shri. *The Life Divine*. New York: The Grey Stone Press, 1949.

Ayer, A. J. 'What I Saw When I Was Dead.' *The Sunday Telegraph* (28 August 1988): www.philosopher.eu.

Badarayana. *Brahmasūtras*. Trans. Madhva Bhasya. Mumbai: Archish Publications, 2005.

Bailey, Alice A. *The Soul and its Mechanism*. New York: The Lucis Trust, 1930.

Basham, Arthur Llewellyn, ed. *A Cultural History of India*. Delhi: Oxford University Press, 1998.

Bhatta, Kumārila. *Ślokavārttika*. Trans. Gangānātha Jhā. Calcutta: The Asiatic Society, 1908.

Bhattacharya, Ram Shankar, and Karl H. Potter, eds. *Encyclopedia of Indian Philosophies*. 4 vols. Delhi: Motilal Banarsidass, 1987.

Carrico, Mara. 'Branches of the Yoga Tree.' *Yoga Journal*: www.yogajournal.com, 2007.

Chakrabarti, K. K. *Classical Indian Philosophy of Mind: The Nyaya Dualist Tradition*. New York: SUNY Press, 1999.

Chandogya Upanishad. Sacred Books of the East. Trans. Max Müller. Oxford: Oxford University Press, 1879.

Chandogya Upanishad. The Thirteen Principal Upanishads. Trans.

R. E. Hume. Oxford: Oxford University Press, 1931.

Chuang-Tzu. *The Inner Chapters*. Trans. A. C. Graham. London: Mandala, 1986.

Colins, Jeff, and Bill Mayblin. *Introducing Derrida.* Cambridge: Icon Books, 2000.

Dasgupta, Surendranath. *A History of Indian Philosophy.* 4 vols. Cambridge: Cambridge University Press, 1949.

Davies, P. C. W., and J. R. Brown, eds. *The Ghost in the Atom.* Cambridge: Cambridge University Press, 1993.

Dutt, Romesh Chunder. *The Ramayana and The Mahabharata.* London: Dent, 1978.

Dyer, Edward. 'My Mind to Me a Kingdom Is.' *Bartleby.com*: www.bartleby.com.

Eight Upanishads. Trans. Swami Gambhirananda. Calcutta: Advaita Ashram, 1978.

Ganeri, Jonardon, and H. Tiwari, eds. *The Character of Logic in India*. Oxford: Oxford University Press, 1999.

Ganeri, Jonardon. 'The Study of the Self.' *Contemporary Practice and Method in the Philosophy of Religion*. Ed D. Cheetham and R. King. London: Continuum, 2008.

Ganeri, Jonardon. *Semantic Powers*. Oxford: Clarendon Press, 1999.

Hacking, Ian. *Why does Language Matter to Philosophy*? Cambridge: Cambridge University Press, 1975.

Happold, F. C. *Mysticism: A Study and an Anthology*. London: Pelican Books, 1963.

Hawking, Stephen. *A Brief History of Time*. London: Bantam, 1998.

Holy Bible. Douay Version. London: Catholic Truth Society, 1956.

Jackson, A. V. Williams. *An Avesta Grammar in Comparison with*

Sanskrit. Stuttgart: Kohlhammer, 1892.

Jaimini. *Mīmamsā Sūtra*. Trans. Ganganatha Jha. Baroda: Oriental Institute, 1933.

Jaimini. *Mīmamsā Sūtra of Jaimini.* Trans. N. V. Thadani. Delhi: Bharatiya Kala Prakashan, 2007.

Jaiminī. *Mīmamsā Sūtras of Jaiminī.* Trans. Mohan Lal Sandal. Allahabad: The Sacred Books of the Hindus, 1923.

Jami. *Masnavi*. Trans. Reynold Alleyne Nicholson. Kharagpur: Digital Library of India, 2015.

Knight, Kevin, ed. *The Catholic Encyclopedia*. New Advent: www.newadvent.org, 2017.

Krishna, Isvara. *Sāmkhya-kārikā of Isvara Krsna.* Trans. Ganganatha Jha. *A Sourcebook in Indian Philosophy*. Poona: The Oriental Book Agency. 1934.

Krishna, Isvara. *Sāmkhya-kārikā of Isvara Krsna.* Trans. Karl H. Potter. *Encyclopedia of Indian Philosophies.* 4 vols. Delhi: Motilal Banarsidass, 1987.

Laine, Joy. 'Udayana's Refutation of the Buddhist Thesis of Momentariness in the Ātmatattvaviveka.' *Journal of Indian Philosophy* 26.1 (1998): 51-97.

Lao-Tzu. *Te-Tao Ching.* Trans. R. G. Henricks. Bodley Head: London 1990.

Manu. *The Laws of Manu*. Trans. Charles Malamoud. *Cooking the World: Ritual and Thought in Ancient India*. Delhi: Oxford India Paperbacks, 1998.

Manu. *The Laws of Manu.* Trans. Georg Buhler. *A Sourcebook in Indian Philosophy*. Ed. Sarvepalli Radhakrishnan and Charles A. Moore. Princeton: Princeton University Press, 1967.

Matilal, Bimal Krishna. *Perception*. Oxford: Oxford University,

1986.

Miśra, Vācaspati. *Tattva-kaumudī*. Trans. Ganganatha Jha. *A Sourcebook in Indian Philosophy*. Poona: The Oriental Book Agency, 1934.

Monier-Williams, Monier. *A Sanskrit-English Dictionary*. 1899. Oxford: Oxford University Press, 1990.

Moore, G. E. *The Refutation of Idealism*. Oxford: Oxford University Press, 1903.

Newman, John Henry. *Loss and Gain: The Story of a Convert*. 1848. London: Longman Green, 1906.

Patanjali. *The Yoga Aphorisms of Patanjali*. Trans. Swami Prabhavananda and Christopher Isherwood. Madras: Sri Ramakrishna Math, 1982.

Patanjali. *The Yoga Sutra of Patanjali*. Trans. J. Haughton Woods. Cambridge: Harvard University Press, 1914.

Potter, Karl H., ed. 'Nyāyakusumāñjali.' *Indian Metaphysics and Epistemology: The Tradition of Nyaya-Vaishesika Up to Gangesa. Encyclopedia of Indian Philosophies Volume 2*. Princeton: Princeton University Press, 2005.

Potter, Karl H., Gerald James Larson and Ramshankar Bhattacharya. *Encyclopedia of Indian Philosophies*. Delhi: Motilal Banarsidass, 1987.

Radhakrishnan, Sarvepalli, and Charles A. Moore, eds. *A Sourcebook in Indian Philosophy*. Princeton: Princeton University Press, 2014.

Radhakrishnan, Sarvepalli. *Indian Philosophy*. 2 Vols. New Delhi: Oxford University Press, 1992.

Rae, Alastair I. *Quantum Mechanics*. New York: Taylor and Francis, 2002.

Rapson, Edward James, ed. *The Cambridge History of India*. 5 Vols.

Cambridge: Cambridge University Press, 1922.

Rig Veda: An Anthology. Ed. and Trans. Wendy Doniger. London: Penguin, 1981.

Rig Veda. Trans. Max Müller. London: Williams and Norgate, 1859.

Rig Veda. Trans. Ralph T. H. Griffith. New York: Motilal Banarsidas, 1992.

Śabara. *Bhasya.* Trans. Ganganatha Jha. *A Sourcebook in Indian Philosophy.* Poona: The Oriental Book Agency, 1934.

Sadhana. *Rabindranath Tagore.* London: Macmillan, 1913.

Sankaran, Ambasamudram. *Some Aspects of Literary Criticism in Sanskrit.* Delhi: Munshiram Manoharlal, 1925.

Sanskrit Religions Institute. *Sri Devasthanam.* Website of the Sanskrit Religious Institute: www.sanskrit.org.

Shakespeare, William. *William Shakespeare: The Complete Works.* Ed Stanley Wells, Gary Taylor, John Jowett, and William Montgomery. Kindle Edition. Oxford: Oxford University Press, 2005.

Sister Nivedita [Margaret Elizabeth Noble], and Ananda Coomaraswamy. *Myths and Legends of the Hindus and Buddhists.* 1914. London: Senate Books, 1994.

Srimad Bhagavatam: The Wisdom of God. Trans. Swami Prabhavananda. Madras: Sri Ramakrishna Math, 1988.

Stcherbatsky, T. *Buddhist Logic.* New Delhi: Munshiram Manoharlal, 1996.

Stoker, Valerie. 'Madhva (1238-1317).' *Internet Encyclopedia of Philosophy*: www.iep.utm.edu.

Sugirthrajah, Sharada. *Imagining Hinduism: A Postcolonial Perspective.* London: Routledge, 2003.

Tharpar, Romila. *Interpreting Early India.* Oxford: Oxford University Press, 1992.

Udayanākārya. *Nyāyakusumāñjali of Udayanākārya*. Trans. N. S. Dravid. New Delhi: Indian Council of Philosophical Research, 1996.

Upanishads. Trans. J. Mascaro. London: Penguin Books, 1965.

Vyasa, Veda. *Bhagavad-Gītā*. Trans. Sarvepalli Radhakrishnan. New York: Harper, 1948.

Wittgenstein, Ludwig. *Philosophical Investigations*. Trans. G. E. M. Anscombe. Oxford: Basil Blackwell, 1976.

Wittgenstein, Ludwig. *Tractatus Logico-Philosophicus*. Trans. David Pears and Brian McGuinness. New York: Routledge and Kegan Paul, 1961.

Zilberman, D. B. *The Birth of Meaning in Hindu Thought*. Dordrech: Reidel Publishers, 1988.